Soviet Bargaining Behavior

Soviet Bargaining Behavior
The Nuclear Test Ban Case

Christer Jönsson

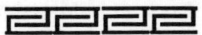

New York COLUMBIA UNIVERSITY PRESS *1979*

Library of Congress Cataloging in Publication Data
Jönsson, Christer, 1944–
  Soviet bargaining behavior.

  Bibliography: p.
  Includes index.
  1. Atomic weapons and disarmament.   2. Russia—
Foreign relations—United States.   3. United States—
Foreign relations—Russia.   I. Title.
JX1974.7.J6   327'.174   78-15875
ISBN 0-231-04606-5

Columbia University Press
New York   Guildford, Surrey

Copyright © 1979 Columbia University Press
All rights reserved
Printed in the United States of America

Contents

Introduction	*1*
Part One A Framework for Analysis	*5*
One / Conceptual Framework	*7*
Two / The Test Ban Negotiations: An Overview	*22*
Part Two East-West Bargaining	*39*
Three / A Typical Soviet Negotiating Behavior?	*41*
Four / In Search of Answers	*55*
Part Three Intra-Bloc Bargaining	*79*
Five / Sino-Soviet Relations as Bargaining Situation	*81*
Six / Intra-Bloc Bargaining: Stage I	*86*
Seven / Intra-Bloc Bargaining: Stage II	*103*
Eight / Intra-Bloc Bargaining: Stage III	*115*
Nine / Intra-Bloc Bargaining: Conclusions	*123*
Part Four Internal Bargaining	*133*
Ten / Soviet Policy Making As Bargaining Situation	*135*
Eleven / Internal Bargaining: Stage I	*143*
Twelve / Internal Bargaining: Stage II	*162*
Thirteen / Internal Bargaining: Stage III	*191*
Conclusions	*209*
Notes	*217*
Bibliography	*245*
Index	*261*

Acknowledgments

"A BOOK," said Marcel Proust, "is a great cemetery in which, for the most part, the names upon the tombs are effaced." And I realize that any effort at retrieving some of the names on the tombs runs the risk of omitting others whose contributions lay buried in this work. Yet a few epitaphs are warranted.

The Department of Political Science at the University of Lund, Sweden, has provided the congenial and supportive environment without which this project could never have been completed. I am indebted to all my colleagues, in particular to Lars-Göran Stenelo with whom I have shared an interest in—and many discussions on—the study of international bargaining.

Among those who have read earlier drafts and offered valuable criticism and advice I wish to mention Vernon V. Aspaturian, Walter C. Clemens, Jr., Alexander Dallin, Alexander L. George, Daniel Heradstveit, Alice L. Hsieh, Roman Kolkowicz, Carl A. Linden, John Sanness, Robert M. Slusser, Jan F. Triska, Arild Underdal, and Ciro E. Zoppo. Ambrose Bierce in his *Devil's Dictionary* defined "gratitude" as "a sentiment lying midway between a benefit received and a benefit expected." Consequently, my thanks to all those mentioned above imply not only the traditional absolution from responsibility for remaining errors and imperfections, but also my hopes for continued collaboration in the future.

I wish to express my gratitude to the Sweden-America Foundation, the Fulbright Commission, and the Siamon Foundation for grants which enabled me to carry out research in the United

States. Thanks to financial support from the Nordic Cooperation Committee for International Politics I have had several opportunities to discuss my research project at conferences in and out of Scandinavia.

Much of the research for this book was carried out at the UN Library at Geneva, Switzerland, and the Hoover Institution Library at Stanford, California. I am impressed by, and gratefully acknowledge, the friendly and efficient service I have received in both places.

Finally, special thanks are due to my wife, Evy, and my children, Lena and Linus, for providing an optimal blend of encouragement and support on the one hand, and much needed diversion from engulfing research problems on the other.

Christer Jönsson

Lund, Sweden
April 1978

Soviet Bargaining Behavior

Introduction

As an example of negotiating methods in practice and of a combination of their different forms—public as well as secret—one may cite the negotiations on the discontinuance of nuclear tests.

(KOVALEV 1968:17)

Soviet–American relations during the Khrushchev era became an active, indeed, a crucial area of Soviet decision-making. . . . Soviet policy toward the United States proved to be bound up with the course of the Sino–Soviet dispute. Furthermore, key questions of Soviet–American relations, especially those that concerned the nuclear-arms race and disarmament, directly involved issues of Soviet internal policy.

(SLUSSER 1967:186–187)

Introduction

⊐ THE NUCLEAR test ban negotiations of 1958–63 have been chosen as the empirical basis of this case study of Soviet bargaining behavior. There are several reasons for this: The test ban negotiations are extremely well documented; they permit observations over a relatively long time span; they have earned a reputation for being the first instance in the history of arms control where serious, detailed negotiations took place; they cover an interesting period in the evolution of the Soviet Union into a superpower and represent, as it were, a microcosm of its foreign policy of that period.

Soviet bargaining behavior will be examined at three different levels of analysis. At a first level Soviet conduct is analyzed in terms of *U.S.–Soviet* interaction. The insufficient explanatory power of this level, which formed the original part of our research,[1] made us explore additional foci of observation.

A recurring game-theoretical idea holds that a negotiation between two parties might be represented as one main game with a number of subgames or "auxiliary games" the playing of which may influence the playing and outcome of the main game.[2] Walton and McKersie include "intraorganizational bargaining" as a basic analytical category in their model of labor negotiations, and also demonstrate its applicability to international negotiations. In the international setting, "intraorganizational bargaining" can, according to Walton and McKersie, be analyzed at two levels: that occurring within an alliance of states, and that taking place within a state.[3]

We shall adopt this perspective and use the labels of *intra-bloc* and *internal* bargaining. Our attention will thus be redirected from the formal East–West negotiations at Geneva to parallel informal intra-bloc bargaining between the USSR and China and internal bargaining between pro-treaty and anti-treaty forces within the Soviet Union. Specifically, at our second level of analysis the hypothesis that Soviet behavior in the East–West negotiations might be a resultant of Sino–Soviet bargaining will be tested, whereas our third level will explore Soviet conduct at Geneva as the outcome of internal bargaining.

While literature on U.S.–Soviet relations, the Sino–Soviet dispute, and domestic Soviet politics, respectively, is abundant, surprisingly few attempts have been made to synthesize or correlate the findings at the different levels of analysis. This study represents one such attempt, focusing on a delimited issue area. Although the categories of analysis are different, our effort bears some resemblance to Allison's noted study of the Cuban missile crisis,[4] insofar as it systematically makes different "cuts" at the same empirical case. The "Allison approach" of examining one issue with alternative analytical lenses has been rather rare up till now, while the reverse—the same analytical lens used on a number of issues—seems to be much more common.

This volume is organized as follows. After the introductory part, outlining a conceptual framework and an overview of the test ban negotiations, Soviet bargaining behavior on the test ban issue is analyzed at the three different levels indicated above. The concluding chapter addresses the intricate question of how our three levels of analysis are interrelated.

PART ONE

A Framework for Analysis

> With rare exceptions bargaining theory has operated in an empirical vacuum. The assumptions about human motivation and behavior have usually been made on the basis of introspection, inspection of special cases, and mathematical tractability. In general, we would have more confidence in the future development of the theory if serious empirical research were to match, in terms of energy and competence, the mathematical efforts of the past 10 years.
>
> (MARCH and SIMON 1958:134)
>
> Although some theoretical work on international bargaining has appeared, the yield of empirical data and its integration with existing theory are almost nil.
>
> (SULLIVAN 1971:361–362)

ONE

Conceptual Framework

◨ THE TWO vignette quotations span a period of more than a decade, during which bargaining models—often involving ingenious mathematics—have flourished, more or less disconnected from the scanty empirical research in the field. Theoreticians have been packing their bags for trips that never took place, and others have set out on trips without any theoretical luggage.

Most existing bargaining models stem from game theory. One debated question is whether game theory is descriptive and explanatory and hence useful as a tool for empirical research. Anatol Rapoport, mathematician and social scientist, writes:

> I think that a categorical disavowal of *descriptive* content is implicit in the entire game-theoretical approach. Game theory is definitely normative in spirit and method.[1]

Rapoport even contends that game theory is more important because of its failures and shortcomings than because of its mathematical success.[2]

Some critics go even further:

> The game theorist is found to be busily stitching down the middle of a seamless garment in the belief that he is holding the whole thing together. His contribution may be ornamental, but it is not structurally necessary.[3]

Such criticism notwithstanding, few social scientists would deny the *heuristic* value of game theory:

It may indeed serve as an indispensable starting point for posing a problem and revealing the essential issues involved.[4]

It has raised and helped to define far more questions than it has answered.[5]

The rewards have thus been indirect, as was the case with the sons who were told to dig for buried treasures in the vineyard. They found no treasures, but they improved the soil.[6]

In the same vein, our conceptual framework has grown out of a critical review of game-theoretical approaches to bargaining and has taken other, complementary approaches into account in the process. The necessity of broadening the theoretical perspective has been stressed by McGrath, who argues that

. . . while negotiation is a relatively unexplored area, there is a lot of *indirectly* related theory and evidence, and we ought to make the most of it.[7]

"BARGAINING" AND "NEGOTIATION": SOME INITIAL DISTINCTIONS

A *bargaining situation* can be said to exist when the following four conditions are met (for simplicity, two actors are assumed):

(1) Both actors perceive the possibility of reaching an agreement in which each actor would be better off, or no worse off, than if no agreement is reached.

(2) Both actors perceive the existence of more than one such agreement which could be reached.

(3) Both actors perceive each other to have conflicting preferences or opposed interests with regard to the different agreements which might be reached.

(4) The ability of one actor to gain his ends is dependent to an important degree on the choices or decisions that the other actor will make.[8]

In short, bargaining situations have two characteristic features: *coincidence of cooperative and competitive elements* (points 1 to 3) and *interdependent decisions* (point 4).

Interdependence of decisions means that each actor has only

partial control over the bargaining situation outcome. The optimal course of action for an actor is contingent on what the other actor does. The actor must attune his plans not only to his own desires and abilities but also to those of the other actor.

Examples of bargaining situations, thus defined, abound in all aspects of social life. The superpower relationship of "mutual deterrence" is a case in point. In fact, most relations between nations can be seen as bargaining situations, as well as such everyday situations as maneuvering a car in a traffic jam or trying to get your partner to follow you through the intricate figures of a tango.

The words "bargaining" and "negotiation" are frequently used interchangeably. In our analysis, however, we shall maintain a distinction between them. The term "negotiation" has a more narrow denotation than "bargaining."[9]

Negotiation refers to a formalized and explicit process, representing just one of several ways in which a bargaining situation may be resolved. Thus, negotiation is but one aspect of bargaining which we may call *explicit bargaining*.

However, we may speak of a bargaining process even when the parties do not sit down at a negotiation table to exchange proposals; when communication is incomplete or indirect. Bargaining may, in fact, be tacit, involving non-verbal acts, in which case "adversaries watch and interpret each other's behavior, each aware that his own actions are being interpreted and anticipated, each acting with a view to the expectations that he creates."[10]

It should be noted that tacit and explicit bargaining are not thoroughly separable concepts.[11] We may find various gradations from completely tacit bargaining up through types of incomplete or indirect communication to the full and direct communication of model negotiations.

We shall be dealing with international negotiations, a special case of social negotiations in that they involve two or more complex social units. It is important to keep in mind that negotiations between nations constitute only part of the manifold relations between those nations. In game-theoretical jargon, an international negotiation is a phase vaguely related to a never-ending "supergame."[12]

This has several implications. One which is significant in this context is that proposals put forward in an international negotiation may represent not an attempt to reach agreement but rather a move in this larger "supergame" or in parallel "subgames." This is, for instance, what Iklé has in mind when he refers to "negotiating for side-effects" such as propaganda or intelligence.[13]

DECISION MAKING IN BARGAINING SITUATIONS

Game theory presupposes rational decision making. Each actor is assumed to make utility x probability calculations and maximize utility. To "game-theoretical man" this means striving for the best possible utility payoff when taking into consideration that the other actor is trying to do exactly the same thing. In zero-sum games this leads to the well-known "minimax" solution: each actor chooses the alternative that involves the least loss if the worst possible outcome should occur; or, from another point of view, maximizes his minimum gain.

The game-theoretical notion of rationality proves problematic from many aspects. First, "rationality" is no simple, straightforward notion. As the environment becomes increasingly complex, more and more sophisticated concepts enter into the definition of rationality.[14] For instance, the appealingly simple criterion of utility maximization undergoes minor modifications and reappears as the "minimax" principle for denoting rationality in zero-sum games. The "minimax" principle applies only to a restricted class of games, and as we move to the complex variable-sum or "mixed-motive" games which best correspond to bargaining situations, no satisfactory definition of rationality, no unequivocal rationality criterion can be given.[15]

There is another problematic aspect of the rationality concept: Does it help us in empirical analysis? It seems that either one needs an omniscient observer, or one has to assume that what the actor selects is always the most rational alternative. Yet this is a circular definition of rationality.[16]

The "rational" actor of game theory is assumed to have perfect knowledge. In order to make a rational choice he must identify the payoffs of both actors. That is, in addition to perceiving all alternative choices available to him and considering all possible outcomes of these choices, he must also know all the constituent elements of the opponent's calculus. Needless to say, these conditions are rarely, if ever, met in real-life bargaining situations. If human imperfection sets a limit to the actor's ability to compute alternative courses of action, the relationship of interdependence introduces an even greater degree of uncertainty. Neither the utilities nor the probabilities the opponent assigns to different outcomes are, as a rule, known to the actor.

Disavowing the assumption of rationality is, of course, not equivalent to accepting an assumption of nonrationality. The only alternative is then to navigate between the Scylla of rationality and the Charybdis of nonrationality. That these are perilous waters has been demonstrated by Snyder whose foreign policy decision-making approach has been criticized both for positing the decision-making process as too rational and for exaggerating the irrationality of the process.[17] Nevertheless, we shall adopt Snyder's assumption of *purposeful behavior*—that activities are more or less explicitly motivated and behavior is not random.[18] This concept is closely related to Simon's notion of "bounded rationality."[19]

Both formulations rest on the observation that the decision-maker has limited intellectual capabilities, limited sources of information, and limited resources which can be allocated to a policy problem. His decisions are based on his considering as best he can a limited number of alternative courses of action.

Any decision, then, includes an element of selection. In contrast to the comprehensive–rational method of game theory, which requires the actor to approach each new problem with a *tabula rasa* and to take into account all aspects of the problem, this approach proposes that the actor possesses a subjective cognitive system, or a system of *images*.

An image can be defined as the organized representation of an object or a situation in an actor's cognitive system.[20] These images, built up as a result of the actor's past experience, include descriptive and evaluative dimensions—images of what has been, what is, and what will be, as well as images of what ought to be.

The system of images serves as a kind of mental and emotional filter, which mediates and orders incoming messages. It determines the actor's focus of attention (what will be perceived?) as well as his interpretation (how will it be perceived?), and it affects the actor's perception both of events and of alternatives open to him.[21]

Whereas game theory tends to postulate an objective reality, this approach assumes multiple subjective realities. It further implies a departure from the simple and unambiguous game-theoretical assumption of perfect knowledge. Uncertainty, following from imperfect knowledge, is regarded as a key element in decision making in bargaining situations.[22] As pointed out earlier, such uncertainty applies especially to the elements of the opponent's calculus.

The supposedly measurable utility/probability dichotomy of game theory is thus replaced by the not as readily quantifiable image concept with mutually interdependent descriptive as well as evaluative and affective components. Either class of components is capable of affecting the other. The principle of *cognitive consonance*[23] further states that such an interrelationship is characterized by a "psychological stress toward consistency."[24] It is, for example, cognitively inconsistent for us to think of people we dislike and distrust making honest, conciliatory moves.

Besides trying to reduce cognitive dissonance when it occurs, an actor may actively avoid or suppress information that might create dissonance.[25] In short, the stress toward cognitive consonance can provide either "occasions for distortion and denial" or "opportunities for learning."[26]

It should be added that an actor may hold inconsistent images without discomfort if he is not compelled to attend to the discrepancy, though he may eventually find himself in a situation that impels him to cope with his image system inconsistencies. Which of the discordant images will then be evoked depends on the contingencies of the situation. A person may, for instance, perceive darkness as both frightening and peaceful. If this person is on his way home through dark streets from a movie, either of the two incompatible images may be evoked depending on whether he has seen a thriller or a comedy.[27]

Cognitive complexity, which normally includes some tolerance of ambiguity and moderately inconsistent images, is usually regarded as conducive to better reality orientation and receptivity to new information, and thus as positively related to an actor's willingness and ability to negotiate.[28]

In the context of bargaining, three types of images seem salient: image of self, image of the opponent, and image of the event or situation being the subject of bargaining (such as arms policy).[29] Decision making involves prediction, and the decision-maker has to act in terms of what "will be" when his act is expected to take effect. In order to do so he must assume a certain consistency in himself and others. Thus, his images of the future, his *expectations*, represent a kind of moving average of past experience projected into the future.[30]

To sum up, our approach represents a movement away from the "objective" world of mathematics in the direction of the "subjective" world of psychology—a substitution of "psycho-logic" for pure logic.

IMAGE AND IDEOLOGY

Images are not the same thing as ideologies, although the concepts are not entirely unrelated. Drawing on the Soviet example, Brzezinski defines ideology as

. . . an action program suitable for mass consumption, derived from certain doctrinal assumptions about the general nature of the dynamics of social reality, and combining some assertions about the inadequacies of the past and/or present with some explicit guides to action for improving the situation and some notions of the desired eventual state of affairs.[31]

As this definition suggests, ideology performs diverse functions. We may distinguish a cognitive function, serving as an "analytical prism,"[32] and a normative function, providing specific policy prescriptions, a "guide to action." In these respects, ideology coincides with images.

But ideology performs additional functions, one of which is to furnish a common political language. Still another related function is legitimation: to legitimize the regime and justify or rationalize changes in policy.[33]

Several students of Soviet ideology maintain that the symbolic and legitimizing functions are becoming relatively more significant than the cognitive and normative ones. In the contemporary world Soviet decision-makers are faced with a host of questions where ideology provides no, or incomplete, cognitive maps and "guides to action."[34]

Yet because Soviet ideology carries a "quasi-religious" aura, allusions to ideology are necessary components of all political moves. For example, Zimmerman notes that, during the Khrushchev era, Soviet specialists on international relations, rather than letting Lenin do their thinking for them, found they could utilize Lenin to legitimate their thinking no matter how un-Leninist those thoughts may be.[35]

Sometimes ideology has to be expanded by extrapolating new principles from old ones or even to be revised in order to justify current policy. We can speak of a kind of "dialectical" relationship between an ideologically oriented party and reality. The ideological party attempts to change reality, and its image of the changed reality may require an adaptation of the ideology.[36] Ideological tenets are, however, not changed at will with retained credibility.

We can think of ideology and images as partly overlapping entities (Figure 1).[37] On the one hand, some images are not manifested in the ideology, such as when a new image has not (yet) caused any corresponding revision or extension of the ideology. On the other hand, some ideological tenets do not represent current images but serve only symbolic and legitimating functions.

The extent to which images and ideology overlap varies with issues and individuals. An analysis by Triska and Finley, for example, suggests that the impact of ideology is greater on long-term

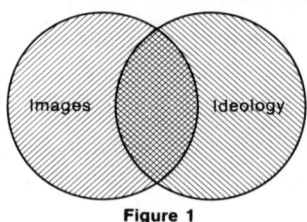

Figure 1

than on short-term questions, and that the images of older Soviet leaders are determined to a greater degree by ideology than images of younger leaders.[38]

The mutual Soviet and Chinese charges of "dogmatism" and "revisionism" respectively indicate that the role of ideology in Soviet and Chinese images may also differ. From our viewpoint, the twin Communist sins of "dogmatism" and "revisionism" can be schematically depicted (Figure 2).

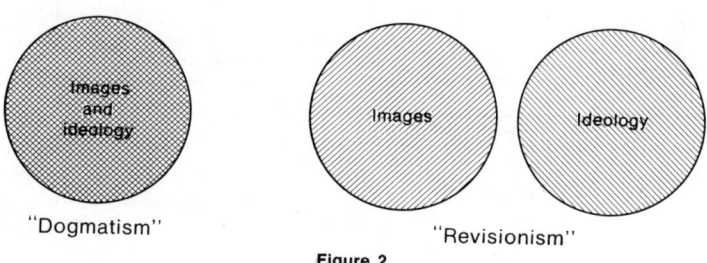

"Dogmatism"   "Revisionism"
Figure 2

THE BARGAINING PROCESS

Each actor comes to the bargaining process with certain initial expectations, and as soon as bargaining begins each actor is in a position to test his initial expectations. This mechanism can be represented schematically as a "closed loop system." (Figure 3).[39]

In this model the decisional output from one of the actors serves as informational input into the other actor's decision-making system. Insofar as expectations are adjusted we may speak of a dynamic process, comparable to a learning process.[40] In the light of his current expectations, actor A makes a decision. This decision is used by actor B to test and either validate or modify his expectations. Actor B's decision, made on the basis of his validated or modified expectation, is then taken into account by actor A who in turn uses it to test his initial expectations, and so on.

Each actor's decision has the double function of (a) influencing the other actor's behavior, and (b) communicating and/or hiding information about his own expectations. A few comments on the character of these decisions—or "moves" as they will be called in the following—seem warranted.

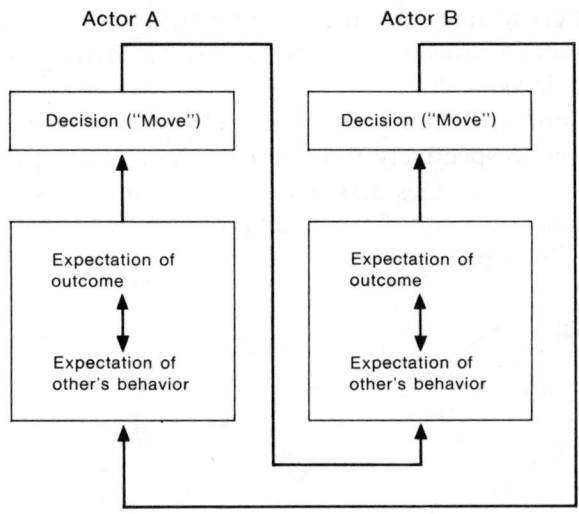

Figure 3

BARGAINING "MOVES"

From such parlor games as chess, game theory has borrowed the notion of "moves" to denote the sequential acts of players, which are the units in the players' respective strategies. In chess, a move means changing the position of one of the pieces according to given rules. In negotiations, the typical move consists of an explicit *proposal*, backed up by some kind of *arguments*.

Proposals and counterproposals are exchanged. Revision of a previous proposal so that it more closely approximates the other actor's position is usually referred to as a *concession*. On the other hand, a *retraction* is a proposal further removed from the other actor's position than the previous proposal.[41] Since negotiations involve both cooperative and competitive dimensions, "concessions" and "retractions" can not always be unequivocally defined, and disputes whether a revision of position should be regarded as a concession or as a retraction are not uncommon in negotiations. A proposal may also represent a combination of concession and retraction. This is very common in so-called package proposals.[42]

Arguments have the double function of revealing one's own

expectations and attempting to modify the other actor's expectations. They represent efforts to convince the other actor, to make him see things as one sees them; in other words, to induce him to adopt one's image.[43]

In addition to submitting proposals and arguments, bargaining actors may employ what Schelling calls *strategic moves*. A strategic move is a move that induces the other actor to choose in one's favor. It constrains the other actor's choice by affecting his expectations of one's own behavior.[44]

A strategic move frequently used is the *commitment*. Schelling describes the art of commitment as "the power to bind oneself."[45] A commitment is a move to underscore one's current proposal by making it more difficult to yield from it. An actor, in making a commitment, eliminates some of the choices open to him.

Commitments may be either *unconditional* or *conditional*. Troops, burning the bridges behind them, display their determination to fight by physically excluding a retreat. Negotiators may try to convince their opponents that a binding public opinion at home renders a change in position impossible. In both instances, unconditional commitments are employed.

Conditional commitments make one's course of action contingent on what the other actor does. Commitments are made to the other actor, and are controlled by the other actor; they imply a relinquishment of the initiative and may take the form of *threats* or *promises*.

Conditional commitments may, in turn, be backed up by unconditional commitments to demonstrate sincerity and resolve. A state threatening war puts its armed forces on the alert. In older times, the exchange of hostages served as commitments to promises. Similarly, threats and promises in negotiations can be emphasized, for example, by publication.

Conditional commitments also include *warnings* and *encouragements*—the "weaker" counterparts of threats and promises. "If you choose *a*, the *natural* consequences will be *b*" expresses either a warning or an encouragement, when *b* to the other actor is respectively undesirable or desirable. The difference between warnings and encouragements on the one hand, and threats and promises on the other hand, thus lies in the role played by their initiators in the causation of the predicted consequences.[46]

A few general observations about commitments should be noted in this connection. First, strong commitments typically consist of both verbal statements and nonverbal acts; in other words, of both explicit and tacit bargaining. Thus, commitments exceed the borderline dividing negotiations from other forms of bargaining, according to our initial distinctions.

Second, not only must a commitment be *communicated* but *made credible* as well. A commitment will be ineffective if it is possible for the other actor to be unavailable for messages or to destroy the communication channels. For example, children are skilled at avoiding the receipt of a warning glance from a parent, knowing that if they perceive it the parent is obliged to punish noncompliance. In negotiations where records are kept, the receipt of verbal communication cannot be avoided. But a communication problem still exists, since there is no simple, universal, unequivocal way for persons or nations to assume commitments.[47]

If a commitment is communicated, the problem of *credibility* still remains. Whether or not a commitment will be believed by the other actor depends on a number of factors. In the first place, the verbal component of a commitment conveys varying degrees of *finality* (cf. for instance the conditional commitments "if you do *a*, I shall undoubtedly do *b*" and "if you do *a*, I might very well do *b*") and *specificity* (cf. "if you attack Berlin, I shall strike back at Moscow" and "if you do something rash, I shall respond in kind").[48] The point is that any loopholes you leave yourself, if they are visible to the other actor, reduce the credibility of the commitment.[49]

Further, the other actor may assess your proposals in terms of *continuity* (do your proposals show some similarity over time?) and *consistency* (are all your proposals on this occasion or over a period of time compatible and not contradictory?).[50]

The other actor's assessment of the credibility of your commitment is to a large extent determined by his image of your behavior. Does he see you as *reliable*? That is, does his past experience of your behavior lead him to conclude that you usually mean what you say? In other words, what is your "bargaining reputation" with him?[51]

In the event of threats and promises, the other actor also estimates whether you have the *capability* to carry out the threatened or promised action.[52] The *internal cohesion* of a collective actor, such as a state, may also enter into the other actor's credibility estimate. A commitment apparently reflecting a broad consensus within the actor is assumed to be more credible than a commitment about which there is visible internal disagreement.[53]

A final observation concerns the loss of flexibility which follows from incurring a commitment. The committed actor runs the risk of establishing an immovable position and thereby provoking the likelihood of stalemate or breakdown.[54] In order to retain flexibility, a committed actor needs to find ways of *abandoning his commitment* without affecting negatively the credibility of his future commitments. A concession may mark a prior commitment as a fraud, and make the other actor skeptical of any new pretense at commitment. Hence, abandonment of a commitment is usually accompanied with a rationalized reinterpretation of the original commitment. As a rule, this involves references to changes in the situation brought about either by external events or by developments internal to the negotiating process, such as changes in the other actor's argumentation or changes in the relationship between the actors.

This technique of "casuistry" (to adopt a term used by Schelling) can also be used to *release the other actor from a commitment*. In that case, one must seek a rationalization by which to deny oneself too great a reward from the other actor's abandonment of his commitment to make it easier for him to make a concession. Conversely, it might sometimes be in one's interest to *convince the other actor that he has made a commitment* although he himself denies that he is committed.[55]

In brief, various possible components of an actor's commitment tactics are discernible. To begin with, *his own commitments* must be communicated and made credible to the other actor. Further, the actor may use "casuistry" to release himself from a commitment already made to retain flexibility without losing credibility.

In addition to this, he can make efforts to influence *the other actor's commitments*. Two conceivable situations are to the point: (1) when he does not want the other actor to be committed, but the other actor either has already made or is expected to make a commitment; and (2) when he wants the other actor to be committed, but the other actor has not made or is not expected to make any commitment. In the first case, he must convince the other actor that a commitment is not or will not be received and/or believed; in the other case, he must convince the other actor that, in his view, a commitment has been received and believed.

A NOTE ON MATERIAL AND METHOD

The test ban negotiations are exceptionally well documented. Verbatim records are available from all the forums in which the test ban was negotiated with the single exception of the final Moscow talks in July 1963. These verbatim records constitute the main source for our first level of analysis.

The analyses of intra-bloc and internal bargaining are based mainly on Chinese and Soviet press material and official documents. Although it is not possible to point to any formal, explicit negotiations on the test ban issue between the Soviet Union and China or within the USSR, our contention is that the intra-bloc and internal aspects of decision making on this issue can be viewed as bargaining processes of a semi-tacit nature. The moves of the parties were indirectly and incompletely communicated—by way of *"esoteric communication,"* a well-documented phenomenon in Communist intercourse.[56] Messages often have deeper meanings than the manifest content and are directed to other than the ostensible audiences. This means that the "esoteric" moves in Sino–Soviet intra-bloc bargaining and Soviet internal bargaining pose the same type of decoding problems as the moves in diplomatic negotiations.

The verbal statements of an actor in a bargaining situation

raise the same validity problem for the researcher as for the other bargaining actor. "Does he mean what he says, and does he say what he means?"

The researcher—as well as the receiver of the communication—must make inferences at two levels.[57] First, he must determine what message the actor is trying to convey. He runs the double risk of either overlooking significant nuances of the message or overestimating its significance and finding hidden meanings where there are none. We can, for instance, recall Metternich's reputed reaction to the death of a Russian ambassador: "I wonder what he meant by that."[58]

Second, both the researcher and the receiver must estimate whether the message is to be believed or taken as deception. The researcher thus faces a credibility problem which is parallel to that of the bargaining actors. Just as there is no sure way for an actor to make a commitment credible, there is no unequivocal criterion by which the researcher—or another actor—can make credibility estimations.

Insofar as written documentation constitutes the basis of our analysis, our method can be called content analysis, with the qualifying addition that it is *qualitative* rather than *quantitative*.

Our previous discussion of the credibility problem points to the need of taking noncontent contextual factors into account. The ordering of the different parts of the message as well as the time of the communication and the events preceding and accompanying it may be highly relevant in reconstructing the meaning which the actor intended to convey.[59]

The dangers of making inferences on the basis of frequencies are particularly conspicuous in bargaining situations, since repetition is a commitment technique, to be manipulated by the actors. It could even be argued that there is often a negative correlation between frequency and importance in bargaining. Assertions rarely used and not expected have greater impact than "debased" frequent assertions.[60] *Changes* in assertions rather than their frequencies are of main interest, for bargaining is a process of gradual and often subtle adjustments.

TWO

The Test Ban Negotiations: An Overview

IN ORDER to provide a basis for the subsequent analysis of Soviet bargaining behavior, this chapter will give some background information about the test ban negotiations generally, and Soviet moves in particular.[1]

THE BARGAINING SITUATION

The accelerated tempo of nuclear testing in the mid-1950s was one of the more dramatic symptoms of an emerging *technological* arms race, focusing on what is called in civil life "product improvement" rather than multiplication of existing weapons.[2] Nuclear weapon tests played a significant role in this "product improvement."

Testing can affect the development of nuclear weapons by facilitating changes in two crucial ratios. First, an increase in the *yield-to-weight* ratio would mean lighter weapons with increased accuracy; necessary, for example, for the development of antiballistic missiles (ABM) and tactical nuclear weapons. Second, a decrease in the *fission-to-fusion* ratio would reduce the amount of radioactive fallout. A fission reaction produces a large amount of intensely radioactive byproducts, whereas a fusion reaction does not. In thermonuclear weapons a fission reaction is used as a "trigger" to detonate a fusion reaction. By minimizing the proportion of explosive energy derived from fission, "cleaner" bombs could be developed and the unequivocal line between nuclear and conventional weapons would become blurred.

A ban on nuclear testing would be one possible way to control the technological arms race. In other words, such a ban would constitute an *arms control* measure.[3] In what respect did the test ban issue in the mid-1950s represent a *bargaining situation?* To simplify, the two main actors, the United States and the USSR, had two basic options: either to continue testing and thus accelerate the arms race, or to control the arms race to a certain extent by discontinuing nuclear tests. This mutual twofold choice resembles the well-known mixed-motive game called "prisoner's dilemma" (Figure 4).

Prisoner's Dilemma

	U.S. stop testing	U.S. continue testing
USSR stop testing	+1 / +1	+2 / −2
USSR continue testing	−2 / +2	−1 / −1

Figure 4

Each actor is assumed to reason as follows: If I continue testing, I may preclude lagging behind my opponent in weapons development and I might even come out ahead. On the other hand, continued testing promises to be costly in terms of absorbing resources that could be used elsewhere, and it does not safeguard me against a technological breakthrough by my opponent. These drawbacks probably outweigh the possible gains in security derived from continued testing.

If, however, I cease testing and my opponent continues, I shall be worse off, because then my opponent will reap the gains of new weapon developments while I lag behind. A mutual agreement to stop testing would alleviate the economic burden and also the fear of technological breakthrough. In addition, it might make it harder for other states to acquire and try out nuclear weapons.

In other words, the nuclear testing issue involved common as well as divergent interests and interdependent decisions. Among the mutual benefits of a test ban, the following were emphasized by U.S. and Soviet spokesmen:

—reducing the danger of radioactive fallout;
—impeding further development and improvement of nuclear weapons;
—preventing the accession of nuclear weapons by additional states;
—contributing to détente and facilitating further disarmament measures;
—alleviating the economic burden of the arms race.[4]

While the United States and the Soviet Union were aware of their common interest in test cessation, they expressed differing opinions over the details of such an agreement from the time the test ban question became the focus of attention. To mention but two basic points at issue, the United States originally advocated an internationally controlled test ban as part of a broader agreement on disarmament, whereas the Soviet Union spoke in favor of a separate test ban and denied the need for international control.[5]

The interdependence of American and Soviet decisions is illustrated by the prisoner's dilemma matrix. A unilateral choice by either actor could have either positive or negative consequences depending on the other actor's choice, and the best course of action for either actor depends on the other actor's behavior.

THE NEGOTIATIONS

Nuclear disarmament had since 1946 been the subject of several international conferences, although it would be an exaggeration to say that serious, detailed negotiation had taken place. Disarmament proposals were initially focused on banning the *production* and *use* of nuclear weapons. Testing was seen as an intermediary stage between research and production and did not at that time attract any significant interest.[6]

The year 1954 may be considered the watershed of the nuclear test ban issue. In March that year the United States conducted a noted thermonuclear test on the Bikini Atoll which caused unexpectedly widespread radioactive fallout affecting in particular the crew of a Japanese fishing boat. The dramatic "Bikini incident" added fuel to widespread anxiety about fallout and crystallized attitudes long germinating in several countries.

The Soviet Union was the first nuclear power to incorporate test suspension into its disarmament proposals. The Soviet scheme for comprehensive disarmament of May 10, 1955, included discontinuance of tests in its first stage, and in the spring of 1956 the Soviet Union proposed a test ban as a separate measure independent of any agreement on other disarmament problems.

In 1957 the test ban issue was first debated between the Soviet Union and the Western powers in the UN Subcommittee of the Disarmament Commission.[7] No agreement was reached, and nuclear tests continued at an accelerated rate throughout 1957.

On March 31, 1958, the Soviet Union unilaterally suspended testing, calling on the Western powers to follow suit, but reserving the right to resume testing should the Western powers do so. The United States and Great Britain at the end of April initiated the most intense test program that had occurred up to that time. In his correspondence with Premier Khrushchev, President Eisenhower drew attention to the fact that this series of tests had been announced for a long time and further proposed that technicians from both sides should study the specific control measures necessary for an agreement on the limitation or suspension of testing. Khrushchev reluctantly agreed to such a conference.

Experts from the United States, Canada, France, and Great Britain conferred with experts from the Soviet Union, Poland, Czechoslovakia, and Rumania at Geneva from July 1 to August 21, 1958. After discussions, which forced the scientists into the role of negotiators, the experts agreed on a report. The establishment of a workable and effective control system was considered technically feasible. In an exchange of notes immediately after the experts' conference, the governments of the United States, Great Britain, and the Soviet Union agreed to begin negotiations at Geneva on October 31, 1958, in an effort to reach agreement on the discontinuance of nuclear weapon tests on the basis of the experts' report.

There were three distinguishable stages in the test ban negotiations: the first extending from the outset of the political negotiations until the fall of 1960, the second until late 1962, and the third until the signing of the Moscow treaty on August 5, 1963. This delineation of periods hinges on two key events in Soviet–American relations: The U-2 incident in May 1960 and the Cuban missile crisis in October 1962. Though basically unrelated to the test ban issue, these events had a considerable impact on the test ban negotiations, as will be analyzed in further detail later.

Stage I

Controversies over procedural matters seem to haunt international negotiations, from the half-year long dispute on the order in which the delegates should enter and be seated at the Peace of Westphalia in 1648, to the tenacious discussions on the shape of the negotiation table for the Vietnam peace talks in 1968. The test ban negotiations had their share of procedural controversy. First, there was disagreement over the name of the conference. The USSR spoke of test "cessation" as the subject to be discussed; the United States employed the term "suspension." As their choice of words suggests, the Soviet Union anticipated a permanent, the United States a temporary test ban. A non-controversial solution to the terminological issue was found in an informal discussion after the first meeting when agreement was reached on the neutral word "discontinuance." Differences remained, however, on the underlying issue of the duration of the treaty.

A second procedural controversy, which required ten meetings to settle, arose on the agenda of the conference. The Soviet Union proposed an agenda according to which an agreement to discontinue nuclear testing would first be concluded and a control system discussed afterwards. The Western powers advocated the opposite order. The deadlock was broken in an informal meeting, when both sides agreed to a "rotating agenda." The conference would deal with the topics proposed by each side in alternating two-day periods. In the future course of the negotiations, this arrangement was quietly abandoned, and each side brought up proposals or discussed issues raised by the other side as it pleased.

In reality, control questions became the focus of attention during this first stage of negotiations. One main reason for this was the U.S. introduction of "new seismic data" in January 1959, challenging the findings of the experts' conference. These data, obtained from a series of underground tests in Nevada, indicated that it was more difficult to distinguish earthquakes from underground nuclear explosions than had previously been assumed. The number of annual unidentified earthquakes which would generate a seismic signal equivalent to that of a 5-kiloton explosion was now thought to be 1,500 instead of the 20–100 mentioned in the experts' report. In addition, the United States later in 1959 brought the "decoupling" theory into the negotiations, according to which one could muffle or "decouple" underground explosions by conducting them in large cavities, thus making detection extremely difficult.

The Soviet reaction was firmly negative. The USSR emphasized that the negotiations had an agreed basis in the experts' report. Accusing the United States of going back on its previous agreement, the Soviet chief negotiator, Mr. Tsarapkin, repeatedly stated that, as far as his country was concerned, invalidating the experts' report was out of the question.

The controversy over the "new seismic data" had an impact on a number of outstanding agenda items. The purported difficulty of detecting and identifying underground tests implied the necessity of increasing the *number of control posts* and/or the *number of inspections*. Negotiations on the *comprehensiveness* of the treaty were also affected, since one way of getting around the difficulties related to underground tests was to leave such tests out of the treaty.

Although the United States did, in fact, propose a partial ban not including low-yield underground tests, and did induce the USSR to make concessions in that direction, a comprehensive treaty was the focus of Soviet negotiators for the major part of this first period.

The Soviet Union initially envisaged a tripartite, comprehensive test ban treaty of unlimited duration and without conditions. This was not significantly altered by its concessions in regard to peaceful detonations and a partial treaty combined with a moratorium on low-yield underground tests. The acceptance of U.S. demands to leave peaceful detonations out of the treaty was circumscribed by such safeguards as to eliminate any tests with the remotest military significance, and the Soviet proposal for a moratorium included such provisions as to exclude the possibility of test resumption at the expiration of the moratorium.

Control questions have over the years been notorious stumbling blocks in Soviet-American disarmament and arms control negotiations. In June 1957 while at the London Disarmament Conference, Soviet negotiators agreed for the first time to control over a test ban, and the experts' report was the first recorded agreement on international control in the history of East–West arms control negotiations.

The controversy over control in the test ban negotiations centered around two crucial and interrelated questions: (1) Should there be *national* or *international* control? (2) Should the control system be based on *reciprocity* or *impartiality?*

At the outset of the political test ban negotiations, the USSR took pains to demonstrate that it preferred national control and that it had already made a major concession by accepting the experts' report and would not allow any control beyond that recommended by the experts.

The Soviet Union adamantly refused to accept the U.S. proposal for dealing with control as the first item on the agenda: "The control system will depend on the kind of decision we take on the question of the cessation of tests, and not vice versa."[8]

Time and again Mr. Tsarapkin declared that international control was conceivable only within the framework of a comprehensive, permanent test ban. Often this took the form of warnings or threats (if no comprehensive and permanent ban, then no agreement on control).

Soviet expectations of outcome could thus be summarized as a degree of international control (a) which did not transcend the experts' recommendations, and (b) which operated within the parameters of a comprehensive, permanent test ban. Behind this lay apparent Soviet expectations that the United States (a) wanted more international control than envisaged by the experts, and (b) wanted this possibly for intelligence purposes.

Soviet suspicions of U.S. intentions to seek more extensive control than already agreed upon, reflected in insinuations early in the negotiations, were strengthened by the U.S. introduction of the "new seismic data." On the whole, however, the Soviet Union showed considerable restraint in dealing with the intelligence aspect of control. The United States was hardly ever openly accused of being motivated by intelligence aims, either at the negotiation table or in the Soviet press.

A control system may be based on two principles. One is the principle of *impartial* verification by persons who are expected not to favor a principal party to the agreement. The second approach might be termed the *reciprocal* principle, which is applicable particularly when there are two parties to the agreement. In that case, the two parties control each other, and each party determines whether the other party is living up to the agreement.[9]

In the test ban negotiations the United States proceeded from the impartial approach, the Soviet Union from the reciprocal approach.

When we speak of controlling one another, there is no question of impartiality; partiality is of the essence. . . . To see that another Power does not violate the treaty or secure a military advantage . . . means, of course, to be in the highest degree partial in the operation of control.[10]

Soviet expectations of outcome, derived from the principle of reciprocity, could be summarized as (a) East–West parity in all facets of the control organization with (b) minimal involvement of countries other than the original parties, especially nonaligned ones. The United States was expected (a) to strive for superiority within the control organization, (b) possibly with the help of third countries.

As for the proposed Control Commission, the Soviet Union persisted in its demand for an equal number of seats for the two sides and decisions by unanimity. Having initially questioned the need to include additional countries in the Commission, the USSR never went beyond one seat for nonaligned countries. The insistent U.S. demands for numerical plurality in combination with majority decisions reinforced Soviet expectations that the United States was trying to gain superiority and put the USSR in a minority position.[11]

The Soviet Union saw the demanded veto in the Commission as the weapon of the minority, a means to achieve parity. This was manifested in its professed willingness to give up the veto in return for a composition of the Commission that would safeguard East–West parity.

In brief, Soviet expectations of parity and minimal third-country involvement provided a rather broad settlement range with leeway for concessions, but expectations of U.S. behavior made the USSR alert, and perhaps oversensitive, to any arrangement that could, in one way or another, tip the balance in favor of the West and put the Soviet Union in an inferior position.

At any rate, during the initial stage of the test ban talks control aspects were negotiated in greater detail than ever before, and unprecedented rapprochement occurred. Despite the differences generated by the "new seismic data" mutual concessions were made on several agenda items. Agreement was reached on a preamble, seventeen articles, and one annex for the prospective treaty. Several of these were of a purely formal nature, others had greater substance. On virtually all the outstanding issues a narrowing down of the initial differences was accomplished during this period.

The negotiations took place against the background of a voluntary moratorium on nuclear testing by the three participating states. To be sure, the Soviet Union did carry out some test explosions just after the opening of negotiations in Geneva, following the intensive series of U.S.–British tests earlier in 1958.

However, after November 3, 1958, the USSR suspended testing. On the eve of the conference, President Eisenhower stated:

[I]n order to facilitate the detailed negotiations the United States is prepared, unless testing is resumed by the Soviet Union, to withhold further testing on its part of atomic and hydrogen weapons for a period of one year from the beginning of the negotiations.[12]

The Soviet tests in November did not elicit any U.S. test resumption. At the expiration of the one-year commitment, President Eisenhower on December 29, 1959 issued the following ambiguous statement:

> Although we consider ourselves free to resume nuclear weapons testing, we shall not resume nuclear weapons tests without announcing our intention in advance of any resumption. During the period of voluntary suspension of nuclear weapons tests the United States will continue its active program of weapon research, development and laboratory-type experimentation.[13]

Much Soviet criticism was directed against this statement. Yet the USSR reiterated its commitment not to resume testing unless the West did.

Stage II

On May 1, 1960, an American U-2 plane on an intelligence mission was shot down over Sverdlovsk. The scheduled summit meeting in Paris was wrecked even before it had begun. Reverberations of the ensuing crisis in Soviet–American relations were gradually to be discerned in the test ban negotiations. The impact was first felt as a standstill in the negotiations. Very few proposals and no concessions were exchanged during the latter half of 1960. Instead, much time was spent on arguments about whose was the next move, with each side accusing the other of rigidity. Simultaneously, the marked Soviet optimism just before the U-2 incident evaporated.

On April 14, Mr. Tsarapkin spoke of "the favourable atmosphere which now distinguishes the recent stage of our negotiations from their earlier stages." He added: "We consider that our optimism here is not excessive but well grounded in the facts of the present stage of our negotiations."[14] On June 2, the tone was different: "Over the past year—since May 1959 down to the present—the results of our work has been almost nil."[15]

On December 5, 1960, the Geneva conference went into recess for almost four months. As negotiations were resumed, the Soviet Union began making retractions. First, it proposed that the chief executive officer of the control organization should be replaced by a "troika" modeled on the 1960 proposal for reorganization of the UN Secretariat. The Soviet Union also began hinting at solving the test ban issue within the framework of general and complete disarmament (GCD). A formal proposal to that end was submitted by Khrushchev at the Vienna summit meeting in June 1961. The Soviet Union furthermore demanded that France be included in the negotiations and wanted to make the entry into force of a treaty conditional on the signature of France.

The deteriorating negotiation climate, fomented further with imperfectly veiled Soviet threats to break up the conference, suffered a final blow on August 30, 1961, when the USSR resumed nuclear weapon tests. After an unsuccessful U.S.–British attempt to achieve at least a nationally controlled ban on atmospheric tests, both Western powers resumed testing, and the test ban conference on January 29, 1962 adjourned *sine die*. A period of intensive testing ensued. From September 1961 through 1962 more than 170 nuclear tests were conducted by the nuclear powers. This figure should be seen in relation to the pre-1961 total of approximately 280 tests.[16]

The test ban issue was transferred to the Eighteen-Nation Committee on Disarmament (ENDC) which convened at Geneva on March 14, 1962.[17] The ENDC established a subcommittee to consider the test ban issue, consisting of the three former negotiation partners, the United States, the USSR, and Great Britain. Both sides initially repeated their old positions, and the Soviet reluctance to consider a separate test ban continued. In an effort to accelerate the negotiations, the eight nonaligned members of the ENDC submitted a joint memorandum outlining the main provisions of a prospective test ban treaty. In informal discussions prior to the formal presentation, both the U.S. and the Soviet delegation reacted to the memorandum with "vigorous opposition."[18] In the ENDC, they duly welcomed the initiative. The text of the memorandum was deliberately ambiguous and resulted in an "exercise in exegesis,"[19] where both sides took the memorandum to vindicate their respective positions.

During *stage I* the Soviet Union was apparently ready to accept the amount of international control recommended by the experts. However, when the Western powers in connection with the Soviet test resumption in September 1961, made a proposal for a nationally controlled ban on atmospheric tests, this was by the USSR taken as a pretext for proposing that national control should apply to all tests except underground ones, later including also these.

Although the U.S.-British proposal served as a pretext, the Soviet shift seems to have been associated with the strengthening of Soviet military defense following the U-2 incident. The four-year program of U.S. air reconnaissance had demonstrated Soviet vulnerability, and had also cast doubts on Soviet ICBM claims. It was becoming increasingly clear that the Soviet Union had not built up its missile force at the pace it had claimed.[20] In the wake of the U-2 incident, Soviet references to its strategic missile capabilities fell far short of the extreme claims of late 1959 and early 1960, and by the fall of 1961, U.S. estimates of the number of operational Soviet ICBMs amounted to 3.5 percent of the 1959 estimate.[21]

In 1961, the Soviet Union announced the first explicit increases in defense spending since 1955. The relationship between the renewed emphasis on defense in the wake of the U-2 incident and the renouncement of international control was alluded to in the ENDC, when Mr. Zorin characterized USSR opposition to international control as "one of the measures for the defense of its security,"[22] and said, "Security considerations demanded that we gave preference to the idea of national control."[23]

The Soviet image of international control over a comprehensive ban was also revised in *stage II* to comprise international control only within the framework of GCD. This revision was first manifested in Khrushchev's proposal at the Vienna summit meeting in June 1961, for solving the test ban issue and GCD conjointly. It was also reflected in the Soviet September 1961 proposal for a nationally controlled partial treaty combined with a moratorium on underground tests "until agreement is reached on a system of control over underground explosions *as a constituent part of an international system of control over the implementation of a programme of general and complete disarmament.*"[24]

The revisions in Soviet expectations of outcome seem to have been founded on changing expectations of U.S. behavior. The classical charges that the United States was seeking "control without disarmament" made their entry into the negotiations, and the ambiguity over possible U.S. intelligence motives disappeared. American control schemes were now characterized as a "demand for the establishment of a system of international intelligence, of international espionage in the territory of the Soviet Union and certain other states."[25]

Equating control in circumstances short of GCD with espionage became a prominent Soviet theme both in the negotiations and in the press. Soviet suspicions of U.S. intelligence aims, accumulated in disarmament negotiations and vindicated by Eisenhower's "open skies" proposal, were reinforced by the U-2 incident.[26]

During *stage I* the Soviet Union had showed willingness to add some elements of impartiality to its reciprocal model of a control organization, and had made concessions to that effect. Soviet expectations in *stage II* apparently changed to comprise strict application of reciprocity: "Only if both sides take part *in each control operation at all levels, in all sections of the control system*, can impartial, objective and fair investigation, and conscientious control, be guaranteed."[27]

The most dramatic manifestation of this strict reciprocity was the "troika" proposal. Soviet expectations of East–West parity and minimal third-country involvement were combined in the demands for a veto in the administrative council and deprivation of the only potentially influential position for nonaligned representatives in the control organization. The behavior of UN Secretary General Dag Hammarskjöld in the Congo crisis reinforced Soviet distrust of nonaligned officials and thereby third party involvement: "The events in the Congo, however, have made us cautious; they taught us sense, as the saying goes."[28]

Compare, for example, the following two Soviet statements, the first one from *stage I*, the other from *stage II*:

We still consider, however, that in the neutral countries it will always be possible to find a person, a really neutral person, who can be used for the job of carrying out the duties of administrator.[29]

Every person must needs display sympathy for some particular country or some particular system. There is no person who would be completely impartial and neutral towards both the social and economic systems that now exist in the world.[30]

Stage III

During two weeks in October 1962 the two superpowers stood face to face in the Cuban missile crisis, and probably brought the world closer to a catastrophic war than ever before since the advent of the nuclear age. The peaceful resolution of the crisis represented a new turning point in U.S.–Soviet relations.

In his correspondence with President Kennedy during the crisis, Khrushchev specifically mentioned that a peaceful solution of the conflict "might be a good beginning and, specifically, facilitate a nuclear test ban agreement."[31] A few days later, Mr. Tsarapkin in the ENDC subcommittee stated, "[W]e should take advantage of the favourable momentum developed in connexion with events in Cuba to resolve the deadlock in the negotiations here."[32]

Khrushchev in December wrote to President Kennedy:

With the elimination of the Cuban crisis, we delivered men and women from the threat of the military use of lethal nuclear weapons that directly confronted the world. Can we not solve the far simpler problem of the cessation of test explosions of nuclear weapons in time of peace? I think that we can and must do so.[33]

Soviet references to the solution of the testing issue conjointly with GCD disappeared, and the renewed interest in a separate test ban first found expression in Soviet concessions on control. The USSR espoused the idea of automatic seismic stations—"black boxes"—to complement existing manned national control posts. Furthermore it abandoned its long refusal to consider inspection at all, and entered a discussion on the number of annual inspections.

In August 1962, what was to become known at Geneva as the "numbers' game" began with an American offer to reduce the annual quota of inspections from twelve to twenty to eight to ten. Four months later, the Soviet Union proposed the figure of two to three inspections a year.

The proposal was described as a concession to the United States, and the Soviet view was still that there was no practical need for inspections. Moreover, the proposed figure was considered to meet Western demands. U.S. Ambassador Dean was cited to have mentioned the figure of two to four inspections in private discussions with Soviet Deputy Foreign Minister Kuznetsov in New York on October 30, 1962. The same figure was allegedly suggested by the American nuclear scientist Wiesner in simultaneous conversations with his Soviet colleague Fedorov.[34]

When the United States saw this move as a starting point for a new round of negotiations on the number of inspections, the USSR withdrew its offer and temporarily returned to its former position: inspection in the absence of GCD equals espionage. This line of reasoning was, however, not pursued with particular force, either at the negotiation table or in the press. Soviet expectations of outcome turned from possible solutions of the control problem to the evasion of the control problem by means of a partial treaty.

The Soviet Union initially negotiated on the basis of a comprehensive treaty. When, however, the negotiations threatened to bog down due to the traditional controversies over control questions, the Soviet Union announced its willingness to settle for a partial ban.

As a result of an exchange of correspondence between the heads of government of the United States, Great Britain, and the USSR during April–June 1963, arrangements were made for high level discussions in Moscow in July. The Moscow talks began on July 15 in a favorable atmosphere. The "hot-line" agreement had been reached in June, discussions between U.S. and Soviet scientists on the peaceful uses of atomic energy had been resumed, and the Soviet Union had stopped its organized jamming of BBC and

Voice of America broadcasts. After only ten days of negotiations a three-environment ban was initialed and, on August 5, 1963, the treaty was signed in Moscow by the foreign ministers of the three countries.

Considering the dominant role that the prevention of U.S. underground testing had until then played in Soviet expectations, the acceptance of a partial ban must be seen as a major shift of position. Compare, for example, the following Soviet statements:

Oct. 28, 1959:
But no kind of agreement on cessation of tests which did not stipulate cessation of tests of underground nuclear explosions would be worth a penny. It would not be worth the paper on which it was written.[35]

Nov. 1, 1962:
[O]ur Western colleagues are very much mistaken if they think that the Soviet Union can be satisfied with an agreement which would permit the continuance of nuclear weapon tests underground or in any other environment.[36]

Aug. 5, 1963:
This treaty [the partial test ban treaty] constitutes a document of great international significance, and its conclusion signifies an important success for all people of good will, who in the course of many years have conducted an active struggle for the cessation of nuclear tests, for disarmament, and for peace and friendship between the peoples.[37]

What adjustments of expectations lay behind this abrupt change? As we have seen, military considerations loomed large in Soviet expectations of U.S. behavior during the first two stages. The United States was expected to resume tests and thereby gain military advantages. It seems that such military considerations had by 1963 fallen into the background, and that the increased interest in East–West détente following the Cuban missile crisis prevailed.

Fears of an American technological breakthrough were apparently alleviated. The USSR even claimed to have made a breakthrough in the field of ABM (anti-ballistic missiles) following the test resumption in 1961.[38] The Soviet Union had, furthermore, started underground testing in early 1962, and claimed to have obtained "not inconsiderable results" with respect to reducing the fission-to-fusion ratio crucial to the development of "cleaner" bombs.[39]

The decreased military importance of continued testing was obliquely referred to by the Soviet representative in the ENDC, as he in June, 1963 remarked that the United States kept testing "even though they themselves admit that further nuclear explosions virtually have no longer—for the United States—any serious military importance for the development of nuclear weapons."[40]

As the military aspects were played down in Soviet argumentation, references to a test ban as a détente measure came to the forefront. This shift of emphasis became evident immediately following the Cuban missile crisis. Khrushchev's letter to Kennedy of December 19, 1962, concluded: "By achieving a speedy solution of this question [test ban] . . . we can facilitate the preparation of a disarmament treaty and proceed with even greater confidence to the solution of other urgent international problems—of which, unfortunately, we have no lack."[41]

Introducing his proposal for a partial ban on July 2, 1963, Khrushchev said that such a ban would, in addition to removing the fallout danger, "undoubtedly also contribute towards a general improvement of the international climate and the easing of tension and will consequently facilitate the search for mutually acceptable decisions and the solution of other international problems."[42]

After the conclusion of the partial test ban treaty, its role as a "good beginning" or "first step" toward East-West détente was to become the pervading theme of Soviet commentators. The argument, favored at the outset of the negotiations, that a test ban would halt further weapons development was, however, conspicuously absent in Soviet commentaries.

In our terms, after having earlier treated nuclear testing as a "game" in its own right, the Soviet Union now evidently looked upon a test ban primarily as one move in the "supergame" of U.S.–USSR relations.

PART TWO

East-West Bargaining

I have not observed as yet . . . that the Soviet diplomatists and commissars have evolved any system of negotiation that might be called a diplomatic system. Their activity in foreign countries or at international conferences is formidable, disturbing, compulsive. I do not for one moment underestimate either its potency or its danger. But it is not diplomacy: it is something else.

(NICOLSON 1954:120–121)

As Lenin repeatedly demonstrated, Soviet socialist diplomacy has nothing in common with imperialist diplomacy . . .

(I. LEMIN, in *MEMO* 1961 (4):17)

THREE

A Typical Soviet Negotiating Behavior?

◨ BOTH WESTERN and Soviet analysts tend to explain Soviet behavior in East–West negotiations in terms of Soviet idiosyncrasies. The purpose of this chapter is to set forward some prevalent assumptions about a characteristic Soviet negotiating behavior to be tested subsequently. We cannot claim to have made an exhaustive survey, although we do maintain that our inquiry is based on a representative sample of the literature on this subject.[1]

Several of the assumptions subsequently referred to emanate from rather old studies, and the objection could be raised that they are outdated and irrelevant for our purposes. However, these assumptions of long standing still seem to be current. A compilation of Western writings on Soviet negotiating behavior made by a subcommittee of the U.S. Senate in 1969 concludes that "many insights provided by those earlier studies are surprisingly valid to this day" while noting the lack of "really incisive analyses based upon more recent negotiating efforts."[2]

Philip Mosely's article from 1951 on Soviet bargaining behavior is probably the work most frequently cited by other authors on the subject. In fact Arthur Dean, chief U.S. negotiator in the final stage of the test ban negotiations, holds that Mosely's article "should be the *vade mecum* of Western diplomats."[3] Similarly, a paper written in 1972 by Steibel draws heavily on Mosely's article and the early works of Leites without offering any empirical evidence as to the current validity of old assumptions.[4]

Soviet literature on diplomacy has also been consulted for counterbalancing views of Soviet negotiating behavior.[5] Soviet sources are not very outspoken on the subject, and it has been impossible to find Soviet allegations to balance every Western assumption.

This chapter will thus deal with common assumptions about the following aspects of Soviet negotiating behavior: expectations of U.S. behavior, expectations of outcome, moves, commitment tactics, and perception of the relationship between the negotiation "game" and the "supergame" of world politics. Our survey of the assumptions will issue in questions to be answered in the following chapter.

SOVIET EXPECTATIONS OF U.S. BEHAVIOR

"Ethnocentric perception" is a commonly observed phenomenon in international relations.[6] When systematic differences are perceived between one's own group and another, it is usual that one's own group is considered superior or, at least, more normal.

The image of the Soviet Union as peaceful is deeply ingrained in the Soviet population at large. Above all, it is conditioned by memories of World War II horrors. "After what we went through in World War II, how could we be anything but peaceful?" is an often heard line of reasoning.[7]

Rapoport traces the origin of this Soviet self-image prior to World War II:

> Already in the interwar period, and especially in the 1930s, a self-image crystallized in the Soviet people the core of which was a heroism of a new kind. . . . Communist ideology, as it developed in the Soviet Union, created a channel for identifying with the nation, hence with the state, in other than military contexts. It promoted a heroics of work, especially of construction, that gave rise to an entirely new form of patriotism. . . . Thus the Soviet peoples saw themselves as a peace-loving nation, wholly immersed in the task of "building a better life," asking only to be let alone. If this self-image needed any reinforcing, the events of World War II certainly supplied it.[8]

The corollary of the peaceful Soviet self-image is the image of the United States as threatening and aggressive. This is qualified to apply only to the decision-makers acting in the name of the United States, whereas the mass of the American people are peaceful but deluded by their leaders. This image is derived, in part, from memories of a number of U.S. actions, such as the postwar establishment of bases around the Soviet borders, the intervention in Korea, and, above all, the U.S. alliance with West Germany.[9]

The observation that the same stereotyped images, *mutatis mutandis*, are held by the United States, has induced the psychologist Urie Bronfenbrenner to formulate the "mirror-image" theory. What is black-and-white in one's image system becomes white-and-black in the other's images, just as, when any object is held up to a mirror, what originally appeared as left-and-right appears in the mirror as right-and-left.[10]

The danger of mirror images lies in their tendency to be self-confirming and thus to give rise to vicious circles of self-fulfilling prophecies. The actors become prisoners of their own images in a way reminiscent of individual paranoid behavior.[11]

For Soviet representatives the hostile intentions of the foreign world have been axiomatic.[12]

Bolshevik doctrine stresses the use of deception as an enemy device and the danger of not perceiving this. . . . Hence, a high degree of political insight includes a high degree of suspiciousness.[13]

The Soviet diplomat feels himself like a traveler by night in the forest who must be constantly on the watch for the smallest sound or sight of treachery.[14]

As these quotations indicate, there was in the 1950s a considerable degree of consensus among Western observers of Soviet negotiating behavior: Soviet negotiators would expect hostility and be highly suspicious of any negotiating partner, especially the United States. Such expectations seem quite logical if we accept the "mirror-image" theory.[15]

Two chief U.S. negotiators in the test ban negotiations, James Wadsworth and Arthur Dean, also testify to the continued currency of this view of Soviet expectations:

It seems to me that suspicion is ingrained in the Russian makeup. . . .[16]

The expectation of hostility, which arises from Communist theory and is reinforced by a selective reading of history, permeates every aspect of official Soviet diplomatic behavior.[17]

A 1972 study cites "native Russian fear and hostility" and "the modern Communist doctrine of class struggle" as decisive elements "that form the Soviet world view of negotiations."[18]

The prevailing portrayal of Soviet expectations of U.S. negotiating behavior can be reformulated as a question:

QUESTION 1: *Were Soviet expectations of U.S. behavior invariably characterized by suspicion and anticipated hostility?*

SOVIET EXPECTATIONS OF OUTCOME

One of the difficulties of Soviet–Russian vocabulary is that the word "compromise" is not of native origin and carries with it no favorable empathy. . . . "Compromise for the sake of getting on with the job" is natural to American and British people, but it is alien to the Bolshevist way of thinking and to the discipline which the Communist Party has striven to inculcate in its members.[19]

They are not disposed by education and professional training to work out compromise solutions with bourgeois representatives.[20]

A country like the United States whose preoccupation is commercial is inherently predisposed toward compromise. . . . On the other hand, a country which makes its living primarily from the production and consumption of goods . . . is equally predisposed toward exclusive possession and the denial of compromise.[21]

The assumption that compromise is excluded from Soviet expectations of outcome is an often reiterated theme of Western observers. If this is the case, then what kind of outcome do Soviet negotiators expect?

To a Western nation, the basic purpose is to reach an agreement by compromise. To Communists, at least to date, negotiation is part of a grand strategy aimed at the eventual total defeat of the other side. They may negotiate with no intention whatever of reaching agreement *except on their own proposals.*[22]

TYPICAL SOVIET NEGOTIATING BEHAVIOR? 45

[I]n any negotiation Communists, if we are to believe that they are the Marxist-Leninists they claim to be, are out to *secure their total objectives* and do not regard any compromise as a permanent solution.[23]

Wedge and Muromcew, who have studied Soviet behavior in disarmament negotiations in the 1962–1963 period, suggest another type of outcome which may enter Soviet expectations:

[T]he Soviet equivalent for compromise is to be found in bartering, especially when quantitative values are involved. Any concession has to be on a quid pro quo basis.[24]

If we then turn to Soviet literature on diplomatic negotiation, a different picture appears. The searching for and acceptance of compromises is alleged to be basic to contemporary Soviet diplomacy.[25] Bogdanov describes the Soviet attitude toward diplomatic negotiations in the following terms:

Negotiations presuppose mutual search for solutions acceptable to both sides, mutual concessions and compromises, because only by way of such methods is it possible to eliminate disagreements between sovereign, independent states. In the process of international cooperation, states have to enter mutual concessions and compromises. But these must be reciprocal, of mutual advantage, and voluntary.[26]

The importance of compromises is further emphasized by Deborin: "Without such compromises there can be no peaceful coexistence. . . . He who denies compromises, also denies peaceful coexistence."[27]

The connection between the acceptance of compromises and the proclamation of peaceful coexistence as the general foreign policy line in 1956 is elaborated in greater detail by Stepanov. Having noted that Stalin, in effect, avoided the question whether compromises could be used in foreign relations,[28] he continues:

Under the present circumstances, there has been an enhancement in the role—and a broadening in the range—of the possible use of mutual concessions and compromises between states with different social systems. . . . To be sure, the character of compromises has changed for the Soviet Union: from having been forced and unavoidable they have turned into being voluntary compromises based on equal rights, acceptable to the same extent to both sides.[29]

Stepanov seems to imply that the changes in the global distribution of power had an impact on Soviet expectations of outcome insofar as compromises were re-evaluated.

The American and Soviet versions obviously differ. The role of compromises in Soviet expectations is the point at issue, and we can formulate our second question thus:

QUESTION 2: *Were compromises included in Soviet expectations of outcome?*

SOVIET MOVES

Concessions as Signs of Weakness

The widely held assumption that the Soviet Union does not expect compromises as outcomes of negotiations implies a Soviet unwillingness to make concessions. In addition, several Western authors hold that the negative Soviet image of concessions also has an effect on the way the Soviet Union reacts to an opponent's concessions. Leites, for instance, in both his early and later writings, stresses the Soviet inclination to interpret a concession by the opponent as "an indication that more, and perhaps more important, advantages can be gained by unrelenting exertions."[30] Other authors have elaborated the same theme:

Few of us have any idea how much perplexity and suspicion has been caused in the Soviet mind by gestures and concessions granted by well-meaning Americans with a view to convincing the Russians of their friendly sentiments. Such acts upset all their calculations and throw them way off balance. They immediately begin to expect that they have overestimated our strength, that they have been remiss in their obligations to the Soviet state, that they should have been demanding more from us all along.[31]

A concession, an accommodation, is evidently regarded as a sign of weakness and will only increase the opponent's demands.[32]

The Soviet negotiator is worried, puzzled, scornful, and suspicious when the Western negotiator tries out a series of minor variations to see if the opposing positions cannot be brought closer together. To him it means only that the Western representative was "not serious" in the first place. If he is willing to shift as quickly from his original position it must mean that he did not hold it in earnest to begin with and that he can eventually be forced all the way over to the Soviet position, provided the Soviet negotiator will only display "principled steadfastness" long enough and vigorously enough.[33]

In the last quotation, Mosely argues that an American concession would cause the Soviet Union to press its original proposal with more vigor. The first two quotations imply that the Soviet Union might even respond with a retraction. From this we find a departure point for our third question.

QUESTION 3: *Did the Soviet Union respond to US concessions by either continuing to put forth its original proposal or making a retraction?*

"Red Herring"

Related to the alleged Soviet averseness to concessions is a negotiating technique ascribed to the Soviet Union which is known as "red herring."[34] It involves "first, to make startling and extravagant demands; then, when these had stirred up sufficient anxiety, to withdraw some of them, and to demand a concession in return."[35]

The example used by Joy to illustrate the "red herring" technique[36] throws some light on what is to be considered a "startling and extravagant demand": Two men are discussing the sale of a car. The seller demands $1,000, whereas the buyer offers $700. The seller then proposes that the buyer agrees to buy all his future cars from him. After having argued for this proposal for an extended period of time, the seller withdraws it, if the buyer agrees to pay $1,000 for the car. The seller depicts this move as a great concession on his part.

In other words, a "red herring" involves a conspicuous *retraction* from the initial proposal (the proposed purchase of all future cars as opposed to the original $1,000 demand in the example above). This retraction is later withdrawn (back to $1,000). The withdrawal is described as a concession and is accompanied by a demand for concessions in return. This provides the basis for a fourth point of analysis.

QUESTION 4: *Was the retraction-concession pattern known as "red herring" a negotiating technique frequently used by the Soviet Union?*

SOVIET COMMITMENT TACTICS

Publicity

The Soviet Union is said to negotiate by way of commitments. Publicity is considered to be a favored commitment technique. The Soviet Union employs

> ... the customary tactic of publicly announcing major disarmament moves through an authoritative source before submitting them formally at negotiations.[37]

> The Soviets negotiate by acts and not by debate, offer and counteroffer. ... Publicity is the lifeblood of such an operation ... the purposes of the Russian leaders demand the spotlight, for the spotlight makes an act out of a speech.[38]

Incidentally, this is a point where Soviet authors tend to coincide with Western observers: "Soviet diplomacy attaches great importance to the publicity of the proceedings of conferences and a broad illumination of their work in the press."[39] Accordingly, we formulate the next question for analysis as follows:

QUESTION 5: *Did the Soviet Union prefer to negotiate by way of commitments, using publicity as a favored means?*

"Head Against Stone Wall"

According to Western observers, Soviet predilection for negotiation by way of commitments makes for a special negotiating method, sometimes referred to as the "head-against-stone-wall" technique.

> During the course of negotiation it is often clear that the Soviet negotiators are under compulsion to try for a certain number of times to secure each Soviet point, no matter how minor. After trying up to a certain point and finding that the demand cannot be put through the Soviet representative has often given in, only to turn to the next item in dispute, over which a similarly prolonged period of deadlock ensues.[40]

> They tend to present fully elaborated positions, keeping ready for substitution under certain circumstances other positions, which are put forward with the same finality.[41]

> It is also said that the Soviets employ a strategy of sustained frustration punctuated by concessions to the demands and requests of other parties.[42]

In our terminology, this technique apparently involves commitments to each proposal, repetition of the same proposal for an extended period of time, and then abandonment of the commitment followed by a commitment to a new proposal. This suggests another point of inquiry.

QUESTION 6: *Did the Soviet Union rely primarily on the "head-against-stone-wall" technique, i.e., a cycle of commitments and abandonments of commitments?*

Lack of Continuity

A "head-against-stone-wall" negotiating technique would, according to our previous reasoning, have serious consequences for the credibility of the negotiator. The lack of *continuity*, which this technique implies, would soon affect negatively the *reliability* of the negotiator. Western authors, however, argue that the Soviet Union disregards the credibility aspects as it employs this technique.

The sudden abandonment of a position long and stubbornly defended is another Soviet negotiating trait.[43]

He [the Soviet negotiator] will repeat his arguments endlessly, may emphatically deny facts or connect unrelated issues, and then may reverse his position *without regard to what he said in previous meetings*.[44]

If his [the Soviet negotiator's] instructions are changed, he will unexpectedly change his position in the middle of a conference without explanation or embarrassment.[45]

Soviet diplomatic literature does not support the thesis of Soviet disregard of the credibility problem: "Backing down from something said (or written) entails a loss of prestige and international confidence which never passes without consequences for anyone."[46] These conflicting contentions can be refined into:

QUESTION 7: *Did the Soviet Union abandon its commitments without regard for continuity or other credibility aspects?*

Informal Meetings

Related to the assumption that the Soviet Union prefers to negotiate by way of commitments are denials of Soviet interest in informal meetings. The significance of informal meetings is that they exclude virtually all possibilities of incurring commitments. No written records are kept, and the meetings are typically surrounded by secrecy.

[P]rofessional private contacts and confidential exchanges of views on a personal basis, practices which have led to many fruitful negotiations in the past, even between states in disagreement with each other, seldom operate in relations between the Soviet and non-Soviet worlds.[47]

Soviet experts and diplomats cannot participate in an informal day-to-day exchange of information, comments, and tentative recommendations concerning policy. Until Moscow has sent instructions they can say nothing at all, for they may fail to express the exact nuance of thinking or intention which has not yet been formulated at the center, and transmitted to them.[48]

Modern Soviet diplomatic literature provides an antithetical view:

Such semi-official talks provide opportunities to find out ways to compromise solutions, which is usually difficult to achieve in plenary sessions.[49]

[I]t is obvious, that in the world such as it is—and realistic, prudent diplomacy deals with the very realities of such a world—talks behind closed doors are in a number of instances inevitable and even useful.[50]

Our next question can thus be formulated as follows:

QUESTION 8: *To what extent did the Soviet Union avoid informal meetings?*

Agreement in Principle

Several Western authors have commented on a Soviet "tendency to rely upon reaching an 'agreement in principle,' without spelling out in sufficient detail all the steps in its execution."[51]

Insistence on broad agreement preceding concurrence on the specific measures needed to implement the object of agreement has long been a characteristic of Soviet negotiatory tactics.[52]

Soviet delegates disregard the spirit of Talleyrand's advice to negotiators: "On s'arrange plus facilement sur un fait que sur un principe." Instead, they keep the conversations on the level of general principles just as long as possible, knowing that this makes for endless debate and gives frequent opportunities for rhetorical fireworks.[53]

Time and time again—and certainly this is clear in the Soviet insistence on an agreement on disarmament first, with details of inspection and such matters to come later—Soviet negotiators will press for a general agreement, often on a principle, such as being for "peace," to which it is very difficult to object, and will charge bad faith when this is refused.[54]

As these quotations indicate, the "absolutistic and deductive Soviet approach"[55] is assumed to have several advantages from the Soviet point of view:

(1) It gives an opportunity to avoid serious, detailed negotiation and stall for time, which is then seen to be in the Soviet interest.[56]

(2) If the opponent does not give his consent to an agreement in principle, the Soviet Union can charge bad faith ("You don't want an agreement"). This can be exploited for propaganda purposes.

(3) If the opponent accepts an agreement in principle, the Soviet Union retains its freedom to propose details which are unacceptable to the opponent.

This leads us to another point of analysis.

QUESTION 9: *Were Soviet efforts to extract "agreement in principle" from the opponent frequent?*

"GAME" AND "SUPERGAME"

Propaganda

We have earlier pointed out that an international negotiation can be seen as one phase in the "supergame" of the manifold relations between the states involved, and that a move in the negotiation may be more related to the "supergame" than to the negotiating game proper. Iklé calls the deliberate use of such moves "negotiating for side-effects" and cites propaganda as one prominent side-effect.[57]

Soviet negotiators have earned a reputation for employing international conferences for propaganda purposes.[58]

In negotiating with Russians it is always necessary to bear in mind that they are not really interested in impressing their immediate interlocutors. Soviet diplomacy, even in the narrowest sense, is directed towards influencing foreign public opinion rather than foreign Governments.[59]

In the West, it has become habitual and almost axiomatic to characterize Soviet negotiating behavior as propagandistic. Such assertions, however, raise more questions than they answer.

First, it must be made clear what is meant by "propaganda." As a foreign policy means, propaganda is often contrasted with diplomacy. Propaganda is *one-way* communication directed toward the *people* in other countries, whereas diplomacy is two-way communication between governments.

It should be noted that this distinction is not upheld in Soviet writing on diplomacy: "The documents of Soviet diplomacy have two addresses: they are directed to governments as well as to peoples." [60]

The alleged Soviet use of propaganda in negotiations is closely related to the assumption about Soviet preferences for commitments, especially publicity. And, in a sense, propaganda can be conceived of as a component of commitment tactics. For instance, the Soviet press conferences during disarmament negotiations in the ENDC (Eighteen-Nation Committee on Disarmament) are described by Zorin as "helping the public to discover the maneuvers of the opponents of disarmament and mobilizing public opinion in support of the cause of disarmament." [61]

Western writers on Soviet propaganda in negotiations rarely clarify whether propaganda is used as a *means* to obtain favorable terms of agreement or is seen as an *objective* in itself. This ambiguity is well illustrated in the following statement: "Khrushchev has recognized that 'a primary condition for progress in disarmament is the mobilization of the people, their growing pressure on the imperialist governments.' Not agreement but agitation here seems to be the goal." [62]

In an immediate perspective, this conclusion from Khrushchev's statement seems feasible. But in a long-range perspective, agitation or propaganda may just as well be seen as a means to achieve agreement. Western authors often imply that propaganda rather than agreement is the principal Soviet objective of negotiation, and few tend to regard Soviet propaganda as a means to reach agreement.

In light of these considerations, our tenth line of questioning is two-phased.

QUESTION 10: (a) *Were Soviet propaganda attempts frequent in the negotiations?* (b) *If so, was propaganda rather than agreement the primary Soviet objective of the negotiation, or was propaganda at least equally a means of achieving agreement?*

The Effect of Tension

We have dealt with the assumption that a predominant Soviet objective in negotiations is to affect the "supergame" of world politics by means of propaganda. But the interrelationship between "game" and "supergame" works in two directions. How, then, does the "supergame" affect the negotiating game?

Specifically, how does the level of tension in East-West relations affect Soviet negotiating behavior?

[A] negotiation over the statute of Tangier bogs down in Paris; this may be a repercussion of a crisis which has arisen in Vienna or of a note delivered in Warsaw. Bolshevist mythology is full of "chain-reaction" concepts of causality.[63]

An unfavorable turn in the relations between the Soviet Union and the western world on the leading international political questions of the day is quickly reflected on a variety of "technical" committees concerned with other questions. This contrasts sharply with the conduct of international relations among the western powers.[64]

More recent studies have cast doubts on the thesis that international tensions would have immediate repercussions in Soviet negotiating behavior. Jensen's study of postwar disarmament negotiations indicates that Soviet negotiating behavior is rather insensitive to tensions.[65] Hopmann's quantitative study of the final phase of the test ban negotiations (March 1962–July 1963) concludes that these negotiations were more affected by the behavior taking place within the negotiations than by events outside, but that the Soviet Union was more directly affected by external actions than were the United States and Britain.[66]

And so we can formulate our final question in the following manner.

QUESTION 11: *What effect, if any, did international tension have upon Soviet negotiating behavior?*

SUMMARY

From our survey of the Western literature emerges a picture of a unique and extraordinary Soviet negotiating behavior. Sometimes Soviet conduct is subsumed in the larger categories of "Communist,"[67] "totalitarian,"[68] or "Eastern"[69] negotiating behavior, but it is always seen as essentially different from Western negotiating behavior. Leites, for example, contrasts "Eastern barbarism" with "Western civilization,"[70] and Steibel maintains that East-West negotiations mean "not alone a clash of specific objectives, but a confrontation between two very different negotiating systems."[71]

The Western view of Soviet negotiating behavior shows a high degree of consistency. First, there seems to be considerable consensus among Western observers. This can in part be explained by the fact that they apparently draw heavily on each other as can be seen from the frequent references to each other's works. Second, the set of assumptions about Soviet negotiating behavior discussed in the previous sections displays a considerable degree of internal consistency. They all add up to a picture of Soviet *inflexibility*. And the alleged Soviet concern with objectives other than agreement, especially *propaganda*, is another theme.

It should be noted that most of these assumptions are based on impressionistic and anecdotal evidence, and in some cases on personal negotiating experience. Examples of *systematic* investigations of Soviet negotiating behavior by *non-partisan* observers are hard to find.

FOUR

In Search of Answers

IN THIS chapter Soviet behavior in the test ban negotiations will be scrutinized in an effort to obtain answers to the questions raised in chapter 3.

SOVIET EXPECTATIONS OF U.S. BEHAVIOR

QUESTION 1: *Were Soviet expectations of U.S. behavior invariably characterized by suspicion and anticipated hostility?*

The period after Stalin's death entailed a "psychological revolution"[1] in Soviet foreign policy. Developments in weapons technology and growing Soviet military strength provided the basis for a changed Soviet image of the U.S.–USSR relationship, epitomized and given ideological sanction at the 20th congress of the CPSU in early 1956.

Khrushchev then declared that war was no longer inevitable, thereby revising an old Marxist–Leninist tenet. And as a positive correlate of the thesis of the non-inevitability of war, the idea of "peaceful coexistence" was brought forth. At the same time, it was carefully pointed out that this ideological revision was based on the view that the aggressive nature of imperialism had not changed, but that its capabilities had. This development would in the early 1960s be labelled "the third stage in the general crisis of imperialism." Its distinctive feature was that there was no longer one dominant power in the world. The modern epoch was "post-imperialist" in the sense that imperialism no longer determined to a significant degree the course of international relations.[2]

Previous shifts in the international distribution of power had transferred leadership from one capitalist state to another, but now the development was from capitalism to socialism and communism. And these two camps were headed by the United States and the Soviet Union which were unique in that they were full-fledged thermonuclear powers and world powers with global interests.[3]

This ideological revision was apparently based on an image of the U.S.–USSR relationship which resembled Western ideas of "mutual deterrence," although this term was anathema in Soviet political language. A vivid expression of the deterrence idea was given by Khrushchev:

The tiger is a beast of prey and will remain one as long as it lives, but everyone knows that a tiger will never attack an elephant. . . . To continue the simile, it must be said that the Soviet Union, the countries of the socialist world, are today a much tougher proposition for the imperialists than the elephant is for the tiger.[4]

The Soviet Union was catching up with the United States in the nuclear field, and the Sputnik space shot in 1957 even suggested a Soviet lead in rocket technology. This profound change in the power configuration justified the elevation of "peaceful coexistence" into a key concept in Soviet ideology. But was the portrayal of imperialists—and the United States in particular—as invariably aggressive really unaffected by the new situation?

There are several indications that the Soviet image of the United States did, in fact, undergo significant changes. Traditionally, the state was seen as a mere instrument of the ruling capitalist class. The relationship between polity and economy was considered to be one of subordination. But around 1960 the word *srashchivanie* (interdependence) came into use to characterize this relationship, and the term "state monopoly capitalism" was substituted for "monopoly capitalism." Soviet authors began to ascribe an autonomy to the American government hitherto undetectable in Soviet commentary. The role of various "lobbies" and interest groups was recognized.

Furthermore, reference was made to "sober" forces or "realists" in the U.S. ruling group. "Sobriety" or "realism" came gradually to refer to those who recognize a common stake in the avoidance of nuclear war.[5]

On the basis of the foregoing, it seems fairly obvious that the new situation created by the "thermonuclear duopoly" promoted the image of the U.S.–USSR relationship as one of struggle *and* cooperation[6] known as "peaceful coexistence," and gave impetus to corresponding modifications of the Soviet image of the United States. As a game-theoretician would have it, the opponent in a "mixed-motive" game must be credited with other qualities than the opponent in a zero-sum game.

We can sum up the dual Soviet images stemming from the notion of "peaceful coexistence" thus:

Soviet Images
U.S.–USSR: conflict - cum - collaboration
U.S.: aggressive and conciliatory
within U.S.: "madmen" and "realists"

How were these images reflected in Soviet expectations of U.S. behavior in the test ban negotiations?

During *stage I* the common stakes in a test ban were frequently referred to by the Soviet Union. At the same time, suspicions were voiced as to American designs especially in regard to control questions. Distinctions were made between forces in favor of, and forces against, a test ban within the United States, corresponding to the "realists"/"madmen" dichotomy. The Pentagon and the Atomic Energy Commission (AEC), backed up by financial interests, were singled out as the most powerful adversaries, while individuals such as Hubert Humphrey and Adlai Stevenson were identified as advocates of a test ban.

Soviet statements carefully avoided associating President Eisenhower and his administration with the opponents, and some press reports suggest that Eisenhower was counted among those favoring an agreement. For example, two *Pravda* articles in early

1960 contrasted the views of American test ban opponents with an Eisenhower statement characterizing the Soviet quota proposal as a "step forward."[7]

Evidently, the Soviet Union saw U.S. behavior in the test ban negotiations as a result of the struggle between those opposite forces.[8] The test ban opponents were perceived to be steadily gaining ground during the first years of negotiation, and accordingly, Soviet suspicions increased. "Only deeds can dispel our doubts," Mr. Tsarapkin said in August 1959.[9] However, a number of U.S. "deeds" (especially the "new seismic data" and Eisenhower's statement releasing the United States from the moratorium) reinforced rather than dissipated Soviet doubts.

Suspicions accumulated during *stage I* came to dominate Soviet expectations during *stage II*. In our discussion of the problems involved in holding incompatible images, we noted that a specific situation may impel the actor, in coping with perceived inconsistencies, to evoke one of the conflicting sets of images. The U-2 incident seems to have been a key catalyst in evoking the "conflict side" of the dual Soviet image of the United States.

The Soviet Union no longer emphasized, and in some cases they even denied, the common gains of a test ban. And whereas the USSR had earlier showed a willingness to give the United States the benefit of the doubt, now the enemy image definitely prevailed ("you want to resume tests," "you want control for intelligence purposes," "you want a dominant position in the control organization").

The entire course of the negotiations in Geneva proves that the Western Powers pursue the aim of actually legalizing those types of nuclear tests in which they are interested, and of establishing an international control body which would be an obedient tool in their hands and, in fact, would be an appendage to the general staffs of Western Powers. Hypocritical statements of the representatives of the United States and Great Britain about the termination of tests and the international control have proved to be nothing but camouflage.[10]

Behind this adjustment of Soviet images was a perceived shift in the balance of forces within the United States: The adversaries of a test ban had finally triumphed. Soviet references to American forces in favor of a test ban dwindled in the negotiations as well as in the press, and the distinction between the adversaries of a treaty and the administration was no longer strictly upheld.

A comparison of two newspaper articles, one from *stage I*, the other from *stage II*, illustrates this change. On April 3, 1960, *Izvestiya* wrote: "[T]he adversaries of a ban on nuclear weapon tests still have a considerable influence and weight in the American government."[11]

Seven months later, the same paper spoke in more categorical terms: "In reality—and this is now becoming increasingly clear to many—the peaceloving statements by US representatives are made in order to hide the fact that *the ruling circles of the United States are adversaries of an agreement on the cessation of nuclear weapon tests.*"[12]

At Geneva, Mr. Tsarapkin said: "It is obvious that militaristic considerations have finally gained the upper hand in the United States, that the Pentagon, the Atomic Energy Commission, and various concerns and monopolistic organizations interested in the arms race and the continuance of the cold war have prevailed."[13]

During *stage III*, the "conflict-cum-collaboration" image returned. The collaboration theme was especially emphasized in Foreign Minister Gromyko's speech before the Supreme Soviet in the wake of the Cuban missile crisis:

> The crisis in the Carribean has demonstrated once again how closely the destinies of the contemporary world are intertwined with the relations between the Soviet Union and the United States of America. History has so developed that without mutual understanding between the USSR and the USA not a single serious international conflict can be settled, agreement cannot be reached on a single important international problem.[14]

And at Geneva, Mr. Zorin again referred to common interests in a test ban: "We have no illusions in this regard; nevertheless, we think that the United States, the United Kingdom, and France should be no less interested than the Soviet Union in the prohibition of nuclear weapon tests."[15]

The distinction between "madmen" and "realists" regained

prominence, and the peaceful solution of the Cuban missile crisis was explained in terms of a victory of "realists" over "madmen" within the United States.[16] In the ENDC, Mr. Zorin expressed the hope "that there are in the United States enough powerful and farsighted forces which will be able to ensure an agreement."[17]

The image conveyed during *stage II* that the United States wanted as much control as possible for intelligence purposes was now more discriminating. Khrushchev in his interview with the editor of the Italian paper *Il Giorno* in April 1963 referred to "certain American circles" who wanted "under the guise of the inspections, to set up reconnaissance centers on the territory of the Soviet Union."[18] In the negotiations, these circles were identified: Pentagon, CIA, AEC, and the NATO staffs were alleged to be interested in exploiting control for intelligence purposes.[19] On the other hand, the Soviet Union also made references to persons and groups in the United States who considered national control sufficient.[20] Mr. Tsarapkin once spoke of the control-for-intelligence policy, "which found particularly favourable soil first within the government of President Truman and then in the government of President Eisenhower."[21] The Kennedy administration was not mentioned, which suggests that Kennedy was now at least not counted among those who were craving for excessive control.

President Kennedy's American University speech of June 10, 1963, seems to have vindicated Soviet expectations of a "realist" recovery in the United States. The speech, which contained ideas and formulations strikingly similar to the Soviet idea of "peaceful coexistence" was published in the Soviet press and favorably commented on by Khrushchev. And the Soviet press coverage of the internal U.S. test ban debate after the conclusion of the treaty singled out pro and con forces—individuals as well as groups—within the United States.[22] Thus, the "mixed-motive" image of the United States was restored after the temporary relapse into a "zero-sum" image during *stage II*.

In short, our question must be answered in the negative: Soviet expectations of U.S. behavior were not unchanging over time. Neither were they characterized exclusively by suspicion and anticipated hostility. Rather, Soviet expectations, flowing from the idea of "peaceful coexistence," contained dual elements—conflict as well as cooperation—with the conflict aspect predominant during *stage II*.

SOVIET EXPECTATIONS OF OUTCOME

QUESTION 2: *Were compromises included in Soviet expectations of outcome?*

Early in the Geneva negotiations, Mr. Tsarapkin declared: "[N]egotiation carries with it the obligation to seek a compromise, to make mutual concessions and to attempt to come to terms."[23] And Soviet behavior during *stage I* indicates that compromise was, in fact, included in Soviet expectations of outcome. The Soviet Union made concessions in relation to its initial proposals on all agenda items during this period, and (partial) compromise solutions were reached concerning parties to the treaty, duration of the treaty, the Control Commission, and the Administrator (chief executive of the control organization).

The issue of control post staffing provides excellent illustrations of Soviet thinking in terms of compromises. Although the Soviet Union vied for an overwhelming majority of host-country nationals at the posts, it showed great readiness to make concessions. In January 1959, Mr. Tsarapkin spoke of one "or any agreed number" of foreign controllers, suggesting two or three. Half a year later, having proposed four to five controllers, he said: "If you have some other ratio in mind, just name it, and we will try to reconcile our points of view and your approach."[24]

After the proposal for six to seven controllers, Mr. Tsarapkin stated: "This matter has not yet been completely settled, but it must be admitted that there also it appears possible to reach a decision satisfactory to all the parties to these negotiations."[25]

The trajectory of concessions actually made suggests a compromise solution at a 50–50 distribution between the two sides. Such a distribution was, incidentally, proposed by the USSR with respect to "headquarters" (the technical section of the Commission)[26] and inspection groups.[27]

Our conclusion that compromise was included in Soviet expectations during *stage I* is corroborated by Jensen's quantitative study of "the propensity to compromise" in the test ban negotiations, expressed in terms of a weighted net balance of concessions and retractions. He assigns numerical values ranging from 1 to 5 to all concessions, and from −1 to −5 to all retractions. This gives the following scores for *stage I*:[28]

	USSR	USA
Oct.–Dec. 1958	14	10
Jan.–May 1959	27	22
June–Aug. 1959	22	4
Sept.–Dec. 1959	6	0
Jan.–Apr. 1960	9	14
May–Aug. 1960	2	10

If Soviet behavior during *stage I* suggests that compromises were included in its expectations of outcome, the behavior during *stage II* rather implies expectations of *non-agreement*. There are several indications of this:

(a) We have found no Soviet concessions during this stage, but several retractions.[29] The Soviet proposal for making a test ban conditional on a GCD solution can be interpreted as a way of signalling a lack of interest in the test ban negotiations. In other words, the original image ("any attempt to link the question of the cessation of tests with other questions of disarmament is tantamount to deliberately forcing a deadlock on this question")[30] remained constant; what had changed was the Soviet interest in a test ban agreement.[31] At any rate, this was the way the Soviet move was perceived by the other negotiating partners.

Similarly, the "troika" proposal was introduced in the negotiations several months after the UN debate had made it perfectly clear that the Western powers were not going to accept such a formula. The Soviet demand for French participation in the negotiations was made more than one and a half year after the first French nuclear test, at a time when the French government had firmly committed itself not to take part in any test ban talks.

(b) The previous searching for mutually acceptable solutions was replaced by remarkable Soviet immobility throughout *stage II*.

In November 1960, Mr. Tsarapkin said: "We have submitted compromise proposals to you and are waiting for you to accept them."[32] And in May 1961: "If you . . . have nothing to say, if you do not wish to accept the compromise proposal of the Soviet Union, I can do nothing to help you."[33] And still in early October 1962: "[D]o not wait for anything new in our position and do not expect any changes."[34]

"It is up to the West" (*delo za zapadom*) was the Soviet catchword of this period both in the negotiations and in the press.

(c) According to Western estimates, the Soviet test series initiated in September 1961 must have taken a minimum of six months, and more likely a year or more to prepare.[35] Thus, during *stage II* the Soviet Union negotiated against the background of planned test resumption.

(d) The Soviet Union communicated in various ways the low priority assigned to test cessation. After the spring of 1961, the USSR repeatedly hinted at breaking off the negotiations. The common gains of a test ban were downgraded, and a Soviet government memorandum of September 26, 1961, alleged that

. . . a treaty on the cessation of tests concluded in isolation from a solution of the general problem of disarmament and against the background of a continued nuclear armaments race would not merely not promote the cause of peace but might even have the opposite consequences and serve as a cover for the preparation of a nuclear war.[36]

Foreign Minister Gromyko in his report to the Supreme Soviet in April 1962 did not even mention test cessation among practicable partial disarmament measures.[37]

We may thus conclude that the outcome expected by the Soviet Union during *stage II* was non-agreement. However, compromise reentered Soviet expectations in *stage III*, when a test ban was given higher priority than previously. To cite but one indication of this: In February 1963, Mr. Zorin in the ENDC dealt with test cessation at length before mentioning a non-aggression pact and nuclear-free zones, whereas only three months earlier the order of attention had been just the opposite.[38]

Soviet statements on test cessation after the Cuban missile crisis communicated renewed optimism: "It can be said without exaggeration that never before have there been such favourable conditions for solving the problem of the prohibition of nuclear tests as there are at the present time."[39]

The Soviet Union again made concessions, and the immobility of the previous stage was broken: "We believe that the existing differences can be overcome if we seek for a compromise on a mutually acceptable basis."[40]

The acceptance of "black boxes" and two to three annual inspections was explained thus: "[I]n actual fact we agreed to something which, in view of the efficiency of national systems for detecting nuclear explosions, is superfluous and unnecessary for control over a treaty. But a compromise is a compromise."[41]

Our answer to question 2 is that compromises were included in Soviet expectations during *stage I* and *stage III*, whereas the Soviet Union did not seem to expect agreement during *stage II*. Soviet expectations of outcome were thus closely correlated with its expectations of U.S. behavior. Compromises were conceivable when the "mixed-motive" image of the United States prevailed, but the "zero-sum" image of *stage II* precluded agreement.

Lloyd Jensen has introduced the hypothesis that the marked shift in Soviet expectations of outcome in *stage II* was a manifestation of "approach-avoidance" behavior: "[I]f one is ambivalent about a goal when he is at a distance from that goal, there is a tendency to approach; near the goal the tendency to avoid is greater."[42] Whereas Jensen ignores expectations of the other actor's behavior, our hypothesis is that Soviet expectations of outcome were strongly affected by expectations of U.S. behavior.

SOVIET MOVES

QUESTION 3: *Did the Soviet Union respond to U.S. concessions by either continuing to put forth its original proposal or making a retraction?*

During *stage I* we have found concessions rather than retractions or immobility to be the typical Soviet response to U.S. concessions. This coincides with Jensen's observation that "until December 1960 there was a strong tendency to reciprocate concessions" in the test ban negotiations.[43]

The picture we get for *stage II* differs significantly. Immobility and, in one case, retraction were the typical Soviet responses. The only response identified as a concession represented an agreement to one part of a U.S. package proposal combined with non-agreement to the other parts.

As for *stage III* it is difficult to discern any decisive pattern of reciprocity. We have recorded no Soviet retraction and several Soviet concessions during this stage. However, except for the proposed two to three yearly inspections, these Soviet concessions could hardly be characterized as immediate responses to U.S. moves.

Consequently, the test ban negotiations do not bear out the assumption that Soviet negotiators invariably regard concessions as signs of weakness and respond by retractions or immobility. Such a response pattern was observable, however, during *stage II*, a period when the Soviet Union apparently was not expecting agreement.

QUESTION 4: *Was the retraction-concession pattern known as "red herring" a negotiating technique frequently used by the Soviet Union?*

As discussed above, "red herring" involves a conspicuous retraction that is later withdrawn, the withdrawal being accompanied by a call for concessions in return. Examples of this negotiating technique were hard to find in the test ban negotiations.

A number of conspicuous retractions were indeed made by the Soviet Union during *stage II*. Yet when this was the case, they were not used as levers to ply concessions from the United States. The demand to include France in the negotiations and the linkage with GCD were both discreetly dropped, as *stage III* began. No efforts were made to exploit the "troika" proposal, which achieved nothing but the burial of the administrator issue.[44] When the USSR dropped its insistence on national control and introduced the idea of "black boxes," it did, in fact, couple this with a call for U.S. abandonment of all inspection demands.[45] However, the very day that these calls for U.S. concessions were made at Geneva, Khrushchev sent a letter to Kennedy in which he consented to two to three inspections a year.[46] The "red herring" potential went without being tested.

On the other hand, we can discern a pattern that does bear some resemblance to the "red herring" technique in the Soviet "veto list." Abandonment of the veto in the Control Commission was offered in return for concessions on various aspects of the control organization. However, the "veto list" was no *retraction* inasmuch as unanimity was the decision-making procedure *originally* proposed by the Soviet Union. Our conclusion must be that "red herring" was not a characteristic Soviet negotiation technique in the test ban negotiations.

SOVIET COMMITMENT TACTICS

QUESTION 5: *Did the Soviet Union prefer to negotiate by way of commitments, using publicity as a favored means?*

Most Soviet proposals in the test ban negotiations were published in the Soviet press. However, with respect to the use of publicity as a means of commitment, a few additional observations should be noted:

(a) We have found only two instances of publication of a proposal prior to its introduction at the negotiation table: the acceptance of a limited number of peaceful detonations in February 1959,[47] and the proposal for "black boxes" in November 1962.[48] In the latter case, the idea had been discussed informally between the two sides earlier.

(b) Several proposals, especially during *stage I*, were not published at all in the Soviet press. The proposal for fifteen control posts on Soviet territory was not covered in the press. The Soviet idea of a predetermined annual inspection quota was given wide publicity, but the proposed figure of three was not mentioned. Also not mentioned was the Soviet acceptance of four other states in addition to the three nuclear ones as members of the Control Commission. The unanimity principle was referred to, but not the specified "veto list" or the Soviet concessions in regard to the veto. There was no mention in the press of negotiations on the question of an administrator until the "troika" proposal was put forward. And the exchange of concessions on the staffing issue was not at all reported. This pattern suggests that the Soviet Union did, in fact, avoid establishing commitments on control questions by means of publicity during *stage I*.

(c) In general, the press paid more attention to the shortcomings of the Western proposals than to the merits of the Soviet proposals. More space was devoted to repudiating the Western position than to advocating the Soviet position. This was especially marked during *stage I*.

(d) If we look at how Soviet proposals were first introduced, we find that the major share of the proposals were submitted at the negotiation table by the negotiator. The exceptions are rather few: a package proposal of November 28, 1961, was brought forward in the form of a government statement. Some proposals identified with Khrushchev were introduced either in direct communication with the American President or in speeches to non-Western audiences. The "quota" proposal in 1959, linkage with GCD in 1961, and the readiness to consider a comprehensive ban with "black boxes" and two or three inspections in late 1962 are all instances of such direct executive communication. In point of fact, the "quota" proposal was the only one not previously hinted at in the negotiations. The 1962 call for extending national control to underground tests and the proposal for a three-environment ban coupled with a non-aggression pact in the summer of 1963 are the only instances of proposals introduced in speeches to non-Western audiences.

Taking these observations into account, it would definitely be an exaggeration to say that the Soviet Union used publicity as a favored means of commitment in the test ban negotiations.

QUESTION 6: *Did the Soviet Union rely primarily on the "head-against-stone-wall" technique, i.e., a cycle of commitments and abandonments of commitments?*

The "head-against-stone-wall" technique was said to involve a cycle of (1) firm commitment to each proposal, (2) repetition of the proposal for an extended period of time, and (3) abandonment of the commitment followed by a commitment to a new proposal. In our answer to the previous question we discounted publicity as a favored Soviet commitment means. Furthermore, we have not found Soviet proposals to be typically accompanied by firm commitments of any kind. In fact, a considerable number of proposals were obliquely probed before being formally introduced: the proposed quota of two to three inspections was hinted at more than a year in advance; similar noncommittal prior notices were given of the linkage with GCD, the "black box" idea, the abandonment of a moratorium on underground tests as a prerequisite for a partial ban, and the renewed offer of two to three inspections.

In general, the Soviet Union did not commit itself exceedingly to its proposals. The conditional commitments incurred had low finality and specificity. Most of them consisted in linking two different agenda items (e.g., "if you agree to the quota principle, we shall not demand a veto on inspections").

Except for *stage II*, it cannot be said that the Soviet Union kept repeating its proposals for an extended period of time. During *stage I* the relative continuity and immobility on agenda items dealing with the scope of the treaty was counteracted by a conspicuous mobility on control items. For instance, within one year the Soviet Union had moved from 1 to 2 to 13 to 14 controllers from the other side at each control post. During *stage III* the final treaty was hammered out within a period of ten days.

This pattern was broken in *stage II* when Soviet behavior was reminiscent of the "head-against-stone-wall" technique: The USSR established commitments, though not particularly strong ones, to its retractions and repeated the same proposals throughout the period. The commitments were abandoned after the Cuban missile crisis, and the negotiating process, as it were, started anew.

With the exception of *stage II*, our question must be answered in the negative: We have not found the "head-against-stone-wall" technique to be a characteristic trait of Soviet behavior in the test ban negotiations.

QUESTION 7: *Did the Soviet Union abandon its commitments without regard for continuity or other credibility aspects?*

Nowhere, not in a single record of our official meetings, will you find any contradiction or change in our position in any respect, except for those cases where we have gone forward to meet you and have put forward official proposals in that regard.[49]

This assertion by Mr. Tsarapkin in June 1960 applies fairly well to Soviet negotiating behavior during *stage I*. The gradual Soviet concessions were coupled with claims of continuity: the USSR remained committed to its original proposals, concessions were made solely in order to seek a mutually acceptable agreement. When the Soviet Union, in May 1960, backed down on some of its concessions, "casuistry" was employed to show that the Soviet position had not changed.[50]

Nor can it be said that the Soviet Union ignored the credibility aspects of its conditional commitments during this period. To mention one example: employing threats and promises, Mr. Tsarapkin had since the beginning of 1960 made a Soviet proposal for the number of inspections conditional on U.S. acceptance of a quota on a political basis (not based on the number of seismic events). The tabling of the proposal for three inspections in July 1960 was accompanied by "casuistry": Mr. Tsarapkin alleged that the condition had been fulfilled, that the United States was perceived to have implicitly accepted a political quota.[51]

Soviet continuity was broken in *stage II*, when drastic retractions were made. There again the Soviet Union resorted to "casuistry" in an effort to demonstrate continuity. In addition to referring to the changed international situation, Mr. Tsarapkin said, about the demands for national control, that Soviet agreement to the experts' conclusions had already been a concession, and in regard to the "troika" proposal that the Soviet Union had always had doubts about a single administrator.

Claims of continuity also accompanied the renewed offers of

some elements of international control (two to three inspections, "black boxes") in *stage III:* national control was still regarded as sufficient; these offers should be seen as efforts to meet the other side. In short, Soviet behavior in the test ban negotiations does not corroborate an assumption of Soviet disregard for continuity or other credibility aspects.

QUESTION 8: *To what extent did the Soviet Union avoid informal meetings?*

Only with great reluctance did the Soviet Union consent in 1958 to joint expert discussions on control. At the experts' conference the informal committee meeting became the tool by which agreement was reached.[52] The positive experience of the experts' conference seems to have predisposed the Soviet Union in favor of such off-the-record discussions.

The initial skirmishes over the conference title and agenda were both solved in informal meetings. The Soviet Union also agreed to a Western proposal for an informal working group on the staffing of control posts. Experts from both sides participated in three different technical working groups during *stage I*; one penetrating the problems of detection of tests at high altitudes, another with the assignment of working out objective criteria for inspection, and a third entrusted to draft a joint research program on underground test detection.

These technical working groups never managed to overcome the differences between the two sides created by the "new seismic data." When the Western powers, after the eight-nation memorandum and again after the Soviet proposal for "black boxes," called for new technical discussions, they met with Soviet refusal.

It could be compared, for example, to a demand that research into the effect of tobacco smoking in the origin of cancer of the lungs or cardiovascular disease should be handed over to the tobacco-companies. Anybody could foresee what would be the results of such research.[53]

Behind this refusal obviously lay the Soviet image of U.S. scientists, built up during the negotiations. Mr. Tsarapkin referred to scientists employed by the Pentagon, the AEC, or the RAND Corporation, having

> . . . directed their efforts and abilities . . . towards creating ever new obstacles in the path to agreement.[54]
>
> Why do you require a meeting of experts, unless you are again planning to press for the establishment of an international system of control posts?[55]

If technical discussions were consequently ruled out in the Soviet view after 1960, diplomatic off-the-record contacts were nevertheless maintained throughout the negotiations and were institutionalized in the co-chairmen meetings of the ENDC. In a plenary session Mr. Zorin testified to the value of these informal discussions: "[W]e consider these meetings useful for finding acceptable ways of reaching agreement."[56]

This view was shared by his American colleague in these meetings, Mr. Dean: "On such occasions it was possible for my Soviet opposite number and myself to talk dispassionately and intelligently about a number of controversial topics, to explore each other's meanings and interpretations, and to get down to detailed drafting."[57]

Thus evaluation of the material brings us to the conclusion that categorical avoidance of informal meetings was not characteristic of Soviet negotiating behavior in the test ban talks.

QUESTION 9: *Were Soviet efforts to extract "agreement in principle" from the opponent frequent?*

A simple frequency count would no doubt reveal extensive Soviet use of the phrase "agreement in principle" in the test ban negotiations. Soviet demands that broad agreement precede the consideration of specific details were common. This "deductive" approach seems to be basic to Soviet conceptions of negotiation. In connection with one Soviet demand for "agreement in principle" Mr. Tsarapkin stated:

> If we insist on first reaching agreement on the basic questions this is not due to any personal considerations of ours, but is a natural requirement for conducting negotiations in a normal and businesslike manner.[58]

Mr. Tsarapkin also commented on the differences from the Western approach:

You are proposing to work on the details before agreeing on the foundation. This is tantamount to putting up a building without a foundation or a framework. Such a building will, however, collapse while it is still under construction.[59]

On a "macro" level, the Soviet approach manifested itself in efforts to obtain a U.S. commitment to test cessation before detailed negotiations started on the different agenda items. Such efforts were made already in the experts' conference and were renewed in the initial meetings of the political conference. Why order a blueprint when we don't even know if we are going to build a house, Mr. Tsarapkin asked, vividly delineating the likely sequence of negotiations in the absence of an agreement in principle:

It is as though we started to argue here on how to preserve a bearskin when the bear itself was still in the woods. We would be arguing about whether to put the bearskin in the refrigerator or to pack it in moth-balls in a trunk at home. In the end, we would disagree with you on which brand of moth-balls to buy and from which firm. The bear would be in the woods, alive and well, and we would have fallen out among ourselves over moth-balls.[60]

No agreement in principle on test cessation was reached, and as a prediction of the actual course of the test ban negotiations, Mr. Tsarapkin's statement merits attention.

The "deductive" Soviet approach recurred on the "micro" level. On a number of individual agenda items the USSR called for agreement in principle. The typical pattern was then (a) Soviet commitment to a principle, (b) calls for U.S. commitment to the principle and, after a period of time, (c) efforts to convince the United States that it in fact had committed itself to the principle.

Three agenda items can be cited as notable examples of this Soviet approach: the number of inspections, the composition and decision making of the Control Commission, and the staffing of control posts. On the issue of inspection, the Soviet Union in early 1959 proposed an inspection quota, i.e., a predetermined number of annual inspections on the territories of the nuclear states, whereas the United States demanded that the number of inspections be dependent on the number of earthquakes or "unidentified events." The Soviet Union committed itself to the quota principle, refused to be drawn into a discussion of figures until the United States, too, had made a commitment to the principle, and after several months proclaimed that it interpreted the absence of U.S. objections to the quota idea as an agreement in principle.

As for the Commission, the USSR established commitments to the two principles of "parity" and "agreed decisions," calling for U.S. recognition of the principles. When the United States agreed to unanimity decisions on some questions and stated that it did not seek a privileged position in the Commission, this was taken to mean that "the disagreement between us is no longer a disagreement on principle but a disagreement on the degree to which the principle should be applied."[61]

The principle of "two sides" or reciprocal control was invoked on the staffing issue. The Soviet Union tried to convince the United States that the latter's proposals, envisaging Americans in key positions at the posts in the Soviet Union and vice versa, implied recognition of the principle of reciprocal control.

The use of this "deductive" approach on the "micro" level sometimes involved elevating a rather concrete question into a matter of principle. The proposal for "black boxes" was introduced in this way: "We are proposing to you an idea. . . . If you accept this idea in principle, we will set about working out the details with you."[62]

The more concrete the issue, the more ambiguous becomes the "deductive" approach. Rather than reflecting an approach of general application, calls for "agreement in principle" then tend to be a commitment technique, the employment of which is ruled by expediency. The Soviet reaction to an American proposal for permanent inspection teams is illuminating in this context: "[W]e must have perfectly clear ideas about this subject. You do not expect that your partner in the talks will agree to the inclusion in the treaty of just a general provision, about which he has no detailed and clear idea."[63]

In summing up, though we must affirm that the Soviet Union frequently sought to attain "agreements in principle" in the test ban negotiations, it is at the same time significant that the absence of an agreement in principle on test cessation did not prevent the Soviet Union from extensive—albeit abortive—negotiations on control.

"GAME" AND "SUPERGAME"

QUESTION 10: (a) *Were Soviet propaganda attempts frequent in the negotiations?*
(b) *If so, was propaganda rather than agreement the primary Soviet objective of the negotiation, or was propaganda at least equally a means of achieving agreement?*

Although our material does not permit a full answer, a few observations, bearing on these questions can be made. To begin with, the USSR willingly deprived itself of important propaganda potentials. The Soviet Union never pressed its original demand for a public conference, and the delegations agreed informally to closed sessions before the opening of the conference. In light of such behavior, it seems improbable that propaganda was the primary Soviet objective of the negotiation.

In order to see whether propaganda was employed as a means of achieving agreement, an examination of Soviet publications and radio broadcasts to foreign audiences would be necessary. Such an analysis has not been possible to conduct within the compass of this study, though the area is no doubt a worthy subject for inquiry. What can be said on the basis of our material is that the test ban negotiations did not occupy a prominent position in the Soviet dailies *Pravda* and *Izvestiya*. For instance, we have found only three editorials in both papers dealing with the test ban issue in the course of the negotiations. This contrasts with the abundance of editorials after the conclusion of the treaty.

The more inclusive forum of the ENDC would seem to provide greater opportunities for propaganda. Also, in the ENDC the habit developed to give press conferences after the sessions. However, test cessation was mainly discussed in the three-power subcommittee and in the informal Soviet–American co-chairmen meetings. The Soviet Union refused to expand the membership of the subcommittee. And the final negotiations in Moscow were kept closed to the public. Kovalev's retrospective explanation of this is noteworthy:

What if the Moscow negotiations were carried on in public and the adversaries of an agreement on a three-environment test ban among the American "madmen" had greater concrete possibilities to influence the settlements in the Moscow negotiations? What if they had the possibility to develop their activity not within the framework that was presented to the U.S. Senate—to accept or reject the final positive result of the negotiations—but within the framework of another choice—to accept or reject this or that position, proposal, or concession, when the outcome of the negotiations was still obscure? Would it not under such circumstances be easier for the adversaries of a test ban to achieve their purposes? Of course, it would.[64]

The Soviet willingness to forgo propaganda potentials thus seems to have been connected with the "dual" image of the United States. The Soviet objective of strengthening "sober" forces in the United States through negotiations called for propaganda restraint.

In a study of arms control and disarmament propaganda in Soviet periodicals in English, Clemens and Griffiths note an antagonistic propaganda line just prior to the Moscow talks, which contrasted with the previous and subsequent propaganda restraint. They find it "difficult to avoid the impression" that this shift was at least in part aimed at covering the Soviet left flank against internal and external criticism from "orthodox" Communists.[65]

The foregoing suggests that Soviet willingness to remove negotiations from public forums preceded by a hardened propaganda line may be an indication that the Soviet Union sought agreement.[66]

We have, in short, raised more questions than are answerable within the limits of our material. However, our study does suggest that it might be worthwhile to turn more attention to an inquiry into Soviet employment of propaganda as a means of achieving agreement in negotiations rather than taking Soviet propagandistic objectives for granted.

QUESTION 11: *What effect, if any, did international tension have upon Soviet negotiating behavior?*

In an attempt to avoid all the subtle problems of measuring degrees of international tension, we will restrict our discussion to two unambiguous peaks in East–West tension in the 1958–1963 period: the U-2 incident and its aftermath in 1960, and the Cuban missile crisis in 1962. Both involved direct Soviet–American confrontation.

Both tension periods did have an impact on Soviet behavior in the test ban negotiations, but their effects were quite disparate. Whereas the U-2 incident resulted in a chain of retractions and a period of inflexibility, the Cuban missile crisis resulted in concessions and renewed flexibility. As demonstrated earlier, these two crisis situations produced shifts in Soviet expectations of U.S. behavior and, indirectly, the expectations of outcome. Thus the negative impact of the U-2 incident (you want intelligence; international control is impossible and a test ban undesirable) as well as the positive impact of the Cuban missile crisis (you do not want war; a test ban is a desirable détente gesture) can be accounted for.

Our tentative conclusion is that it hardly makes sense to speak of any one direct and unequivocal effect of international tension upon Soviet negotiating behavior. Rather, the circumstances of international tension affect Soviet *expectations*, and may evoke different images, as the test ban negotiations demonstrated.

SUMMARY

In Western studies of Soviet foreign policy there has been a tendency to mystify, to portray Soviet behavior as unique and extraordinary. Winston Churchill's characterization of Soviet policy as "a riddle wrapped in a mystery inside an enigma" has acquired fame. Bridging of the gap between simplified, "tailor-made" models of Sovietologists and more generic models and methods for the study of foreign policy has only recently begun. Over the last decade there has been a development from approaches stressing the uniqueness of Soviet behavior toward more comparative approaches; from hostile "ultra-hard" images of the Soviet Union toward more differentiated and conciliatory "mixed" images.[67]

In this part of our study we have tested a number of widely

held assumptions about the idiosyncrasies of Soviet negotiating behavior that can be said to reflect the mystifying tendency. We found Soviet negotiating behavior to be less unique and extraordinary than has generally been assumed. Specifically, Soviet behavior was found to be more flexible and less propagandistic than could be anticipated after consulting Western observers.

The eleven assumptions dealt with in this investigation appear to be lagging behind in the evolution of the study of Soviet foreign policy and seem to stem from hostile images of the Soviet Union bred in the cold war climate. De Rivera points out that the traumatic experiences immediately after World War II, when expectations of continued U.S.–Soviet cooperation were shattered, may have had a lasting impact:

The scars of this sobering encounter are still with us today, in part because the realization of Soviet differences worked towards the selection of "tough minded" negotiators; and in part because of negotiators who "converted" to a belief in the intransigency of the Soviet Union—with all the rigidity that sometimes accompanies conversion.[68]

The unavoidable conclusion emerging from our study is that it does not seem very meaningful to speak of any one unique, invariable Soviet negotiating behavior. We have observed significant changes in Soviet behavior in the test ban negotiations; several of the assumptions about unique Soviet negotiating methods applied reasonably well during *stage II*, while Soviet behavior in *Stages I* and *III* did not confirm the assumptions. This would suggest that the Soviet Union employed distinct negotiating methods only when it was not interested in an agreement. But, as Pipes has put it, "whenever they happen to be interested in a settlement, Communist diplomats act in a traditional manner, efficiently and undeterred by difficulties."[69]

Modifications in Soviet images of the United States were found to be correlated with changes in manifest Soviet negotiating behavior. The psychological stress toward consistency epitomized in the principle of cognitive consonance could be observed in the Soviet image system, as Soviet images of outcome were adjusted in accordance with the modified images of the United States. In addition, the hypothesis that cognitive complexity may be conducive to an actor's willingness and ability to negotiate seems to be confirmed by Soviet behavior. It was during periods when it displayed a dual, partially inconsistent image of the United States that the Soviet Union engaged in serious negotiations, whereas the more consistent "enemy" image evoked after the U-2 incident coincided with apparent Soviet unwillingness to seek an agreement.

However, our analysis of East–West bargaining does not provide us with any definite answer as to why Soviet images changed after the U-2 incident and again after the Cuban missile crisis. In order to throw additional light upon this question, let us now turn to our two other levels of analysis.

PART THREE

Intra-Bloc Bargaining

. . . one day it will make an interesting and instructive exercise for somebody to make a detailed study of Soviet foreign policy between 1958 and 1963 in the light of what everyone now knows about the Sino–Soviet quarrel.

(CRANKSHAW 1966:274)

The formation and development of the world socialist system gives special significance to the question of correct relations between Marxist–Leninist parties . . . socialist equality not only means having equal rights to take part in working out collectively the common policy but also entails equal responsibilities for the fraternal Parties of socialist countries for the destinies of the entire community. . . . We do not close our eyes to the fact that . . . different interpretations of the forms and methods of our cooperation may occur in the relations between socialist countries. . . . All this necessitates constant efforts to find ways and means to enable us to settle the differences arising, from positions of principle and with the least damage to our common cause.

(CPSU letter to CPC, March 30, 1963, in GRIFFITH 1964:252–253)

FIVE

Sino–Soviet Relations as Bargaining Situation

◲ WE HAVE studied Soviet behavior in the test ban negotiations as responses to U.S. behavior, mediated through the Soviet system of images. Now, as we shift the level of analysis, we shall test the hypothesis that Soviet negotiating behavior at Geneva might be the result of intra-bloc bargaining between the Soviet Union and China.

Several Western observers have suggested—more or less explicitly—that Sino–Soviet relations during the period under study may be analyzed as a bargaining situation.[1] In this perspective, the Soviet Union and China are regarded as interdependent actors having common as well as divergent interests.

Interdependence

Stalin's death marked the beginning of the end of unquestioned Soviet dominance and supremacy within the Communist system. In 1956 the Cominform—the last vestige of a hierarchically organized Communist bloc—was liquidated, and a new concept of intra-bloc organization came into use: that of a "commonwealth" of socialist countries (*sodruzhestvo sotsialisticheskikh stran*), implying a more informal, loose association.[2] Whereas loyalty to the Soviet Union had earlier been the touchstone of "proletarian internationalism," references to mutual respect for the sovereignty and national interests of the socialist states now entered definitions of "socialist internationalism," the aspect of "proletarian internationalism" applicable to relations among Communist party-states. Persuasion and maneuvering gradually replaced the stern centralism of the Stalin era: "While still predominant, Moscow now has to bargain rather than command. Bargaining leaves a lot of room for imbalance of power and should not be confused with equality."[3]

Interdependence rather than subordination characterized in particular China's relationship with the Soviet Union. The Chinese Communists owed their victory to their own strength, and ever since the traumatic experiences of Stalin's Kuomintang policy, the Chinese Communists had been "an ally but not a satellite" to Moscow.[4]

Common Interests

Communist and non-Communist observers alike for a long time saw the common ideology of the USSR and China as the unshakable foundation of a strong community of interests. Zagoria, for example, wrote in 1962: "One cannot stress too much that the partners to the Sino–Soviet alliance are dedicated to a common purpose and bound together by a common ideology."[5] However, as Sino–Soviet differences accumulated, the unifying role of ideology was de-emphasized. And in the preface to a new edition of his book, Zagoria two years later admitted:

. . . the common ideology which I expected to set limits on the conflict operated rather to sharpen it. Indeed, one of the lessons to be drawn from this dispute is that ideologically oriented powers such as Russia and China have much greater difficulty in harmonizing differences of view and interest than do the more pragmatic non-communist powers which are accustomed to having and to adjusting conflicting interests.[6]

Other authors, too, have stressed the fact that a common ideology makes pragmatic compromises more difficult and may aggravate rather than mitigate conflicts.[7] In game-theoretical jargon, a common universalistic ideology tends to spiral conflicts into "zero-sum games."

On balance, it seems that the main element binding the two

alliance partners together, at least in 1958, was the common interest in a strong and united front vis-à-vis the West. Both parties realized that unity was a decisive factor of strength and that a split would weaken the position of the socialist bloc in relation to the non-Communist world.[8] A Chinese 1958 statement may illustrate this:

> The greater the solidarity between the communist movement and the socialist countries, the more powerful we shall become. On the other hand, should there be divisive forces among us, our strength would be dissipated. Then, even if we possessed such a powerful weapon as intercontinental ballistic missiles, we would not be able to overwhelm the enemies, we might even be overwhelmed by them.[9]

Brzezinski has suggested that the need for unity served as a kind of hostage in Sino–Soviet relations:

> In the bargaining process between them, *unity* plays a role analogous to that of a hostage restraining both Parties. In a situation involving the exchange of hostages . . . , one may threaten the life of a hostage, but such a threat can be effective only as long as the hostage is alive; once dead, the threat of killing the hostage has lost all effectiveness. The same applies to unity. . . . [A]s long as the hostage is alive (i.e., unity of sorts is maintained), the asymmetry of strength between the two partners is diminished (or disappears altogether): it makes the weaker stronger, the stronger weaker.[10]

Conflicting Interests

Whereas the Soviet Union and China thus had a common stake in a cohesive and strengthened socialist bloc, their divergent interests grew out of conflicting preferences as to the distribution of authority and capabilities within the bloc and the posture toward the world outside the bloc.

The test ban issue touched on several critical areas of Sino–Soviet disagreement. Lowenthal as early as 1959 pointed to the nuclear test ban as the "least publicly discussed and most important" divisive issue.[11] Clemens has made the following retrospective assessment:

> If one sought to compare the importance of the nuclear test ban with other issues exacerbating Sino–Soviet relations prior to July 1963, it

would be difficult to point to any other that so consistently gnawed at what both sides regarded as their vital interests, whose symbolic and material significance was so great in itself, or whose ramifications penetrated so many areas of the dispute.[12]

The test ban issue involved Sino–Soviet disagreement about the distribution of nuclear capabilities as well as differences as to the correct policy toward the West.

THE ANALYSIS OF SINO–SOVIET BARGAINING

Article IV of the Sino–Soviet Treaty of Friendship, Alliance, and Mutual Assistance of 1950 reads: "Both High Contracting Parties will consult with each other in regard to all important international problems affecting the common interests of China and the Soviet Union, being guided by the interests of consolidating peace and universal security."[13] And the joint communique after Khrushchev's visit to Peking in August 1958 referred to the mutual "obligation to regular and all-round advance consultation."[14]

Although intra-bloc bargaining obviously did take place between the USSR and China on the test ban issue, it seldom took the form of explicit negotiations and consultations. The extent and content of direct Sino–Soviet contacts are subject only to speculation, and our analysis will have to concentrate on "crypto-public"[15] bargaining moves.

As in our analysis of East–West bargaining, we shall focus on the images and expectations of the actors. Thus, after identifying the major "moves" in the intra-bloc bargaining, we shall try to reconstruct Chinese images (a) of the test ban issue, and (b) of U.S. behavior. Under (a) we shall place the test ban issue in perspective and also discuss Chinese images of

—disarmament and arms control in general;
—the nuclear proliferation issue;
—China's nuclear development.

Under (b) will be included an analysis of Chinese images of

—U.S. attitudes to détente and arms control in general and the test ban issue in particular;

—differences within the U.S. leadership;
—what strategy to follow vis-à-vis the United States.

These Chinese images will then be compared with the Soviet counterparts. Our periodization of the test ban negotiations, based on observable changes in Soviet negotiating behavior, will be used here, too, in order to finally assess the impact of intra-bloc bargaining on Soviet negotiating behavior at Geneva.

SIX

Intra-Bloc Bargaining: Stage I

Major Moves: Stage I

1958	March 31	The Soviet Union suspends nuclear testing.
	April 4	Khrushchev sends letter on test ban issue to Chou En-lai—belated answer.
	May 24	Warsaw Pact meeting in Moscow. Speech by Chinese observer differs markedly from Khrushchev's speech.
	May 27	The Military Committee of the CPC Central Committee assembles for unprecedented eight-week session.
	July	Experts' Conference starts. China issues ultimatum to the United States, threatening to break up U.S.–Chinese ambassadorial talks.
	July	Middle East crisis reveals Sino–Soviet differences over strategy vis-à-vis the West.
	July 31	Khrushchev goes to Peking for unannounced three-day visit.
	Aug.–Sept.	Taiwan Strait crisis.
	Sept. 30	The Soviet Union resumes nuclear testing—immediate Chinese support.
	Oct.	The publication of Mao Tse-tung's *Imperialists and All Reactionaries Are Paper Tigers* starts anti-U.S. campaign within China.

1959 Jan. 27	21st CPSU congress opens. Khrushchev presents proposal for Asian atom-free zone—Chinese reaction slow and ambiguous.
April–June	Chinese military goodwill mission to East European countries headed by Marshal Peng Teh-huai.
June 20	The Soviet Union, according to later Chinese charges, abrogates defense technology agreement and refuses China sample nuclear bomb.
Aug. 2–16	Lushan plenum of CPC Central Committee. Dismissal of Marshal Peng Teh-huai.
Sept.	The Soviet Union takes neutral stand in Sino–Indian border incidents. Khrushchev visits the United States.
Sept. 30	Khrushchev visits Peking.
1960 Jan. 14	Khrushchev announces reduction of Soviet conventional forces.
Jan. 21	China declares itself unbound by disarmament agreements without its own signature.
Feb. 4	Warsaw Pact meeting in Moscow issues statement on foreign policy stressing need for East-West negotiations. Speech by Chinese observer indicating disagreement not reported in East European media.
April 19	China publishes "Long Live Leninism!"

THE 1958–60 period was characterized by highly esoteric communication in Soviet and, especially so, in Chinese media. Moreover, several Soviet and Chinese acts entailed significant communication in the Sino–Soviet dialogue pertaining to the test ban issue.

It should also be noted that there were frequent opportunities for bilateral high-level talks during this period. However, a number of important steps were apparently taken without prior coordination or consultation. The Soviet test suspension on March 31, 1958, is a case in point. Chou En-lai, in a belated official reaction to this Soviet move, stated that "the Chinese Government *has been informed* of this decision by the Soviet Government."[1] And whereas President Eisenhower went to Europe to consult his allies before receiving Khrushchev in the United States in September

1959, Khrushchev, significantly, did not go to Peking until *after* his talks with Eisenhower.

CHINESE IMAGES OF THE TEST BAN ISSUE

Western observers have often emphasized the declaratory Chinese support of test cessation and of Soviet moves in the test ban negotiations into 1959.[2] However, a closer scrutiny of Chinese statements reveals certain nuances that seem to signal a lack of enthusiasm over test cessation. To be sure, in 1957 Peking supported the Soviet test ban proposals to the London Disarmament Conference and condemned the U.S. attempt to link a test ban with other issues as "hopelessly complicating the question."[3] But by the end of 1957 Chinese commentaries had established a theme that was to reappear throughout the 1958–60 period and that came close to the U.S. line condemned earlier. Support was given to a ban on the testing *and* use or manufacture of nuclear weapons. In other words, a test ban was not primarily seen as a separate measure in its own right but as a part of comprehensive nuclear disarmament.

[W]hat is wrong with an agreement between the Soviet Union, the United States, and Britain on *ending nuclear weapons tests and prohibiting the use of such weapons?* [4]

All over the world calls are heard for general disarmament, *prohibition of the tests and use of nuclear weapons.* [5]

We take a firm stand for universal disarmament and *the prohibition of the testing and use of nuclear weapons.* [6]

On the face of it this shade of difference may seem insignificant. But the frequency of such phrases [7] and the fact that the same mode of expression was, as we shall see later, used by the opponents of a test ban in the Soviet Union go to indicate that these nuances should not be dismissed lightly. In a 1963 statement the Chinese have dated the beginning of Sino–Soviet divergencies on the test ban issue to 1956 when the Soviet Union "divorced the cessation of nuclear tests from the question of disarmament."[8] While this retrospective judgment cannot be taken at face value (the date may, for instance, be set too early), it does point in the same direction as our analysis of the, at best, qualified Chinese support of Soviet test ban proposals.

China signaled that it was less than enthusiastic about Soviet efforts to achieve a test ban agreement in other indirect ways as well. Soviet consent to the American proposal for holding an experts' conference in July 1958 did not meet with full Chinese endorsement,[9] whereas the Soviet decision to relieve itself from its unilateral test suspension met with prompt and "unreserved support."[10]

On the nuclear proliferation issue China and the Soviet Union were not at one. Khrushchev sent a letter to Chou En-lai on April 4, 1958 spelling out the rationale behind the Soviet decision to suspend testing. There he dwelt on the proliferation argument: "If the tests are not terminated now, other countries may develop nuclear weapons within a certain space of time and then it will, of course, be more difficult to reach agreement on ending tests thereof."[11]

In his belated answer dated April 13, Chou En-lai, while supporting the Soviet move in general terms, made no mention of the proliferation aspect.[12] Chinese statements during the summer of 1958 pointed out that the United States planned to increase its exchange of nuclear weapons information with Britain and France,[13] and reports appeared in the Chinese press on American shipments of nuclear weapons to Japan, South Korea, Taiwan, and West Germany.[14] These comments could be read as reminders to Moscow that the United States, on its part, did not consider nuclear sharing incompatible with negotiating a test ban. When Khrushchev in his speech to the 21st Party Congress in January 1959 revived the concept of an Asian atom-free zone, the Chinese reaction was slow in coming and ambiguous in wording.[15]

It is evident that the Chinese reluctance to come out unequivocally for a test ban and against proliferation can be attributed to its determination to acquire a nuclear capability of its own. In 1955 the Soviet Union had made a commitment to aid China in peaceful nuclear research and development, and the following year Chinese scientists began taking part in nuclear research at Dubna, outside Moscow. According to Chinese revelations in 1963, neither denied nor confirmed by the Soviet Union, Soviet nuclear aid took on a military dimension in October 1957, when an "agreement on new technology for national defense" was concluded.[16] And by late 1957, Chinese statements revealed considerable optimism about further Soviet nuclear weapons assistance.[17] An indication of Chinese expectations can be found in the new training program for the Army, promulgated in January 1958:

> The new programme of combat training is based on our strategic policy, the peculiarities of our terrain, the glorious traditions of our Army, the experience of training practice of the past few years, *and the development of modern military techniques and military science. Soviet advanced experience in this field is also incorporated.* . . .
> [T]he object of training in the future should be to continue improving modern military technique and to learn the co-ordination of the various branches of the Army *in combat under the modern conditions of atom bombs, chemical warfare, and guided missiles,* as well as in other complicated situations, so that the Army may be ready at all times to deal with any emergency.[18]

After an interim period, in which the training program was not approved or even heard of, a new Chinese military line gradually emerged in mid-1958 which represented drastic changes.[19] Slavish reliance on the Soviet Union and blind following of foreign experience were condemned. Man, not weapons technology, was to be considered the decisive factor in modern war.[20]

All the same, there were Chinese statements at this time indicating that China would develop its own nuclear weapons "in the not distant future."[21] Although the wording was typically ambiguous as to the expected Soviet contribution to this Chinese nuclear weapons program, the optimism of late 1957 had apparently evaporated.

> We should and absolutely can master, in not too long a time, the newest technology concerning *atomic energy in all fields.* . . . There are people who think that as long as we receive assistance from the Soviet Union and other fraternal countries, there is no need for us to carry out more complicated research ourselves. This way of thinking is wrong. . . . Because of the natural conditions of China and the characteristics of her

construction work, *there is in fact no possibility for us to make wholesale use of the existing experiences of other countries.*[22]

On June 20, 1959, the Soviet Union dissipated Chinese uncertainty about the extent of Soviet aid by unilaterally abrogating the agreement on defense technology and refusing to provide China with a sample bomb, according to later Chinese charges.[23] Developments a few months later suggested that the ambiguity in Chinese statements on nuclear strategy up till then had been partly due to internal differences within the Chinese military leadership. A number of high-level militaries including Marshal Peng Teh-huai, the minister of defense, were dismissed at the Lushan plenum of the Central Committee in August. Peng Teh-huai, who made an open, broad attack on the policy of the Party at the plenum, is believed to have favored greater reliance on the Soviet Union and was charged with having conspired with the Soviet leadership.[24] According to Chinese statements made during the Cultural Revolution, these cleavages had repercussions in the political leadership, where Liu Shao-chi is supposed to have represented "right opportunist" viewpoints, opposing China's independent nuclear program and favoring reliance on the Soviet nuclear umbrella.[25]

CHINESE IMAGES OF U.S. BEHAVIOR

If Sino–Soviet disagreements on the test ban issue were implicit and largely latent during the 1958–60 period, differences in their respective images of the United States were more articulate and easier to discover.

At the root lay divergent images of the international distribution of power. In the Chinese view, the success of Sputnik in 1957 marked a "qualitative," irreversible change in the balance of power—"the East wind was now prevailing over the West wind."[26] Another recurring Chinese figure of speech was that of the West as "the setting sun in the afternoon" and the East as "the rising sun in the morning."[27] In other words, the West was considered inferior and bound to become weaker and weaker, while the already superior East would grow ever stronger.

Soviet estimates, on the other hand, were less definite and more circumscribed.[28] Chinese media made several oblique references to these divergencies in outlook:

[R]ight up to the present, there are still many people who over-estimate the strength of imperialism and the reactionaries, and under-estimate the strength of the revolutionary forces. They only see the superficial strength of imperialism and the reactionaries, but do not notice the actual weakness of imperialism and the reactionaries.[29]

It is the reactionaries that should fear the revolutionary forces, and not vice versa. At present, there are quite a few people who still fail to see this, who still cherish superstitions and illusions, who still stand in awe of the imperialists in general and the US imperialists in particular.[30]

The fact that imperialism was moribund did not mean that it had become harmless, in the Chinese view.

The nearer the imperialists and the reactionaries are to their demise, the more desperate their struggle becomes.[31]

[A]s Chairman Mao said, "in human history, all reactionary forces that are about to be extinguished invariably fight desperately against the revolutionary forces." Isn't there a Chinese saying that says: "A cornered beast will put up a desperate fight?"[32]

This image of moribund but still aggressive imperialism was epitomized in Mao's "paper tiger" theme: imperialists could be slighted strategically, since in the long run they were doomed; but tactically they should be taken seriously.[33]

Accordingly, no genuine détente measures could be expected from the United States: "one can no more hope to get the United States to give up its policy of creating tension than one can expect 'a cat to keep away from fish.' "[34]

After Khrushchev's visit to the United States in September 1959, Chinese statements on inherent American aggressiveness assumed a defensive character. The more conciliatory U.S. policy line, epitomized in the "Camp David spirit" and publicized in Soviet commentary, was discharged as a change in tactics—a "smokescreen" or "calculated fake"[35]—while the aggressive goals remained unchanging. The United States was "talking peace while preparing for war." American imperialism had not, and would not, "lay down the butcher's knife to become a Buddha," to use a favorite Chinese slogan of the period.[36]

Furthermore, the Chinese denied any sudden change in American policy: "In reality, this tactical change on the part of the US, instead of beginning only a few months ago, may be traced two years back to the time shortly after the launching by the Soviet Union of the first man-made satellite."[37] Finding itself in an inferior position militarily, the United States was employing this change in tactics in order to "try to get enough time to reinforce their armament; at the same time, they try to use peace to bewilder the people, slacken the people's will of fighting against imperialism, disarm the people's vigilance and thereby clear the way for them to start an aggressive war."[38]

By early 1960 Chinese statements began to imply that Khrushchev had, in fact, fallen prey to the American design and was mistaking the tactical changes for changes in the nature of imperialism. A *Jen-min Jih-pao* editorial in January asserted that "an increasing number of people in both East and West have seen through the two-faced tactics of the United States. Even if *it still misleads some people*, this cannot last long."[39]

The pamphlet "Long Live Leninism!" went one step further toward identifying these misled people, characterizing them as "well-intentioned persons who sincerely want to be Marxists, but are confused in the face of certain new historical phenomena."[40]

In keeping with this image of the United States as an invariably aggressive imperialist power, the Chinese denied any genuine U.S. desire to achieve disarmament or arms control generally and a test ban treaty in particular. "The United States is zealous not for disarmament but for an arms drive in preparation for war."[41]

Long before negotiations on test cessation had started at Geneva, the Chinese dismissed American proposals on the issue as "empty talk."[42] A few days after the opening of the experts' conference, *Jen-min Jih-pao* commented:

The United States refused to follow the Soviet example in stopping nuclear tests and played the dual-face trick in respect of the conference of eastern and western nuclear specialists. This is a proof of its unwillingness to ease the international tension.[43]

Assertions that the Western powers had no intention whatsoever to end their nuclear weapons tests and warnings that one should not be deceived by their "empty talk" about test cessation continued to appear in the Chinese press during the fall of 1958.[44] After the test ban negotiations had been in progress less than two months, a Chinese commentary made the following assessment: "as demonstrated at the Geneva Conference what the governments of the U.S. and Britain are interested in is not the discontinuance of nuclear tests and destruction of nuclear weapons, but the continuation of nuclear tests and preparations for a nuclear war."[45]

A year of negotiations at Geneva did not change this image, as indicated by an early 1960 comment: "[J]udged by the progress of the [test ban] conference in the past 14 months, the U.S. and its partner Britain are not prepared to reach any agreement with the U.S.S.R."[46] At the same time it was pointed out that U.S. efforts to prevent a test ban were inseparable from its overall policy of war preparation,[47] and predictions were made about "the U.S. intention to continue its sabotage in the future negotiations."[48]

The Chinese "enemy" image of the United States left no room for significant differences within the U.S. leadership, as did the Soviet "enemy-partner" image.

> Whether the American regime is in the hands of the Democrats representing the interests of one monopolistic bloc or of the Republicans representing the interests of another monopolistic bloc, whether the Secretary of State is Marshall, Acheson, Dulles or Herter, the people in authority remain the tools of American monopolist capital, and to expect them to change the aggressive policy of American imperialism can be likened to angling up a tree or cherishing day dreams.[49]

Consequently, the tactical change in American policy after Camp David had nothing to do with the internal balance of forces in the U.S. leadership but could "be attributed to outside squeeze like what is applied to a tube of toothpaste."[50]

After Khrushchev's U.S. visit, Sino–Soviet differences became most pronounced on the appraisal of President Eisenhower. Portions of Khrushchev's speech in Peking on his return from the United States were deleted from Peking broadcasts, including his "impression that the U.S. President understands the need to relax

INTRA-BLOC BARGAINING: STAGE I

international tensions."[51] And in early 1960 there were several articles in the Chinese press demonstrating that Eisenhower was *not* a "man of peace," and references were made to efforts by "revisionists" to "prettify imperialism and Eisenhower, the chieftain of U.S. imperialists."[52]

From these images of the United States and of the international balance of power the Chinese drew conclusions as to what strategy to follow in relations with the West, which differed from Soviet conclusions.

Soviet as well as Chinese evaluations of the U.S.–USSR military balance had apparently led to the conclusion that the United States was deterred by the novel Soviet military strength. However, they disagreed on the question: deterred from what?

> The point at issue between Peking and Moscow was not whether Soviet power deterred the United States from an *unprovoked* attack on China, but whether the Soviet Union was prepared to use its power to back up China's external objectives and to support effectively revolutionary activity in underdeveloped areas.[53]

In the Chinese view, much active maneuvering, especially in the third world, could be done under the protection of the Soviet nuclear umbrella, while the Soviet image of *"mutual* deterrence" implied avoidance of all types of confrontations that might escalate into nuclear war.

> Some people fear that the face-to-face struggle against U.S. imperialists would invite a world war. The wild aggression and war plans of U.S. imperialists are not the consequences of our struggle against them; on the contrary, our resolute struggles have thrown their aggression and war plans into disorder and forced them to retreat step by step.[54]

These Sino–Soviet divergencies were tied to different images of likely U.S. reactions to a more provocative policy. "To bully the weak and fear the strong" was an old habit of American imperialists, according to a favorite Chinese expression. Any sign of weakness would encourage aggression.

> Some people are of the opinion that we had better not offend the U.S. imperialists and that if they are offended, they will become more frenzied and this will not be in the interests of world peace. . . .

Can peace be secured by refraining from opposing and stopping them and driving them away? Of course not. On the contrary, this will only result in pampering aggression and making the imperialists and reactionaries wilder.[55]

The Chinese on several occasions voiced their displeasure with Khrushchev's behavior in this regard. Right after his visit to Peking on July 31, 1958, *Jen-min Jih-pao* editorials complained about the "soft-hearted pacifist" thinking of "certain persons."[56] In connection with the Lenin anniversary celebrations in April 1960, a Chinese spokesman said:

Whether or not one dares to expose the imperialists, and especially the U.S. imperialists, whether or not one dares to struggle against them, is the touchstone of whether or not he wants to carry out the people's revolution, to win the complete emancipation of the oppressed nationalities and to win a genuine world peace.[57]

The 1958–60 period also offered ample opportunities to test these divergent images. The Middle East crisis of July 1958 provided the first test. As Zagoria puts it, there was throughout the crisis "difference between the degree of risk Khrushchev was prepared to accept and the degree Mao wanted to see him accept."[58] Whereas the Soviet Union responded to the Iraqi coup and the subsequent British and American landings in Lebanon and Jordan with calls for moderation and a summit meeting, Chinese public statements seemed to favor military counteraction, lest the West would become increasingly overconfident and arrogant.[59]

In August 1958, when China initiated a crisis in the Taiwan Strait by shelling the offshore islands Quemoy and Matsu, there were no high-level Soviet expressions of support until the crisis had been substantially reduced and China had offered to negotiate, and even then the statements were ambiguous as to what Soviet action would be taken against anything short of a U.S. attack on China.[60] It has been suggested that the Chinese undertook the offshore islands venture, at least partly, in an effort to demonstrate to Moscow the correctness of their thesis that the United States was deterred from forcefully responding to offensive Communist thrusts.[61]

The fall of 1959 saw another momentous chain of events.

First, the Soviet Union took a neutral stand in the Sino–Indian border dispute, and shortly afterwards Khrushchev made his widely publicized visit to the United States.[62]

The Sino–Soviet differences on the overall strategy to be followed in East–West relations also implied different attitudes to negotiations with the West. The apparent Soviet confidence in the possibility of making gains by negotiations was not shared by the Chinese. It is not hard to find Chinese statements from this period indicating a totally negative attitude to negotiated settlements, notably compromises.

There should be no compromise in dealing with the imperialists because this will end in submission.[63]

With the imperialists we should not compromise; for the imperialists are a bunch of creatures that would submit to force but never listen to persuasion. . . .
[P]eace will be preserved if we fight for it, and it will be lost of we resort to compromise.[64]

On the other hand, counterbalancing statements can be found as well.

We have always advocated the settlement of questions between nations by means of negotiation.[65]

In the struggle against imperialism and its policy of aggression it is entirely permissible and necessary and in the interests of the people of various countries that, wherever possible, the socialist countries conduct peaceful negotiations and exchange visits with the imperialist countries, strive to settle international disputes by peaceful means instead of war, and endeavor to sign agreements of peaceful coexistence or treaties of non-aggression.[66]

It seems reasonable to conclude that Soviet and Chinese views differed in degree rather than in kind, and that the point at issue was the emphasis to be put on negotiations, as compared to other means of influencing the West. Exclusive emphasis or overreliance on negotiations was thought to be harmful by the Chinese. This was well illustrated in 1958 by Chinese reactions to the experts' conference and to the Soviet decision to break its test moratorium, respectively.

On the eve of the opening of the experts' conference, the

Chinese government made a statement urging the U.S. government to resume the suspended U.S.–Chinese ambassadorial talks within fifteen days, or it would be considered that the United States had desired to break up the talks. Comments in the Chinese press stressed that the Chinese people, while "partisans of peace", would "never crave for talks with the U.S. imperialists nor are they afraid of waging a resolute struggle" against them.[67] The timing of the campaign suggests that it was, at least in part, directed against the Soviet conciliatory attitude in respect to the experts' conference and designed to show the Soviet leaders how to conduct negotiations with the West.

This veiled Chinese hint was further clarified in the supportive comments on the Soviet decision to resume tests while negotiating a test ban.

Pressure must be brought to bear on the United States and Britain to achieve a permanent suspension of nuclear weapons tests. . . .
In face of imperialist aggressive forces, mere talk of peace instead of swelling the ranks of peace defenders will only help to add to the ferociousness of the imperialist aggressive forces and endanger peace.[68]

As indicated by these examples, negotiation was seen by the Chinese as a complement to, rather than a substitute for, other more coercive foreign policy means. Negotiations could not, in and of themselves, contribute much to the pursuit of Communist aims. The main weapon should always be popular struggle rather than intergovernmental talks. This was considered valid for arms control issues as well.

The peoples of the world should not be deceived by the U.S. and British Governments' empty talk about cessation of nuclear weapon tests for one year. They must continue an unabated struggle to force these governments at the coming Geneva conference to agree to the permanent cessation of all nuclear weapon tests.[69]

SOVIET AND CHINESE IMAGES: COMPARISON AND SUMMARY

Several Western observers have pondered over a "most puzzling aspect" of Sino–Soviet relations during this period. The Soviet

Union seemed to be pursuing two contradictory courses: nuclear aid to China simultaneous with serious efforts at agreement in the test ban negotiations.[70] China gave declaratory support to Soviet test ban proposals, while at the same time making no secret of its intention to achieve a nuclear capability. Some Western analysts have suggested that the answer to this riddle is to be found in a secret "test ban clause" in the 1957 defense agreement, according to which Peking had to pay the price of supporting a test ban for achieving Soviet nuclear aid.[71] Unbacked by any evidence, such a conspiracy does not seem convincing against the background of growing Sino–Soviet differences.[72] Besides, as we have seen, the Chinese never did give Soviet test ban moves wholehearted support but on several occasions signalled its uneasiness about a test ban.

Our previous analysis would rather indicate that the Soviet Union and China were acting on the basis of divergent expectations at the outset of the test ban negotiations. These expectations can be represented schematically thus:

	Chinese Expectations	*Soviet Expectations*
re test ban issue	low probability of test ban	test ban desirable, plausible
	nuclear capability *with or without* Soviet aid	Soviet control over Chinese nuclear capability
re U.S. behavior	test ban not in the interest of U.S.	test ban might be in the interest of U.S.
	U.S. will not be influenced by negotiations	U.S. might be influenced by negotiations
	no internal differences within U.S. leadership	differences within U.S. leadership that can be exploited by negotiations

Some of these initial expectations gradually eroded during the 1958–60 period. The Soviet Union was evidently searching for an arrangement, combining continued assistance to China with increased Soviet control over China's military potential.[73] In 1958 it "put forward unreasonable demands designed to put China under

Soviet military control," according to later Chinese allegations.[74] Soviet restlessness over the prospect of China's future possession of nuclear weapons was also reflected in its proposals in 1957–58 and again in 1959 for an Asian nuclear-free zone.[75] The danger of being drawn into a conflict started by China must have caused Soviet leaders concern, especially after the Taiwan Strait crisis.[76] Its control efforts having failed, the Soviet Union in mid-1959 cut off its nuclear aid to China. At a closed Warsaw Pact meeting in February 1960, the Soviet representative is reported to have "made it plain, in so many words, that the Soviet Union had not the least intention of giving nuclear arms to China."[77] At Geneva, Soviet confidence in the possibility of inducing "other countries" to join or abide by a test ban agreement evaporated during 1959.

China's low assessment of the probability of a test ban was based on its reiterated estimate that the United States would not agree to such a treaty. Not until after Khrushchev's U.S. visit did the Chinese begin to fear that *the Soviet Union* might make concessions and conclude a treaty behind their back. On January 21, 1960 China pointedly declared that "any international agreement concerning disarmament, without the formal participation of the People's Republic of China and the signature of its delegate, cannot of course have any binding force on her."[78]

Khrushchev had foreshadowed Chinese worries in his address to the Supreme Soviet a week earlier, where he asserted that the Soviet Union "never had and does not have any intention of reaching agreement behind the backs of other countries on matters directly affecting their interests."[79]

Another indication that Chinese worries that a test ban might be imminent did not become acute until the turn of the year 1959–60 is provided by the retrospective Chinese judgment that "there was not yet the slightest sign of a treaty on stopping nuclear tests" in June 1959, when Soviet nuclear aid was discontinued.[80] Western observers have tended to discard this Chinese assessment as insincere and inaccurate, pointing to Western optimism at the time as to the prospects of concluding a test ban treaty shortly.[81] However, the point is how *Chinese* leaders estimated the situation in mid-1959. And it is not implausible to as-

INTRA-BLOC BARGAINING: STAGE I 101

sume that their firm belief that the United States would never agree to a treaty made them discount the probability of agreement until after Camp David, when they apparently became increasingly worried that Khrushchev's susceptibility to U.S. "peace talk" might result in Soviet concessions to the Western position.

The initial Chinese expectation as to a future nuclear capability *with or without* Soviet aid also underwent change. While in mid-1958 apparently still retaining some hope for increased Soviet aid, the Chinese a year later were left with no choice but going it alone. The initial Chinese dilemma is spelled out in a retrospective statement:

True, if the Soviet leaders really practised proletarian internationalism, China might consider it unnecessary to manufacture its own nuclear weapons. But it is equally true that if the Soviet leaders really practised proletarian internationalism, they would have no reason whatever for obstructing China from manufacturing nuclear weapons.[82]

By late 1959 it had become evident to the Chinese (a) that the Soviet Union would not extend any further nuclear aid; and (b) that the Soviet nuclear umbrella would not be extended to deter violent responses to offensive Chinese moves, as the Taiwan Strait crisis and the Sino–Indian border incident had clearly demonstrated.

Thus, by the end of 1959 both the Soviet Union and China must have realized that their initial expectations had not been borne out by events. The Soviet Union, while still expecting and desiring a test ban, realized that it would not be able to keep control over China's nuclear capability. China, while still striving toward an independent nuclear capability, realized that no Soviet nuclear aid was forthcoming and began to fear that a test ban treaty might be concluded. Neither side had changed its image of U.S. behavior.

Against the background of the initial divergencies in Soviet and Chinese expectations, the surprising thing is not that this crisis did occur, but rather that it did not occur earlier. Previous experiences of Sino-Soviet relations seem to have made both sides discount new, contradictory signals.

The Soviet Union may not have taken at face value the new militancy of the Chinese, which contrasted with their international posture of the mid-fifties. And the Chinese concern with Communist unity and eagerness to stress the leading role of the CPSU in 1957 probably seemed reassuring to the Soviet leaders.[83] That the Soviet Union may initially have misjudged the Chinese determination to develop a nuclear capability of its own is also suggested by later polemics where the Soviet side has referred to assurances by Mao Tse-tung as late as September 1958 that China "need not organize the production of such [nuclear] weapons, especially considering the fact that they are very costly."[84]

Chinese leaders, on the other hand, initially "seemed convinced that 'non-antagonistic contradictions' with Moscow would ultimately lead to unity, through their internally tested process of 'unity-criticism-unity.' "[85] Their belief may well have been reinforced by recent experiences where they felt that their criticism had in effect had an influence on Soviet decisions: Poland and Hungary, 1956.[86]

In any case, the mutual re-evaluation of late 1959 obviously called Sino–Soviet unity into question. The "hostage" now was in danger of being killed off.

SEVEN

Intra-Bloc Bargaining: Stage II

Major Moves: Stage II

1960	May 1	U-2 incident.
	May 14–19	Abortive summit meeting in Paris.
	June 5–9	World Federation of Trade Unions (WFTU) meeting in Peking. Chinese delegate attacks Soviet views on questions of war and peace.
	June 20–25	Soviet counteroffensive at Rumanian Party congress in Bucharest. The Soviet Union circulates anti-Chinese letter among delegates.
	Aug.	Soviet technicians leave China.
	Sept. 10	Chinese letter to CPSU responding to Soviet charges at the Bucharest conference.
	Oct.	Volume 4 of Mao's selected works published in China.
	Nov.	Conference of 81 Communist parties in Moscow issues ambiguous joint statement after long discussions.
1961	June 3–4	Vienna summit meeting.
	Aug. 31	Soviet test resumption—immediate Chinese support.
	Oct. 17–27	22d CPSU congress. Khrushchev's speech includes sharp attack on Albania. Chou En-lai, heading the Chinese delegation, abruptly returns home before the

	conclusion of the congress, after having ostentatiously placed a wreath on Stalin's tomb.
Dec. 16–19	Meeting of World Peace Council in Stockholm with heated Sino–Soviet debates.
1962 July	Moscow Peace Conference—subdued Chinese appearance.
Aug.	Tokyo Conference against atom and hydrogen bombs—strong Chinese criticism of Soviet position. Chinese commentary characterizes the meeting as "the most successful conference in 1962 that really represented the will of the overwhelming majority of the people throughout the world." SCMP (2811):33.
Aug. 25	Soviet government, according to later Chinese statements, notifies China of its willingness to enter non-proliferation agreement.
Sept. 3, Oct. 20	Chinese protests against Soviet non-proliferation position

WHEREAS THE Sino–Soviet dialogue in the 1958–60 period was conducted "surreptitiously, at closed meetings, only echoed in subtly diverging public pronouncements,"[1] it now began to lose some of its "esoteric" character. It also transcended the bilateral framework and came to involve the whole international Communist movement. The Sino–Soviet controversy was to a considerable extent carried on in multilateral Communist gatherings, and both sides circulated letters among the fraternal parties. Variations in the type of moves preferred by the two sides could be discerned.

Being physically weaker, they [the Chinese] must prove to Moscow that they are *serious* in their views, that they are even willing to run risks. For this reason, they cannot only communicate informally—that would not carry the necessary weight.[2]

Being the stronger and ideologically more moderate participant in the dispute, Moscow had the advantage in organisational rather than ideological moves.[3]

The Chinese brought the controversy into the open with the publication of "Long Live Leninism!" in April 1960. The CPSU responded to this and other verbal attacks by trying to isolate

China at international Communist conferences, beginning at Bucharest in June 1960.

Behind these differences in behavior lay different ideas as to how the Sino–Soviet dispute might be settled. The Chinese, stressing the sovereignty of each individual party, insisted on unanimity. The CPSU, appealing to the principle of "democratic centralism," favored majority decisions that would be binding on the minority as well.[4] Already in December 1959, Khrushchev had spoken about the need to "synchronize our watches," and on the eve of the Bucharest conference a *Pravda* editorial stated bluntly that "among Socialist countries, there cannot be two opinions on the question of peace and war."[5] Soviet party journals began claiming for the first time that peaceful coexistence represented the general foreign policy line of the *entire* Communist bloc.[6]

The Soviet Union thus chose to put emphasis on the peace–war issue in its efforts to isolate China and rally a majority. And Bucharest saw the beginning of protracted polemical exchanges in which the Chinese as well as the Russians were distorting the arguments of the other side: "The Russians sought to create the false impression that the Chinese were pressing for a global war, and the Chinese sought to create the equally false impression that the Russians had given up the struggle for world revolution."[7] As other Communist parties were drawn into the Sino–Soviet dispute, some of them made attempts at mediation. Other parties thus became involved both as subjects and as objects in the controversy.[8]

By bringing the dispute into a multilateral framework, both sides became increasingly committed to their respective positions. This was particularly evident in the period between the Bucharest conference and the Moscow meeting. The meeting of 81 Communist parties in Moscow of November 1960 managed—apparently after prolonged and tough bargaining[9]—to reach agreement on an ambiguous document.[10] The Moscow Declaration, far from being a compromise in terms of mutual concessions, represented a collation of often incompatible views.[11] This meant that each side could—and indeed did—read into the document what it itself wanted.

The Moscow conference was followed by an apparent lull in the Sino–Soviet dispute, which concealed an escalating "controversy by proxy" involving Albania and Yugoslavia, concomitant with increased Soviet–Yugoslav and Sino–Albanian rapprochement.[12]

CHINESE IMAGES OF THE TEST BAN ISSUE

As the Sino–Soviet dialogue was increasingly channelled into questions of peace and war, the Chinese were impelled to develop their views of disarmament and arms control in greater detail. In February 1960, a Chinese periodical published the most detailed discussion of these problems up till then.[13] On the subject of disarmament it concluded that

> ... to fight for all-round, thorough disarmament is a long-term, complicated struggle against the imperialists, from which we cannot get any result at one stroke. Fundamentally speaking, as long as they live the imperialists will never disarm themselves. Therefore, it is a kind of unpractical fantasy to pin our hope for a lasting world peace on the possibility that the imperialists might agree to, and actually execute, an all-round, thorough disarmament.[14]

After the new Soviet proposal for general and complete disarmament in June 1960, these views were further expounded:

> We support the proposal for disarmament put forward by the Soviet Union. It is, however inconceivable that imperialism will accept a proposal for general and complete disarmament. The purpose of putting forward such a proposal is to arouse the people throughout the world to unite and oppose the imperialist scheme for arms drive and war preparations, to unmask the aggressive and bellicose nature of imperialism before the people of the world in order to isolate as far as possible the imperialist bloc headed by the U.S., so that they will not dare unleash a war lightly. But there are people who believe that such a proposal can be realized when imperialism still exists and that the danger of war can be eliminated by relying on such a proposal. This is unrealistic illusion.[15]

In other words, disarmament *proposals* were seen as having a certain value as tactical propaganda devices aimed at expediting the downfall of imperialism, while disarmament as such was not possible as long as imperialism still existed. The launching of disarmament proposals was but one aspect of the constant struggle against imperialism: "Thus, while striving for general disarmament, it is necessary to strengthen constantly the struggles of all those peoples for national independence and liberation."[16] The Chinese, therefore, were in favor of holding disarmament *talks*, mainly for propaganda purposes; and though they expected no real disarmament to result from negotiations,

. . . it is possible, through struggle at disarmament talks and pressure from various sides, to force imperialism headed by the United States to accept certain disarmament agreements (on the banning of nuclear weapons, for instance). And, if the imperialist countries can be compelled to accept even a partial agreement on disarmament and guarantee its implementation, it will be beneficial to the cause of world peace and so will be welcome to us.[17]

China made it perfectly clear that it did not include a test ban among conceivable and acceptable partial measures. Test cessation was conspicuously absent from Chinese enumerations.[18] The practice of giving support to a ban on the testing *and* manufacture of nuclear weapons was continued.[19]

China supported the new Soviet line at Geneva (linking a test ban with GCD) and immediately endorsed Soviet test resumption in 1961. The low frequency of Chinese statements on a test ban throughout the period, however, seems to indicate a certain lack of enthusiasm about the issue.

Behind this may well have lain continuing and deepening Sino–Soviet disagreement on the proliferation issue. While the Soviet Union began to demonstrate a definite interest in nonproliferation,[20] China abandoned its previous ambiguity on the subject and came out clearly in favor of the spread of nuclear capabilities to socialist states other than the Soviet Union.[21]

Soviet mastery of nuclear weapons has now deprived U.S. imperialism of its monopoly of nuclear weapons. The Soviet Union *and the other socialist countries* should continue to develop their lead in the sphere of atomic energy.[22]

Until the time imperialism agrees to the overall banning of nuclear weapons, *the socialist countries* must have nuclear weapons and nuclear superiority.[23]

China's pro-proliferation argument was obviously, to a great extent, a rationalization of its determination to develop a nuclear capability of its own. According to Crankshaw, during the heated and acrimonious discussions in the preparatory commission of the Moscow meeting in the fall of 1960, many foreign delegates learned for the first time that "one of the real causes of Chinese bitterness . . . had been Khrushchev's refusal to give China nuclear weapons."[24]

In a number of articles during the fall of 1962, ostensibly directed against American policy but with an implied message to Moscow as well, the Chinese made it clear that it considered a positive interest in a test ban or non-proliferation agreement as a threat to its own defense program.

> The reason why U.S. ruling circles are so interested in preventing what they call "nuclear proliferation" is no secret. The Western papers have recently more than once disclosed that Washington is anxious to tie China's hands in developing nuclear weapons, and have even openly stated that this is one of the objectives of the limited ban draft treaty recently put forward by the United States. In the eyes of the U.S. rulers, it would assure U.S. nuclear superiority and make it easier for Washington to use nuclear blackmail if it can prevent China and other socialist countries from possessing nuclear weapons.[25]

> The Kennedy Administration's attitude on the nuclear weapons question calls to mind the Chinese saying that "while a prefectural official has the right to get away with arson, the common people are not allowed to light a lamp."[26]

That grievances over Soviet policy in this regard may have lain behind statements such as these is further suggested by the later Chinese allegation that the Soviet government on August 25, 1962 notified China of its affirmative reply to an American non-proliferation proposal.[27]

In brief, the 1960–62 period saw no substantial changes in Chinese images but rather clarifications and elaborations of images previously held.

CHINESE IMAGES OF U.S. BEHAVIOR

The U-2 incident reinforced Chinese images of an invariably aggressive United States and emboldened the Chinese to sharpen their criticism and drive home their thesis to the Russians with greater force. On May 14, 1960, Mao received Japanese and Latin American visitors and told them that the U-2 incident "further confirmed to the world the following truth: no unrealistic illusions should be cherished with regard to imperialism. Some people had described Eisenhower as a man who loved peace very much. I hope, Chairman Mao said, these people will be awakened by these facts."[28]

Sino-Soviet differences were succinctly summarized in an exchange of allegorical statements in June 1960. The first passage appeared in a *Red Flag* editorial, the second a few days later in Khrushchev's speech at Bucharest:

A wolf is a wolf, and its man-eating nature does not change. An ancient Chinese fable about the Chungshan wolf tells the story of Schoolmaster Tungkuo, who once found a wolf wounded by hunters and saved it by hiding it in his bag. After the hunters had left, he released the wolf from the bag. Instead of showing gratitude, the wolf wanted to devour him. Fortunately a peasant came along who understood well the man-eating nature of the wolf. He lured it back into the bag and beat it to death, and thus Schoolmaster Tungkuo was saved.

It is common knowledge that a wolf is just as bloodthirsty as a lion or a tiger, but he is much weaker. That is why a man fears less meeting a wolf than meeting a tiger or lion. Of course, small beasts of prey can also bite; essentially they are the same, but they have different possibilities. They are not as strong and it is easier to render them harmless.[29]

"Schoolmaster" Khrushchev thus refused to be saved by the "peasant" Mao and persisted in his view that the United States was deterred from aggressive violence by Soviet nuclear strength—an assumption explicitly denied by the Chinese.

Eisenhower is not unaware of the fact that the Soviet Union possesses the most advanced rocket weapons capable of repulsing any aggressors, but all the same he dispatched aircraft to intrude into the Soviet Union to carry out provocations. This shows that U.S. imperialism will never abandon its aggressive and war plans on account of the powerfulness of the socialist camp.[30]

It is sheer deception to say that the imperialists would change their policy if they were made to understand the truth that to commit aggression is to court destruction.[31]

Khrushchev's propagated view of differences within the U.S. leadership with Eisenhower included among the more "sober" elements also came under increased Chinese fire after the U-2 incident.

The "peace" gestures made by U.S. imperialism, and particularly Eisenhower as a fake "peace-lover" did indeed mislead some people and give rise to the illusion that U.S. policy had "changed." . . .
But if his clumsy tricks have failed in the past to mislead many people, how can they deceive anybody today after the further exposure of the true colors of U.S. imperialism?[32]

To think, on the strength of some passing gestures at relaxation put up by the imperialists, that the "cold war" has come to an end and a so-called "new era" has dawned—if it is not a deliberate attempt to prettify imperialism, is at least naive, with no factual basis. There are also some others who say that though not all those who are in power in the imperialist countries have mended their ways, there have emerged among them some "sober-minded" and "sensible" men and this after all is a new thing. . . .
It is true that all kinds of different opinions quarrel among imperialism, but not a single fact can be cited to show that among the bickering groups, there is one which is so "sensible" as not to regard all questions from an imperialist viewpoint.[33]

The advent of the new Kennedy administration did not elicit any changes in Chinese images. Whereas in the Soviet Union at least Khrushchev seemed to look forward to Kennedy's inauguration with wary optimism and displayed a wait-and-see attitude during his first year in office, the Chinese left no doubts about their attitude. The election results were commented thus: "The reactionary nature of the new tool of monopoly capital differs little from the Republican government either in its policies at home or abroad. Of course, to satisfy the needs of monopoly capital, Kennedy's government may continue the trick of really preparing for war while pretending to favor peace."[34]

The Bay of Pigs debacle fortified China's image. Mao is reported to have stated: "U.S. imperialism in its haste to launch aggression against Cuba, has once again revealed its true face before the whole world. This shows that the Kennedy administration is worse and not better than the Eisenhower administration."[35]

This was to become a recurring theme from then on. Kennedy followed the same "dual-face policy" as his predecessor had done and boldly did "what the Eisenhower government wanted to but dared not do."[36] If there was any difference it was that "the deceptive tactics of the Kennedy administration are more cunning, and its gestures more smart."[37] It is evident from Chinese remarks that the "limited war" doctrine of the new administration caused special alarm.

China also gave vent to its displeasure with the less assertive Soviet attitude, and when a U-2 plane was shot down over Chinese territory in September 1962, it expressed the hope that this incident would serve as a "second eye-opener" just as the 1960 U-2 incident had unmasked Eisenhower.[38]

Chinese commentary emphatically denied any significant differences within the Kennedy administration, making Tito the ostensible target of the polemics.

Tito tried to make people believe that only "wise men" are needed to bring about world peace. According to him, "wise men" would not entertain the thought of war. In Tito's eyes, U.S. imperialist leaders, such as Kennedy, are these "wise men."[39]

Tito's contention that military circles exert pressure on governments is a fallacy so crude that it needs no refutation. Any one with common sense knows that military affairs and politics are inseparable and that military methods are only a means of fulfilling political tasks. Whether in the United States or the Soviet Union, the military men are one with the government. Tito's absurd statement, on the one hand, serves to defend the Kennedy administration and to present Kennedy as a "peace lover" different from the Pentagon generals; on the other hand it is insulting to all the militarymen of the Soviet Union and other socialist countries.[40]

A corollary of the unaltered Chinese "enemy" image of the United States was, as before, the expectation that the United States was not interested in any genuine arms control. In June 1960, a *Jenmin Jih-pao* editorial on the new Soviet disarmament proposal bluntly stated: "The imperialist countries headed by the United States will never agree to general and complete disarmament."[41]

With respect to a test ban, an article on the ENDC negotiations stated:

> While doing everything possible to divert the conference from its main task of formulating an agreement on disarmament, the United States made every effort to drag it out by using the question of halting nuclear tests. Here too it reveals its ulterior motives. . . .
>
> [A] nuclear test ban would be acceptable to the U.S. only if it would assure U.S. nuclear superiority.[42]

From these images of the United States, China drew the same conclusions as previously regarding what strategy to pursue toward the West. After the Bucharest meeting and just before the conclusion of the Moscow Declaration, volume 4 of Mao's selected works was published (volume 3 had appeared in 1953). It includes a detailed account of the abortive efforts at "co-existence" between Communists and Nationalists in China. His conclusion, echoed in Chinese media from then on, is that "struggle is the only way" in relations with imperialists and reactionaries. The ambiguous Moscow Declaration was hailed in the Chinese press as "a militant call to combat imperialism."[43]

The Chinese view of negotiations with the West was elaborated in further detail during the 1960–62 period. A concise statement of Chinese expectations of U.S. behavior in negotiations was given by Liu Shao-chi:

> Experience shows that the imperialists, and first of all the U.S. imperialists, are devoid of all sincerity for peace and totally faithless in international dealings. They will not accept negotiations unless they have absolutely no other way out, and even when forced to accept negotiations they still try by every means to obstruct and sabotage them. Even if agreements are reached in negotiations, they can go back on these agreements and tear them up at any moment.[44]

Chinese experiences in the Sino–American ambassadorial talks, in the Korean armistice negotiations, and in the Laos Conference were said to have confirmed these expectations.[45]

The Chinese specifically warned against relying on internal differences within the U.S. leadership in negotiations.

> Facts have proved to the hilt that it is nothing but wishful thinking divorced from the class realities to regard Eisenhower, Herter, and their ilk as forming the sensible group of the American ruling clique who can understand profoundly the necessity of peaceful co-existence, and *to place hope on diplomatic negotiations with them.*[46]

Only in combination with popular struggle could negotiations be useful.

[T]o win world peace, the struggle of the world's peoples and the diplomatic negotiations carried out by the socialist countries should be linked together. It should not be supposed that since diplomatic negotiations are needed the struggle of the people could thus be dispensed with. On the contrary, diplomatic negotiations should be backed up by the solidarity and struggle of the world's peoples. To win world peace, we should mainly rely on the struggle waged by the peoples throughout the world.[47]

The Chinese thus made the priority of the two foreign policy instruments emphatically clear and rhetorically asked "modern revisionists":

Shall we believe the people of various countries or shall we believe the capitalists? Shall we lay our confidence on such unrealistic and illusory basis as believing the nature of the capitalists may change, or though it has not changed the capitalists would relinquish their policy of aggression and war and would have a "genuine wish" for peace?[48]

In keeping with their image of East–West bargaining, the Chinese never endorsed the 1961 Vienna summit. Chinese commentaries prior to the meeting pointed out that Kennedy had no intention to negotiate, thereby strongly implying that there was no sense in Khrushchev's going to Vienna. The meeting itself merited a mere reprint of brief Tass news without comments.[49] And Chinese remarks on the forthcoming ENDC negotiations in early 1962 stressed the necessity "to expose thoroughly and wage a sharp and unremitting struggle against the Kennedy Administration's use of the disarmament talks for political blackmail and its increased moves for war."[50]

SOVIET AND CHINESE IMAGES: COMPARISON AND SUMMARY

As we have seen, Chinese images were clarified and elaborated in greater detail during the 1960–62 period, but no change in images could be detected. It will be recalled that Soviet behavior did indeed change at the Geneva test ban negotiations in this period and that these changes were concomitant with changing Soviet images. The direction of these changes was toward convergence with Chinese images. In fact, Soviet policy toward the West in general hardened, and some Western analysts have suggested that this change in Soviet behavior was a direct response to Chinese pressures.[51]

However, the fact that these changes took place against the background of gradually worsening Sino–Soviet relations represents the puzzling aspect of this period. In Zagoria's words:

> Had Sino–Soviet differences been limited to mere matters of policy, one might have supposed that the hardening of Soviet foreign policy since the summer of 1960, combined with the radical domestic retreat of the Chinese, would have gone some way toward removing or decreasing the causes of conflict.[52]

Zagoria suggests that rivalry over power and authority in the Communist world was at the core of the continuing differences, and on the related issue of the distribution of nuclear weapons Soviet and Chinese images continued to diverge, as we have seen.

Chinese suspicions that Khrushchev was moving toward an accomodation with the West at the expense of China do not seem to have been alleviated by the shifts in Soviet behavior. This became especially obvious in the summer and early fall of 1962, when the Chinese claim to have been informed of a positive Soviet interest in non-proliferation and themselves published a series of articles against non-proliferation; when there were increased attacks on the U.S. emphasis on the test ban issue in the ENDC, usually combined with warnings against being misled by Kennedy's "peace talk"; and when Chinese comments on the Chinese U-2 incident stressed its significance as a "second eye-opener."

EIGHT

Intra-Bloc Bargaining: Stage III

Major Moves: Stage III

1962 Oct.	Sino–Indian border clash—indecisive Soviet position.	
	Cuban missile crisis.	
Nov.–Dec.	Sino–Soviet ideological exchanges occasioned by the anniversaries of the 1957 and 1960 Moscow Declarations.	
Nov. 5	Bulgarian party congress	Sino–Soviet
Nov. 20	Hungarian party congress	conflict
Dec. 2	Italian party congress	recurring
Dec. 4	Czechoslovak party congress	theme.
1963 Jan. 15	East German party congress sees anti-Chinese demonstration—speech by Chinese delegate drowned out by whistles, boos, shouts, and foot-stamping.	
Feb.–March	Sino–Soviet exchange of polemical letters.	
May	Exchange of letters results in agreement to hold bilateral talks in Moscow in July.	
June 6	Chinese protest against Soviet non-proliferation position.	
June 9	The Soviet Union, according to later Chinese statements, notifies China of its objections to U.S. stand on test ban.	

June 14	Chinese letter to CPSU—Chinese efforts to distribute letter within the USSR lead to diplomatic hostilities.
July 5	Sino–Soviet talks open in Moscow.
July 14	CPSU publishes "open letter" to CPC.
July 15	Test ban talks open in Moscow.
July 20	Sino–Soviet talks suspended *sine die*.
July 25	Partial test ban initialed.

WHEREAS THE Sino–Soviet split in the 1960–62 period became visible to all within the Communist movement but was still scantily concealed from the outer world, after the Sino–Indian and Cuban crises in October 1962, it moved closer toward an open, public, total breach and altogether lost its "esoteric" character.

The use of proxies gave way first to quoting explicitly anti-Soviet or anti-Chinese attacks by other parties, and finally to direct and open Sino–Soviet polemics which reached a climax after the signing of the test ban treaty.

After several polemical exchanges at party congresses and in the press, a mid-May exchange of letters resulted in an agreement to hold bilateral Sino–Soviet talks beginning on July 5. These talks started in an ominous atmosphere. In June, the CPC had delivered a "cold, brittle and totally uncompromising"[1] letter to the CPSU and had even tried to distribute it within the Soviet Union. In response, a number of Chinese diplomats and students were expelled from the Soviet Union.

Khrushchev's ostentatious absence as the Chinese delegation arrived in Moscow contrasted with his smiling and joking appearance as he personally opened the test ban talks with Averell Harriman and Lord Hailsham on July 15, while Sino–Soviet talks were still in process. On July 14, the eve of the test ban conference, the CPSU Central Committee published an "open letter" which contained the sharpest anti-Chinese attacks thus far. The fact that the letter was addressed not to the CPC but to all members of the CPSU suggested that the Soviet Union had terminated the dialogue with China and that party relations were *de facto* discontinued.² On July 20, the Sino–Soviet meeting was "suspended" on the motion of the Chinese delegation, and five days later the partial test ban treaty was initialed.

CHINESE IMAGES OF THE TEST BAN ISSUE

The public Sino–Soviet ideological exchanges on war, peace, and disarmament added nothing new to the images already projected. The proliferation issue, however, seems to have been the subject of intensified Sino–Soviet contacts behind the scenes. The Chinese have since referred to three memoranda sent to the Soviet government on September 2, 1962, October 20, 1962, and June 6, 1963, warning that

. . . we would not tolerate the conclusion, in disregard of China's opposition, of any sort of treaty between the Soviet Government and the United States which aimed at depriving the Chinese people of their right to take steps to resist the nuclear threats of U.S. imperialism, and that we would issue statements to make our position known.³

The Soviet Union, on its part, has claimed that it "more than once"

. . . took steps to convince the Chinese government that preventing the spread of nuclear weapons was in the interests of peace, in the interests of all socialist countries, including the interests of the People's Republic of China.⁴

In early 1963 there was a series of articles in the Chinese press on the MLF discussions within NATO, highlighting U.S. efforts to maintain its nuclear supremacy and dominate the alliance as well as France's stand in favor of a national nuclear deterrent. Although the relevant analogies were not drawn explicitly, the implication that China was stating its case for a Chinese nuclear capability was abundantly clear.⁵ That China considered a test ban a measure aimed at obstructing its own nuclear plans was explicitly stated on the eve of the break-up of the Sino–Soviet talks in Moscow⁶ and was further accentuated in the post-treaty polemics.

The fact that the question of a national Chinese nuclear capability was amplified in Soviet responses to Chinese criticism to the Moscow treaty, apart from being an instrumental tactic in the polemics, further suggests that this aspect was at the core of Sino–Soviet differences on the test ban issue.[7]

The previously expressed Chinese view that a test ban should not be separated from general nuclear disarmament was reiterated in the post-treaty polemics. The fact that the test ban agreement was only partial further aggravated the Chinese:

Since even such a step as the banning of underground tests is something very remote, how can the tripartite partial nuclear test ban treaty be counted as a first step? Far from being a first step toward a total ban on nuclear weapons and toward general disarmament, the tripartite treaty has made the realization of these urgent tasks even more difficult.[8]

Chinese commentaries made much of the fact that the Soviet Union had made an abrupt volte-face in agreeing to the treaty. Not only had the Soviet Union abandoned the link with disarmament, it had also gone back on its assurances that it would not agree to anything less than a comprehensive treaty. The Chinese claim to have been notified as late as June 9 by the Soviet government that a partial ban was not acceptable.[9] A few days after the initialing of the treaty, the New China News Agency published the full text of the U.S. draft treaty of August 27, 1962, which is basically identical with the final treaty, along with extensive quotes from the negotiation records showing the negative Soviet reaction to it at the time.[10]

CHINESE IMAGES OF U.S. BEHAVIOR

The Cuban missile crisis fortified China's image of invariable U.S. aggressiveness. It was again pointed out that the shifts in the global balance of forces to the detriment of the United States had in fact not changed its aggressive nature, nor could it possibly be changed.[11] "The more unfavorable the circumstances in which imperialism finds itself, the more it will intensify its attacks on the people."[12] According to Chinese estimates, the United States was "turning ever more arrogant since the Cuban incident."[13]

The Chinese image of the aggressive nature of the United States implied, as we have seen, U.S. hostility to arms control measures generally. How then could the U.S. accession to the partial test ban treaty be explained? Chinese commentary emphasized the link between the omission of underground tests from the treaty and the development of U.S. tactical nuclear weapons to be used in "limited nuclear wars" against non-nuclear countries and oppressed peoples in Asia, Africa, and Latin America.[14]

Khrushchev's "unrealistic illusions" about "sober forces" within the imperalist camp became the target of Chinese scorn after the Cuban missile crisis.

It will be recalled that three years ago, following the "Camp David talks," some persons in the international communist movement made propaganda in a big way about Eisenhower's sincere desire for peace, saying that this ringleader of U.S. imperialism was just as concerned about peace as we. . . .
Now we hear some people saying that Kennedy is even more concerned about world peace than Eisenhower was and that Kennedy showed his concern for the maintenance of peace during the Caribbean crisis. . . .
The intrusion into the Soviet Union of spy planes sent by the Eisenhower administration, the aggression against Cuba by the Kennedy administration, the hundred and one other acts of aggression around the world by U.S. imperialism, and its threats to world peace—have these not repeatedly confirmed the truth that the ringleaders of U.S. imperialism are no angels of peace but monsters of war?[15]

The class character of "wisdom" was expounded in a *Red Flag* article: "There can never be a 'wise policy' which represents the interests of two antagonistic and different classes. Such abstract, super-class 'wisdom' does not exist at all."[16]

After the conclusion of the test ban treaty, the tenor of Chinese statements grew increasingly defiant:

[T]he U.S. imperialists have not become beautiful angels in spite of Khrushchev's bible-reading and psalm-singing; they have not turned into compassionate Buddhas in spite of Khrushchev's prayers and incense-burning. However hard Khrushchev tries to serve the U.S. imperialists, they show not the slightest appreciation. They continue to expose their own peace camouflage by fresh and numerous activities of aggression and war, and thus they continue to slap Khrushchev in the face and reveal the bankruptcy of his ridiculous theories prettifying imperialism.[17]

As for the policy implications of the differing Chinese and Soviet images of the United States, the Cuban crisis to the Chinese signified a touchstone.

Marxist–Leninists deem the attitude one should take towards imperialist aggressors to be a matter of principle. Should one submit gracefully, relinquish sovereignty, and connive at aggression or should one persevere in struggle, defend sovereignty, and oppose aggression? Every revolutionary must take a clear-cut stand on this question, and not the slightest ambiguity should be allowed.[18]

The Soviet Union was accused of "adventurism" as well as "capitulationism" in the crisis, and these twin errors were related to the "paper tiger" concept:

If anyone does not dare to despise the enemy strategically, refusing to look upon imperialism and the reactionaries as paper tigers, either he will give up the revolutionary struggle, make one-sided compromise or accommodation with the enemy, and even surrender shamelessly, or he will take reckless, impudent, and adventurist steps in specific struggles.[19]

Overreliance on nuclear weapons and underestimation of popular struggle were said to lie behind Soviet miscalculations.

Those who blindly believe in the omnipotence of nuclear weapons and sneer at the might of the people's struggle, either recklessly play with nuclear weapons in their own hands, thus making the mistake of adventurism, or fall down on their knees before the enemy's nuclear weapons, thus committing the error of capitulationism.[20]

The Chinese no doubt considered "capitulationism" the graver Soviet sin in the Cuban adventure, as the label of "another Munich" indicates. They still saw a continuous and firm popular struggle against imperialism as the best policy, and meant that events had proven them to be right.

Facts have shown that only through struggle can imperialism be compelled to retreat and a genuine relaxation of international tension be achieved. Constant retreat before the imperialists cannot lead to genuine relaxation but will only encourage their aggression.[21]

The Chinese view of negotiations with the West also crystallized after the Cuban crisis. First, several Chinese statements, outlining how negotiations were *not* to be used, implied criticism of the Soviet position: (1) The long held opinion that negotiations were not to be regarded as the sole, or even the main, means was reiterated;[22] (2) Chinese commentaries after Cuba pointed out that while compromises with the enemy were necessary under certain conditions, it was absolutely impermissible to barter away principles or the vital interests of the people;[23] (3) Peace could never be achieved by negotiations alone;[24] (4) Especially after the conclusion of the test ban treaty, China emphasized that compromises between socialist and imperialist countries would not require oppressed peoples and nations to follow suit, to give up their revolutionary struggle and compromise with imperialism.[25]

Finally, the Chinese view that the masses rather than political leaders or diplomats at the negotiation table were the agents of history was contrasted with perceived Soviet attitudes.

We place our confidence in the great strength of the masses.... In contrast, these persons have no confidence in the masses and pin their hopes, not on the unity and struggle of the masses, but mainly on the "reason" and "goodwill" of the imperialists and on talks between the heads of two great powers.... In their opinion, the course of history and the fate of mankind are determined by two great powers and two "great men".... In their opinion, the statement that the masses are the makers of history is another empty phrase, and every matter under the sky can be settled if the two "great men" sit together.[26]

SOVIET AND CHINESE IMAGES: COMPARISON AND SUMMARY

The Cuban missile crisis evidently had a profound impact on the crystallization of Soviet and Chinese images. While the peaceful unraveling of the crisis vindicated Khrushchev's image of "reasonable" leaders in the United States, the forceful U.S. behavior in the crisis vindicated the Chinese leaders' image of U.S. aggressiveness.[27] More important still, Chinese expectations of Soviet readiness to sacrifice its allies on the altar of East–West détente and superpower hegemony were strengthened by Soviet behavior in the Cuban and Sino–Indian crises.

The Chinese image of U.S.–Soviet collusion developed gradually during this period. After the Cuban crisis there were many references to "great power chauvinism" in Chinese media. The concept was defined as

> ... the practices of greater nations of the world and their peoples in their relations and dealings in international life with a number of smaller nations and their peoples, which depart from the principle of true equality. They consider themselves as great nations and are arrogant with the feeling of superiority, thinking what they have is all good and what they do is right. They impose their will on others, thinking their own countries should enjoy special political, economic and cultural privileges without showing any respect for the rights of other countries.[28]

In a thinly veiled criticism of Khrushchev's behavior, a *Jenmin Jih-pao* editorial stated:

> The minimum demand that can be made of a communist is that he should make a clear distinction between the enemy and his own comrades. He should be merciless toward the enemy and be kindly toward his own comrades. But there are some who do just the opposite.[29]

After Kennedy's American University speech and its favorable reception in the Soviet Union, Chinese media started referring to a U.S.-inspired "great conspiracy" with the Soviet Union as willing accomplice, the essence of which was to isolate China.

> Evidently Kennedy and his brain trusters have perceived recently great signs of hope of achieving "victory without battle." Kennedy declared, with full confidence: "I believe we can help them (the Soviet leaders) to do it (meaning, to adopt a more enlightened attitude)." On what is Kennedy's confidence based? The U.S. Secretary of State Dean Rusk said elatedly a few days ago: In the socialist countries, "there are important changes going on and these are in the right direction." Are not these "changes" the cause for Kennedy's belief in the possibility and need for his "help"? Was he not providing such "help" when he delivered the speech in question?[30]

To the Chinese, the test ban treaty provided the final confirmation of their images of U.S.–Soviet collaboration. The two superpowers, according to the Chinese, shared a "self-conceited belief that they are nuclear overlord, while the overwhelming majority of the countries are to kneel down on the ground and obey orders meekly, as if they were nuclear slaves."[31] The U.S.–Soviet accord was even labeled a "new holy alliance."[32]

NINE

Intra-Bloc Bargaining: Conclusions

◨ IN THIS chapter we shall, first, summarize the findings of our analysis of Chinese images as compared to Soviet images and, finally, address ourselves to the question of what impact intra-bloc bargaining may have had on Soviet behavior at Geneva.

IMAGES IN INTRA-BLOC BARGAINING

We have suggested that ideology and images may be thought of as partly overlapping entities and noted that the frequent charges of "dogmatism" and "revisionism" respectively indicate a difference in the role of ideology in Soviet and Chinese images.[1] Although it would of course be a gross exaggeration to describe Chinese images as exclusively flowing from ideology and Soviet images as devoid of ideological roots, it has generally been assumed that Chinese images are ideologically determined to a greater degree than Soviet images. However, as Clemens has pointed out, a more adequate description may be that different segments of Communist ideology are operational in Soviet and Chinese images:

The Chinese understanding of Leninism derives primarily from Lenin's works written before the Bolshevik *coup d'état*, while Soviet ideologists rely more on the ideas developed by Lenin during the formative stages of the New Economic Policy.[2]

The quotation also suggests a bedrock of self-interest and expediency underlying a great deal of ideological flourish. In other words, the symbolic and legitimizing functions of ideology [3] were salient in the Sino–Soviet dialogue as well. This point will be further elucidated as we go on to summarize the content of Chinese and Soviet images.

Images of the Test Ban Issue

The Soviet and Chinese images of disarmament in general reflected the ideological differences referred to above. Lenin is ambiguous on the subject. The orthodox rejection of disarmament before the downfall of imperialism in his early writing is confounded by more "opportunistic" statements in connection with the 1922 Genoa Conference. [4]

Whereas the Chinese image drew on Lenin's early writing on the subject, the Soviet Union used documents from 1922 to justify its position. The differences can be represented schematically (Figure 5). [5]

Furthermore, after 1956 the Soviet Union accepted the view that partial arms control measures were feasible and advocated a test ban as the most important and practicable partial measure. China, however, continued to be reluctant—as had the Soviet Union been prior to 1956—about anything short of general disarmament or the total prohibition of nuclear weapons.

In addition to these basic differences, the Soviet Union and China throughout the 1958–63 period had contrary images of the specific issue of nuclear proliferation—the aspect of a test ban most central to Sino–Soviet relations.

The Soviet Union, after an initial period of ambivalence, became increasingly worried about the negative consequences of proliferation in general. The Soviet Union—as well as the United States—had to find answers to two crucial questions: (a) how will nuclear sharing affect my control over my ally? and (b) how will the other side respond to my policy?

At the test ban conference the Soviet Union initially expressed confidence in its ability to forestall nuclear testing by "other countries." Behind this confidence seems to have lain the

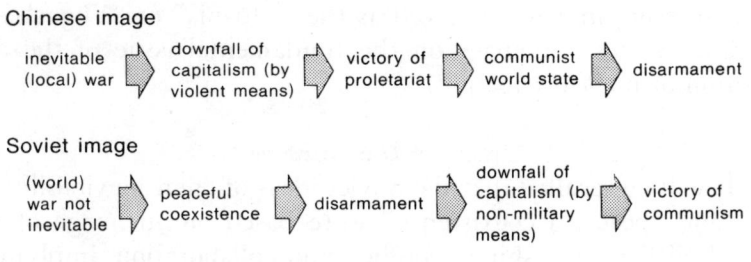

Figure 5

expectation that it would be able to keep control over China's nuclear development. As this expectation was shattered, the professed Soviet confidence in preventing proliferation dwindled at Geneva. From the spring of 1962 the USSR began to express worries about the MLF discussions within NATO and about alleged West German demands for nuclear weapons. The question of what the other side would do came to the fore, and the ensuing dilemma was aptly summarized in a Soviet government statement in the post-treaty Sino-Soviet polemics:

It would be naive, to say the least, to assume that it is possible to conduct one policy in the West and another in the East, to fight with one hand against the arming of Western Germany with nuclear weapons, against the spreading of nuclear weapons in the world, and to supply these weapons to China with the other hand.[6]

China, on the other hand, first avoided the subject of proliferation and then gave explicit support to the spread of nuclear weapons to the socialist countries. We have suggested above that this stand was mainly a rationalization for China's nuclear ambitions, and later developments further corroborate this argument. After the Chinese nuclear detonations in October 1964 and May 1965, China gradually abandoned its proliferation position and began to emphasize the no-first-use principle, arguing that this principle would remove the need for those states not possessing nuclear weapons to develop or import them.[7]

Our analysis of Chinese and Soviet images thus leads us to the conclusion that at the core of Sino-Soviet disagreements on the test ban issue was the question of China's nuclear capability. The test ban issue, in a way, served as the "Albania" or "Yugoslavia" for Sino–Soviet exchanges on the fundamental issue of the distribution of nuclear capabilities.

Images of U.S. Behavior

It will be recalled that the Soviet ideas of "non-inevitability of war" and "peaceful coexistence" were based on an image of the U.S.–USSR relationship as conflict-cum-collaboration, implying a corollary image of the United States as both aggressive and conciliatory—as an "enemy-partner." Soviet images also included notions of "madmen" as well as "realists" within the United States representing these contradictory tendencies.

The corresponding Chinese set of images differed on several scores. Whereas Peking went along with the Soviet 1956 thesis that, owing to the strength of the socialist camp, war was no longer fatalistically inevitable, it never accepted the more far-reaching 1959 formula on the emerging possibility of eliminating world war permanently, even while imperialism remained.[8]

On a general level, there was Sino–Soviet agreement, especially after Sputnik 1957, that favorable conditions for peace existed, but the two sides differed as to the role of the United States on the road to peace. Chinese images left no room for active contributions by the United States. The favorable conditions had been created by a decisive, irreversible change in the global balance of power in favor of socialism, and only through continued strengthening of the socialist camp could the imperialists be kept from carrying out their aggressive plans and be compelled to accept peaceful coexistence. While Khrushchev, in particular, granted the ability of at least some Western leaders to draw the correct conclusions from historical developments, the Chinese repeatedly asserted that history had taught and would teach the imperialists nothing. The denial of a learning process on the part of Western leaders was also reflected in the emphatic Chinese dismissals of the Soviet notion of "sober forces" or "realists" within the U.S. leadership.

In short, China recognized only the "conflict" side of the Soviet "conflict-cum-collaboration" image of East–West relations. In consequence, the Chinese image of the United States was that of an invariably aggressive imperialist power—an "enemy" image rather than the Soviet "enemy-partner" image. Nor was the Soviet distinction between "madmen" and "realists" within the United States included in the Chinese set of images.

Whereas we have found marked changes in Soviet images over the 1958–63 period, Chinese images of the test ban issue and of U.S. behavior remained remarkably stable. The changes observed in Chinese images of the likelihood of a test ban were, as we have seen, based on changing expectations of *Soviet* rather than U.S. behavior.

Why, then, did Soviet and Chinese images differ? In a CPSU letter to the CPC of February 21, 1963, it was stated:

Of course, it is not excluded that in the communist movement there may emerge, and there are emerging, different approaches in understanding certain questions of current world development. This can be explained by the different conditions in which this or that detachment of the international communist movement is working.[9]

Among those different conditions, two factors in particular are amplified by Western analysts: differences in stages of development and in position in the international system.

Stages of Development

In 1957 the Chinese revolution was just ten, not forty, years old. The Chinese leadership was a group of revolutionary veterans, who may be assumed to have looked upon the Soviet leaders as "a group of Russian parvenus, who took no part in any revolution, who were the creatures of Stalin, or those creatures' creatures."[10]

And whereas the Soviet Union was in a stage of development where it needed peace to foster prosperity at home, China was still in a formative stage where it needed the atmosphere of "beleaguered fortress" to justify sacrifices at home.[11]

Western observers often emphasize the parallelism between Chinese images and policies during the period under study and Soviet images and policies in the first decade after the 1917 revolution. Clemens has, for example, pointed to the similarities between Peking's response in 1963 to the test ban treaty and Moscow's reaction in 1922 to the Washington Treaty's limitation on capital ships.

Peking in 1963, like Moscow in 1922, complained that it was not invited to the Great Power negotiations, and that it suffered from a position of general military inferiority to the Great Powers. It denounced the arms control agreements reached as schemes to freeze the *status quo* to the advantage of the Great Powers; pointed out what military forces were *not* included in the agreements (everything except capital ships in 1922, everything but certain nuclear tests in 1963); predicted that the arms race and the danger of war would increase; offered counter-proposals devised purely for their appeal to world opinion, namely, *general* disarmament of all types of weapons and a genuinely international conference to reflect the interests of all states.[12]

Positions in the International System

The differences were here between, on the one hand, an established superpower with global interests and with a stake in the contemporary international system and, on the other hand, an internationally isolated "have-not" country with great power ambitions, aspiring to leadership in the third world.[13]

China was moreover a weaker alliance partner in the bipolar alliance structure, and Brzezinski and Huntington have pointed to striking similarities between French and Chinese images and responses:

In each case, the weaker and more dependent ally (France, China) was a country with an old history, a long tradition in diplomacy and warfare, and an ancient culture. To each, the United States and the Soviet Union were upstart nations, compensating for their lack of culture and background with a heavy-handed reliance on their relative power, wealth, and technological superiority.[14]

Both China and France "had reasons to feel that their interests had not been fully recognized by their more powerful allies,"[15] and both had doubts about the extension of the "nuclear umbrella" in support of their interests.

Finally, whereas Soviet images of the United States grew out of experiences in symmetric superpower relations and the dilemma of mutual nuclear destructiveness and vulnerability, Chinese images were based on experiences of the West in a third world, colonial context. And Chinese Communist experiences with the Kuomintang alliances were not calculated to produce any confidence about the usefulness of negotiations and agreements with powerful bourgeois groups.[16]

THE IMPACT OF INTRA-BLOC BARGAINING

The evolution of the Sino–Soviet controversy over the 1958–63 period could be represented as three different, consecutive "games," as seen by China. In 1958–59 China and the Soviet Union were engaged in direct though semi-tacit bargaining. From early 1960 through 1962 the controversy lost its bilateral character, and the persuasion attempts were directed not at each other but mainly at third parties. Finally, beginning in 1963, China saw itself engaged in a "three-person coalition game"[17] with two actors (U.S., USSR) colluding at the expense of China (Figure 6).

It should be noted that after 1959 it became increasingly uncertain whether any genuine *bargaining situation* continued to exist, as the cooperative element was weakened and the survival of the "hostage" of unity was in doubt.

What was the impact, then, of intra-bloc bargaining on Soviet negotiating behavior at Geneva? We set out to test the hypothesis that Soviet negotiating behavior might be a resultant of Sino–Soviet bargaining. If this hypothesis is true, we should be able to correlate changes in Soviet negotiating behavior to changes in China's influence on the USSR in intra-bloc bargaining. Our

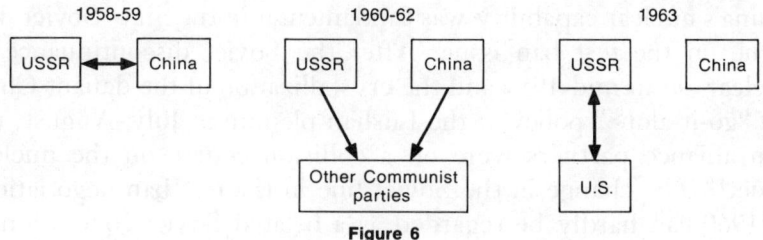

Figure 6

analysis of Chinese and Soviet images furthermore indicates the direction of changes to be expected. Increased Chinese influence should be reflected in less conciliatory behavior toward the West, decreased Chinese influence in more conciliatory Soviet behavior. In order to verify our hypothesis about China's impact, we should thus find the correlation shown in Figure 7. This is closely related

		China's Influence	
		high	low
Soviet Negotiating Behavior	conciliatory		X
	non-conciliatory	X	

Figure 7

to Holsti's hypothesis about a positive correlation between East–West tensions and Sino–Soviet consensus (high East–West tension—high Sino–Soviet consensus; low East–West tension—low Sino–Soviet consensus), corroborated by a quantitative content analysis of selected shorter periods between 1950 and 1965.[18]

However, unlike Holsti's, our analysis of the test ban issue during the 1958–63 period does not corroborate our hypothesis but rather suggests a weak Chinese impact throughout the test ban negotiations. Changes in Soviet negotiating behavior at Geneva do not seem to have been directly related to intra-bloc bargaining.

Soviet behavior in the test ban negotiations underwent distinct changes in the latter half of 1960 and again in late 1962. In 1960 Soviet behavior did indeed change to become less conciliatory, but there are several indicators that this change cannot readily be explained in terms of changes in China's influence.

(1) We have drawn the conclusion that the question of China's nuclear capability was fundamental in the Sino–Soviet dialogue on the test ban issue. After the Soviet discontinuance of nuclear aid in mid-1959 and the crystallization of the defiant Chinese "go-it-alone" policy at the Lushan plenum in July–August, the two alliance partners were on a collision course on the nuclear issue.[19] The change in the Soviet line in the test ban negotiations in 1960 can hardly be regarded as a belated Soviet concession to

Chinese pressures, especially as the differences on nuclear proliferation in general and a Chinese nuclear capability in particular were not removed.

(2) As pointed out earlier, the change of Soviet test ban policy in 1960 took place against the background of continued deterioration of Sino–Soviet relations generally. The Sino–Soviet consensus that, according to Holsti's hypothesis, might be expected as a result of the Soviet shift did not materialize.[20] We shall later argue that the observed changes in Soviet behavior and images can be traced to changes in the balance of power in internal Soviet bargaining, so that Khrushchev's opponents, who held divergent images, came to have a greater say in the formulation of policies. Thus, one partial explanation why converging images and policies did not abate the Sino-Soviet quarrel could be that Khrushchev continued to be the target of Chinese polemics. The Chinese delegation at the Bucharest meeting, for example, repeatedly stressed that the differences were "between us and Comrade Khrushchev" rather than the CPSU.[21] And after November 1961 there was a systematic derision of Khrushchev personally within China.[22]

(3) We have also noted a lack of enthusiasm in Chinese commentary on the new Soviet policy in the test ban negotiations, gainsaying any decisive Chinese influence on the Soviet policy shift.

(4) Finally, if the Chinese had felt they could take any credit for the "positive" change in Soviet behavior in the test ban negotiations after 1960, they would in all probability have indicated so in the post-treaty polemics, in which China scrutinized Soviet test ban policy over the years. No such indication can be found, however.

Soviet behavior in the test ban negotiations changed again after the Cuban missile crisis in late 1962, now to become more conciliatory. According to our hypothesis, this change should have come about *in spite of* Chinese pressures and should reflect low Chinese influence. However, Chinese pressures may, paradoxically enough, have had an unintended positive influence on the Soviet decision to agree to the partial test ban.

The test ban provided a convenient focal issue, once the Soviet leaders had concluded that a breach with China was inevitable. It would focus the polemics on questions of peace and war, where the Soviet Union could count on broad support within the Communist movement and in the third world, and would put China in the uncomfortable position of opposing a "peace move." China's opposition may thus have been an additional argument *in favor of* a test ban in internal Soviet bargaining.

With little prospect of better relations on acceptable terms with its eastern flank, the Kremlin was naturally drawn toward improvement of relations in the West. Khrushchev was probably able to use the increased Chinese attacks to secure support for his détente policy in the internal Soviet debate.[23]

Some Sovietologists have suggested that there might have been greater support for a breach with China than for East–West détente in the Soviet leadership. In that event, China's opposition may have helped the pro-détente forces to muster the necessary support for a test ban.

In any case, China's role in the renewed Soviet interest in a test ban after the Cuban crisis was indirect and marginal and does not alter our conclusion as to low direct Chinese influence on Soviet behavior throughout the test ban negotiations. Our initial hypothesis correlating changes in Soviet behavior to changes in China's influence has not been corroborated. Instead, we have found the correlations shown in Figure 8.

		China's Influence	
		high	low
Soviet Negotiating Behavior	conciliatory		X
	non-conciliatory		X

Figure 8

There remains the possibility that China might have had an indirect impact *via* contacts with Khrushchev's opposition within the Soviet Union. We shall take a closer look at this possibility after our analysis of internal Soviet bargaining on the test ban issue.

PART FOUR

Internal Bargaining

Treating national governments as if they were centrally coordinated, purposive individuals provides a useful shorthand for understanding problems of policy. But this simplification—like all simplifications—obscures as well as reveals. In particular, it obscures the persistently neglected fact of bureaucracy: the "maker" of government policy is not one calculating decisionmaker but is rather a conglomerate of large organizations and political actors.

(ALLISON 1971:3)

Negotiations on disarmament and the prevention or cessation of wars are conducted between governments. It would be a mistake, however, to reduce the study of these problems to a mere study of intergovernmental relations. The class and party struggle and the struggle of peace-loving organizations against militarist groups play a very important part in the solution of the problems of war and peace.

(GORIAINOV and GLAGOLIEV 1965:418)

TEN

Soviet Policy Making As Bargaining Situation

◫ IN OFFICIAL Soviet doctrine, foreign policy is viewed as the continuation of domestic politics. Foreign policy, according to Marx and Lenin, is shaped by the interests of the dominant social group in society.

Similarly, in Western political analysis, one approach or research strategy focuses on the study of domestic sources of foreign policy and "linkages" between national and international political systems.

Both Marxist and Western theories have been applied primarily to the foreign policies of Western states, and have tended to treat the Soviet Union as an exception. According to Marxist theory, the foreign policy of the classless Soviet Union is determined by the interests of the entire toiling people; according to traditional Western analysis, Soviet foreign policy is determined by a single person or a small group of identifiable individuals relatively free from internal restraints or pressures. Only recently have the domestic sources of Soviet foreign policy been submitted to analysis by Western observers.

Our thesis is that "internal bargaining" on the test ban issue took place within the Soviet Union—an "auxiliary game" in relation to the formal East–West negotiations. Our underlying assumption is that the issue of nuclear testing—like most other foreign and domestic policy issues—represented an internal *bargaining situation.* In other words, we view Soviet decision making as a process involving several actors who have converging as well as diverging interests and whose decisions are interdependent.

Soviet official doctrine one-sidedly stresses the common interests and denies conflicts of interests in Soviet society or even within the ruling party. The party knows the "real" interests of the people as a whole, and there is only *one* correct policy flowing from *one* correct interpretation of the doctrine. The notion of "proletarian dictatorship" rules out opposition outside the Party, and the principle of "democratic centralism" neither admits in theory nor permits in practice the existence of oppositional groups or factions within the Party.

In a similar fashion, the concept of "totalitarianism" that for a long time dominated Western analysis of the Soviet political system portrayed the USSR as a monolith with an all-embracing ideology and a stark concentration of policy-making powers, and largely ignored the existence of internal conflict.[1]

It has become increasingly apparent to Western scholars that after Stalin's death "the Soviet political system, when conceived as a monolith, is a myth."[2] The common ideology has proved to leave room for differing interpretations, and evidence of conflicts of interest between individuals and groups within the Soviet elite has accumulated.

To be sure, Soviet doctrine admits the existence of "non-antagonistic contradictions," but Soviet literature provides no empirical references to this type of conflict in Soviet politics.[3] In the West, however, alternative models of the Soviet political system have developed, seeing conflict as a crucial feature of Soviet politics. The "conflict school" is a collective epithet sometimes given to this new approach, in which two main lines of analysis can be distinguished.

Kremlinology focuses on the top-level struggle for power; and recently efforts have been made to apply an *interest group approach* to Soviet politics. According to Kremlinologists, the absence of any rules of succession and the post-Stalin abandonment of terror as a political weapon entail an intensive and permanent power struggle in the top leadership. In addition, advocates of an interest group approach argue that the social, economic, and technological changes associated with the modernization of the USSR have produced potential intermediate participants in the policy-making process.

The "thesis" of the totalitarian school's stress on unity and the "antithesis" of the conflict school perspective suggest a *bargaining* "synthesis."

Lacking a decisive and authoritative leader as both Lenin and Stalin had been, and lacking anything more than a most general consensus on the future course of foreign policy . . . , the Soviet leadership in making foreign policy decisions embarked on a "bargaining" relationship vis-à-vis one another and the reference groups in society to which the members of the elite turned for support.[4]

This also means that the Kremlinological and interest group approaches may be seen as complementary rather than mutually exclusive. In identifying cleavages and controversies within the Soviet leadership, Kremlinologists have tended to emphasize personal alignments. Whereas early Kremlinology tended to overstate the personal power struggle and downgrade policy issues to mere pawns in the fight for supremacy, several modern Kremlinologists express a more balanced view. "Policy is seen as the twin, not the pawn, of power; thus the focus is on the *nexus* of power and policy, and on the combustion produced by their interaction."[5]

Foreign and domestic policy issues in the Soviet Union as elsewhere are interrelated, that is, they come in "clusters."[6] The interlocking nature of domestic resource allocation issues and East–West détente has been especially emphasized and is recognized also in Soviet sources.

The interrelationship of policy issues suggests interlocking patterns of alignment. Some Western authors have sought to place Soviet leaders on a left–right scale according to their position on outstanding issues.[7] Avoiding the ambiguity of the left–right dichotomy in the Soviet setting, we shall adopt Linden's distinction between *"reforming"* and *"orthodox"* forces. According to Linden, the reforming forces, associated with innovation and pragmatic solutions, have a predominantly *internal* policy orientation: They tend to stress internal problems and express belief in the prospects for a stable international environment. The orthodox forces, on the other hand, represent doctrinal continuity and display a more *external* policy orientation: the world class struggle and the permanent dangers from the outside enemy are their rallying points.[8]

Two important conclusions emerge from existing analyses of Soviet interest groups.

1. It has become increasingly obvious that it is a gross oversimplification to think of the institutional-occupational groups studied in terms of internally monolithic and homogeneous entities. Rather, close scrutiny of these groups reveals inner divisions and factionalism. To mention one pertinent example, students of the Soviet military have distinguished at least five different dimensions of intra-military conflicts of interest: inter-service competition; political officers vs. military professionals; traditional commanders vs. technocrats; younger vs. older generation; the "Stalingrad group" vs. the "Stavka."[9]

2. Attention has also been directed to the possibility that two or more groups may have identical or similar interests in certain questions and may act in concert. Again proceeding from the Soviet military, a number of analysts have pointed to a Soviet military-industrial complex, benefiting from and possibly promoting an aggressive foreign policy and the maintenance of interantional tensions. Aspaturian also includes professional party apparatchiki and ideologues in this community of interests, tied together by an understanding of the interdependency between security, heavy industry, and ideological orthodoxy.[10] Wolfe adds scientists to this coalition of sorts, emphasizing the fact that a large portion of the Soviet scientific and technological effort is conducted in close association with military institutions.[11] We thus wind up with a notion of a Soviet "politico-military-industrial-scientific complex."

In short, Western students of Soviet institutional-occupational groups have pointed to the dual possibilities of intra-group conflict and intergroup collaboration. As several authors have suggested, it would therefore seem more appropriate to alter the analytical focus to informal *"groupings"* cutting across formal institutional lines.[12] This becomes imperative if we set out to make a case study of a specific issue. "If we look for patterns of articulation on specific issues, as opposed to the conflicting articulations that arise from specific formal groups, we find signs of shared outlooks and claims which cut across formal groups."[13]

Finally, how does the interest group approach relate to Kremlinology? Leadership conflict is a precondition for interest group activity. Conversely, overt interest group activity indicates a lack of leadership consensus.[14] Furthermore, several authors suggest that Soviet groups have an impact *via* individual members of the highest decision-making body (Presidium/Politburo), who are in a position to influence outcomes, either through active "lobbying" or through decision-makers seeking their expertise and judgment.[15] In other words, interest groups are likely to become involved in leadership struggles. Thus, it does not seem unreasonable to conceive of a *grouping* as a "vertical" entity, including a faction of the top leadership as well as a combination of (factions of) sub-elites sharing common attitudes on a specific issue. Stewart's broad definition may serve as our point of departure: "When similar opinions on the same issue are expressed by more than one individual, this is called, for analytical purposes, a 'grouping.' "[16]

Whereas the focus of attention of interest group analysis is an upward flow of communication from intermediate levels to the central decision-makers, our approach presupposes mutual influence attempts by "vertical" groupings. For traditional group theory, originally intended for the study of "subsystem-dominant" Western political systems, we have substituted an approach more adapted to the "system-dominant" Soviet system.

According to what criteria can groupings be distinguished? Linden maintains that the reformist-orthodox dichotomy holds true also of intermediate groups below the top leadership.[17] Translating this broad notion to the specific issue of test cessation, one would expect to find anti-treaty forces in the orthodox grouping: with their stress on the inevitability of conflict and heavy industry priorities, they are supposedly urging strategic superiority, demanding high defense budgets, and opposing arms control measures. Conversely, the reformist grouping can be assumed to comprise pro-treaty forces. Emphasizing conflict avoidance and the needs of the consumer sector, they would tend to support a deterrence policy based on strategic parity, strive to keep defense spendings down, and advocate arms control.[18]

We shall be looking for reverberations of this cleavage in the following sub-elites: the military, industrial managers, scientists, and the foreign affairs intelligentsia.

The Military

Being one of the main instruments of state power, the military constitutes a potentially powerful sub-elite: "It is both the mainstay of the regime and a principal potential rival for power."[19]

While references to "the continuing resistance of the [Soviet] military to the arms control idea over the years"[20] are frequently found, Aspaturian has suggested possible inter-service differences in attitudes to détente measures.

Khrushchev's periodic calls for troop cuts and reductions for military spending were invariably accompanied by proposals to increase spending for missile and technological development in the military. Since a *détente* and relaxation of tensions would require in any event the maintenance of a deterrent capability, these forces are not threatened, but in fact may be favored, by a relaxation of international tensions. Furthermore, of all the officers in the military, these are the most likely to adjust to peacetime careers without difficulty.[21]

Industrial Managers

The traditional watershed between heavy industry on the one hand, and light and consumer goods industry on the other, appears to be relevant also in this context. It has been suggested that light-industrial managers benefit from (and thus have an interest in) international détente, whereas heavy-industry managers profit from international tension.[22] There is no doubt that light industry has constantly been in a weaker position: disfavored by traditional Soviet economic doctrine, they are geographically dispersed and have little or no access to the levers of power.[23]

Heavy industry, on the other hand, is generally assumed to be in a powerful position—especially so the branches involved in the production of armaments. Soviet defense industry has been relatively insulated. It constitutes a privileged "economy within an economy" with remarkably little spillover into the non-defense sectors.[24] Its executives are portrayed as a group characterized by great continuity and cohesion in combination with expertise and efficiency.[25] Their "symbiotic relationship with the military establishment"[26] is another characteristic feature, according to most Western observers. Although little is known about their part in policy-making, Soviet defense-industry managers seem to have all the potentialities to be a politically influential sub-elite.[27]

Scientists

In early 1958 Khrushchev asserted that Soviet scientists, like their Western colleagues, were demanding test cessation "with increasing insistence."[28] On the other hand, in July 1961 he told John McCloy that he was under strong pressure from his "scientists" to resume nuclear testing in the atmosphere.[29] And in an April 1963 interview with Norman Cousins, he stated: "My atomic scientists have been pressing me hard to allow them to carry on more nuclear tests."[30]

Although Khrushchev's statements cannot be taken at face value but should be seen within the context of Soviet commitment tactics vis-à-vis the West, they nevertheless point to a potentially powerful sub-elite. Whereas the armaments industry supervises its own research and development agencies, the prestigious Academy of Sciences provides the institutional backing for scientists at large.

Foreign Affairs Intelligentsia [31]

This sub-elite includes specialists conducting research in foreign policy, especially at the Institute of World Economy and International Relations (IMEMO). Zimmerman maintains that

> . . . since 1956 in the Soviet Union the study of international relations has been the concern both of specialists in the institutes and of decision-makers at the apex of the state and Party structures. Indeed, one of the major consequences of the Soviet reevaluation of the role and significance of international relations has been the recognition that international relations questions are sufficiently *complex* to warrant attention by

specialists, and that specialists, to the extent that their research is policy-oriented, have a major role to play in the analysis of questions concerning international relations.[32]

Our analysis of internal bargaining on the test ban issue represents an attempt to identify pro-treaty and anti-treaty groupings and reconstruct their images and expectations (a) of the test ban issue, and (b) of U.S. behavior. A first category of material, on which the analysis is based, consists of public statements by individual leaders and sub-elite representatives. A second category of material consists of periodicals ostensibly articulating the interests of different sub-elites. We thus proceed from Lodge's conclusion: "Soviet spokesmen grudgingly acknowledge and Western analyses have demonstrated that specialist journals are vehicles for the limited articulation of elite attitudes."[33]

Among the periodicals used the most important are *Krasnaya Zvezda* (military), *Voprosy Ekonomiki* (industrial managers), *Vestnik Akademii Nauk SSSR* (scientists), and *Mirovaya ekonomika i mezhdunarodnye otnosheniya* (MEMO) (foreign affairs intelligentsia). In addition, we have examined other relevant journals, not primarily representing distinct group interests (such as *Kommunist*, *International Affairs*, and *New Times*), as well as the dailies *Pravda* and *Izvestiya*, on the assumption that these may occasionally reflect the existing balance of forces between different interests and groupings.

Although existing Kremlinological and interest group analyses provide a foundation for our study, we are venturing into areas incompletely mapped. Our undertaking amounts to a *case study* of a specific issue, a type of study frequently called for but less frequently conducted in the Soviet setting. Furthermore, it deals with a *foreign policy issue*, where this infrequency becomes even more pronounced. Our detailed analysis of internal bargaining for each of the three stages of the test ban negotiations will be prefaced by a brief summary of pertinent Sovietological findings as to the *dramatis personae* and their shifting fortunes.

ELEVEN

Internal Bargaining: Stage I

BACKGROUND

IN JUNE 1957 Malenkov, Kaganovich, and Molotov had led an effort to remove Khrushchev from the party leadership. Having defeated the "anti-party group" with the aid of the Central Committee, Khrushchev seemed to have attained unassailable power. In March 1958 he took over the premiership from Bulganin and thus became head of both party and government. The 1958–60 period is also generally described by Sovietologists in terms such as "Khrushchev's ascendancy"[1] or Khrushchev's "consolidation and advance" and "drive for supremacy."[2]

At the same time, careful Kremlinological analysis has suggested that Khrushchev's 1957 victory was incomplete and his power position less than absolute. The victorious coalition of 1957 was diverse and included several who were anti-Malenkov rather than enthusiastically pro-Khrushchev.[3] The members of the "anti-party group" were retained in the party and some of them even remained in high posts.

The "group" issue was not closed with the defeat of the anti-Khrushchev faction in 1957 but continued to be a subject of public debate. Khrushchev was pressing for the full exposure of still hidden members of the oppositional faction. At a Central Committee plenum in November 1958 he exposed ex-premier

Bulganin, who had been removed from the Presidium two months earlier, as a member of the "anti-party group." And the 21st Party Congress in January 1959 unveiled the controversy between Khrushchev and his followers, on the one hand, who opted for the expulsion from the party of "anti-party group" members, and others, such as Suslov, who pictured the issue as closed.[4] No purge occurred, but neither was the matter buried, as a result of the congress.

Khrushchev's drive against his old foes to expand his power was coupled with a program of reform. Challenging traditional economic policy, Khrushchev soon after the 1957 leadership crisis launched efforts to improve the efficiency of Soviet agriculture. The foreign policy corollary of Khrushchev's domestic pro-consumer line was a striving for East–West détente culminating in his visit to the United States in September 1959. On both accounts Khrushchev met with opposition from orthodox members of the leadership, notably Kozlov and Suslov.[5] And upon his return from the United States Khrushchev faced an opposition on the offensive.[6]

While the fortunes of Suslov and Kozlov were rising, some of Khrushchev's close associates were falling from favor. In December 1959 Kirichenko and Belyaev were subjected to public criticism and were reassigned to less important posts. And in March–April 1960 a series of cumulating signs of typical Kremlinological subtlety pointed to the decline of Mikoyan, who was regarded as a staunch Khrushchev supporter on foreign policy matters. One of Khrushchev's challengers in 1957, Molotov, evidently saw it opportune to submit an article to *Kommunist* for its Lenin Day issue at the end of April.[7]

In regard to party-military relations, the 1958–60 period has been characterized as one of relative tranquility with mounting tensions toward the end of the period.[8] In October 1957 Marshal Zhukov had suddenly been ousted from his positions as defense minister and Presidium member, accused of "Bonapartism." Under his charismatic leadership the military had acquired an extraordinary degree of professional autonomy, and the political control machinery in the armed forces was gradually withering away. Zhukov's fall ushered in a period of tightened party control. It also opened the way for the ascendancy of the Stalingrad group, closely associated with Khrushchev, as its followers gradually replaced officers appointed by Zhukov.[9]

In his January 1960 Supreme Soviet speech Khrushchev introduced a plan for reducing the Soviet armed forces by 1.2 million men, tied to a new military doctrine of nuclear-missile deterrence which reduced the role of conventional forces. These new policies met with opposition within the military community to the verge of alienating some members of the Stalingrad group and entailed a general deterioration of party-military relations.[10]

Khrushchev's parallel espousal of the development of nuclear-missile weaponry and East–West détente thus generated internal opposition both within the military and among political leaders, "with the distinct possibility that links might develop or be forged between the two opposition groups."[11]

The 1958–60 period saw the emersion of "a pattern that would characterize Khrushchev's efforts to implement his policy. He would ask for more and have to settle for less. . . . And at the same time he would seek to inject new elements in the party line that would be used as the basis for bolder moves in the future."[12] In other words, Soviet policy-making in general came to include an element of bargaining. In the following we shall attempt to trace the initial stage of the internal bargaining process on the specific issue of nuclear testing.

IMAGES OF THE TEST BAN ISSUE

While test cessation was a measure of high priority in official Soviet declarations throughout 1958, there were also mounting signs of cleavages on this issue. Questions of arms control (including a test ban) and foreign trade were the main themes of Mikoyan's Supreme Soviet election speech in early March. Apart from Khrushchev, Mikoyan was the only one among the top leadership to highlight these themes and, significantly enough, his was the only major election speech not reported in the Army daily *Krasnaya Zvezda*.

The reserved military attitude toward a test ban was further disclosed in connection with the March 31 Supreme Soviet decision to suspend testing unilaterally. A *Krasnaya Zvezda* editorial of April 2, while focusing on the agricultural decisions of the Supreme Soviet, endorsed the test suspension in general and brief terms and subsequently dwelt on West German plans for nuclear armament, quoting the Supreme Soviet statement on that subject in italics.[13] The following day—that is, two days after the decision to halt testing was hailed in other Soviet media—*Krasnaya Zvezda* carried an ambiguous editorial ostensibly welcoming the unilateral Soviet initiative, the major part of which dealt with the negative reaction in the West. Western failure to reciprocate unilateral Soviet peace initiatives in the past was demonstrated, and the passage of the Supreme Soviet announcement that premised resumed Soviet tests in case the Western powers would not follow suit was quoted in italics. The last part of the editorial expressed worries about the possibility of a nuclear armed West Germany.[14]

In his May Day speech, defense minister Malinovsky reiterated the same themes and referred to repeated Soviet proposals "that atomic weapons be banned and *the production and testing* of them discontinued."[15] He thus struck a chord we have detected previously in Chinese commentaries and which was to be employed by other Soviet opponents to a test ban: that of treating test cessation as a part of more comprehensive nuclear disarmament rather than a separate measure in its own right.

On July 1, the opening day of the experts' conference, *Krasnaya Zvezda* made no mention of this event among its foreign news items but chose instead to report on the first atomic reactor in China and renewed U.S. nuclear weapons testing.[16] This veiled hint in combination with the afore-cited material gives an indication of the military's arguments against a test ban: (a) the Chinese nuclear weapons development would be hampered, while plans for equipping West Germany with nuclear arms were not abandoned; and (b) the United States could not be trusted to cease its testing and weapons development.

The monthly journal *Voprosy Ekonomiki*, which is regarded as the mouthpiece of orthodox economists favoring heavy industry,[17] at the same time made some significant omissions. An article in the August issue on the joint efforts of the socialist countries toward peaceful coexistence failed to mention test cessation among the cited examples of practicable socialist proposals.[18] In addition, two articles in the November issue—that is, right after the opening of the test ban conference—dealt with Soviet peace initiatives and disarmament efforts without referring to test cessation.[19]

If there were thus some early signs of reserve toward, if not resistance to, test cessation on the part of the military and heavy industry, there were obviously countervailing forces favoring a test ban. Khrushchev was the one leader to come out unequivocally in favor of a test ban. Some scientists, notably Andrei Sakharov, also opted for test cessation. Sakharov dates his involvement in the nuclear testing issue to 1957 and alleges to have made his views known in memorandums and conference speeches. With the assistance of Igor Kurchatov he made direct pleas to Khrushchev to stop the November 1958 test series.[20]

Both Sakharov and Kurchatov had been actively engaged in developing Soviet nuclear weapons, and Kurchatov, who was known to be closely associated with Khrushchev,[21] is reported to have been in charge of the testing program in 1958.[22] Though demands for test cessation came from other scientists as well, Sakharov and Kurchatov seem to have been the only advocates closely associated with nuclear weapons research and development.[23]

In August 1957 the participation of Soviet scientists in Pugwash conferences was endorsed by the Soviet Academy of Sciences, and a statement calling for the prohibition of atomic weapons and immediate cessation of nuclear weapons tests was signed by 196 Soviet scientists.[24] It should be noted, however, that most Soviet participants in Pugwash conferences in the late fifties as well as most of the signers of the 1957 statement were *not* nuclear physicists and were *not* associated with defense research.

At the turn of the year there were further manifestations of differing priorities given to the test ban issue in the December Supreme Soviet debate and at the January–February 21st party congress.

The Supreme Soviet foreign policy debate centered around two issues: the Berlin crisis and a test ban. Whereas the representative of the scentists, the mathematician A. A. Lavrentev, first spoke at length about a test ban and referred to the Berlin crisis in one brief paragraph only, the military spokesman, Marshal Sokolovsky, dealt exclusively with the Berlin question, making no mention whatsoever of test cessation.[25]

In his opening report to the 21st party congress, Khrushchev advanced the thesis that because of the increased strength of the socialist camp there was "a real possibility of excluding world war from the life of society even before the complete triumph of socialism, even with capitalism existing in part of the world."[26] In the section of the report dealing with disarmament questions, Khrushchev touched on test cessation in just one brief paragraph. His reticence on this issue was shared by most speakers at the congress. Among the few who made any mention of a test ban at all, foreign minister Gromyko used it as one of several examples of Western intractability, and the atomic scientist Kurchatov dwelt on the "extremely successful" 1958 test series necessitated by the Western intransigence.[27] While not explicitly referring to test cessation, defense minister Malinovsky pointed out that all "effective measures for reducing international tension and preventing war" undertaken by the Soviet Union had been persistently rejected or sabotaged by the West. He concluded: "In these circumstances we should be committing a fatal error if we ignored to any degree the sacred duty of constantly increasing the defense capacity of the great socialist motherland."[28]

Against this background of unanimous reticence it seems rather surprising that Khrushchev devoted a large part of his concluding remarks to the test ban issue which he characterized as "one of the important international issues." Khrushchev's diagnosis of the test ban negotiations was pessimistic—"our partners have evidently resolved not to reach agreement"—but ended with a reaffirmation of the Soviet desire and preparedness to reach an agreement. Unlike his treatment of other subjects, Khrushchev's comments on test cessation were reportedly not applauded by the congress.[29] And in the congress resolutions there was only a brief

INTERNAL BARGAINING: STAGE I   149

reference to Soviet measures for "achieving agreement on ending tests *and* totally prohibiting nuclear weapons," a formulation that suggests reservations about the wisdom of a separate test ban.[30]

The impression emerging from the congress of Khrushchev in favor of, yet not strongly committed to, a test ban agreement, opposed by orthodox forces, was to be further reinforced in the months to follow.

In the election campaign for the republican soviets in the latter part of February, Khrushchev was the only leader reported to have dealt with the test ban issue in his speech.[31] And at the annual meeting of the Soviet Academy of Sciences that same month, the geophysicist Fedorov, who had taken part in the experts' conference, made a speech complaining about the passive role of Soviet scientists in world affairs: "Our scientists have to appear more often in the Soviet and foreign press on the most important political issues, for example disarmament, the cessation of atomic weapon tests, and so forth."[32]

Whereas *Krasnaya Zvezda*'s comments on the foreign policy aspects of the party congress focused on the German problem exclusively without mentioning anything about disarmament questions,[33] one editorial made a passing reference to Soviet proposals for "an agreement on the ending of tests *and* the total prohibition of nuclear weapons" responded to by the West with new war preparations.[34] Marshal Sokolovsky in his Army Day article in *Pravda* failed to mention test cessation in a long list of Soviet arms control initiatives.[35]

It is also notable that Kozlov in a number of speeches in the summer and fall of 1959 discussed different Soviet disarmament and peace proposals without ever mentioning a test ban.[36] Another indication of the growing internal opposition to a test ban as a separate measure can be found in the treatment of the issue in the May Day and October slogans of the Central Committee. Whereas demands for immediate test cessation were given sixth and ninth place respectively in the 1958 May and October slogans, in May 1959 these demands were found in tenth place combined with calls for armaments reductions. And the eleventh item on the October 1959 list was a reformulated call for universal disarmament and "the immediate cessation of tests *and* the banning of atomic and hydrogen weapons forever."[37]

Though there were almost no references to test cessation in Khrushchev's public appearances while in the United States in September 1959, he began committing himself more firmly to a test ban agreement upon his return from the American visit. In his report to the Supreme Soviet on October 31, Khrushchev redundantly stressed the necessity of mutual concessions and compromises between states with different social systems. He also expressed renewed optimism in regard to the progress of the test ban negotiations that contrasted with the gloomy picture he drew at the party congress nine months earlier: "These talks have, admittedly, dragged out, but there has nonetheless been definite progress in them and it is to be hoped that they will before long be crowned with success."[38]

The Academician Fedorov once again toed Khrushchev's test ban line in an article in the *Vestnik Akademii Nauk SSSR* entitled "An Agreement on the Cessation of Nuclear Weapon Tests Must Be Concluded without Delay."[39]

In his noted January 14, 1960, speech to the Supreme Soviet, in which he announced the troop cut and formulated the nuclear-missile strategy, Khrushchev again dealt at length with test cessation in the same optimistic tone.[40] He continued to assign high priority to a test ban in a number of speeches and published letters in the months to follow,[41] and from February to April the Geneva negotiations were given an extraordinary amount of publicity in the Soviet press.[42]

During his visit to France in March 1960, Khrushchev gave further indications of his expectations in regard to a test ban. Questioned in a press conference about the interconnection between disarmament issues and the Berlin question, Khrushchev unequivocally assigned first priority to disarmament.[43] Furthermore, he did his best to tone down the significance of French nuclear tests for the test ban negotiations and evaded questions about the inclusion of France in the negotiations.[44]

About the progress of the negotiations Khrushchev stated: "Now there exist differences only in regard to a most insignificant range of problems: underground tests which cannot be registered with any instruments. . . . But on all the other questions we have already agreed."[45] He asserted that the test ban issue would be included in the agenda of the pending summit meeting in Paris "if by that time the necessary agreement on this question has not already been achieved."[46] Back from France, Khrushchev spoke of the possibility that a test ban agreement would come "in the nearest future."[47]

Just prior to the Paris summit (and the U-2 incident) a *New Times* article stated: "News commentators in the U.S. and Britain believe that the summit will make possible early conclusion of a test stoppage treaty. That belief is not unfounded, for at Geneva the representatives of the U.S.S.R., U.S.A., and Britain have prepared the ground for such a treaty."[48]

Available evidence thus suggests that Khrushchev launched an offensive on the test ban issue after his American visit and hoped that an agreement would be sealed at the Paris summit in May 1960. This would have given him a concrete result to demonstrate the correctness of his détente line in the internal and intra-bloc debate. It is evident, however, that Khrushchev's optimistic outlook was not shared by all his colleagues in the Soviet leadership. His explicit commitment to test cessation contrasted with the reticence of other Soviet leaders. In the Supreme Soviet debate of January 1960, the nuclear physicist Kurchatov was the only speaker to share Khrushchev's strong advocacy of a test ban.[49] High-ranking militaries as well as the military press carefully avoided mentioning test cessation throughout Khrushchev's offensive early 1960. And the relatively obscure place of calls for "the discontinuance of all tests *and* for the prohibition of atomic and hydrogen weapons" alongside demands for a German peace treaty as the eleventh item on the list of May Day slogans published in early April 1960 suggests that Khrushchev's priorities did not reflect any broad consensus within the Kremlin.[50]

In sum, the period up to May 1960 saw Khrushchev increasingly committed to a test ban but facing a less outspoken opposition which publicized its views by means of "esoteric communication." Different methods of implicit opposition unfolded during this period. There were the techniques of omitting a test ban in discussions of conceivable peace measures and, when it was mentioned, calling for an end to the testing *and* production of nuclear weapons. Finally, the relative priority assigned to the German problem and the test ban and other arms control issues in public statements seemed to be something of a touchstone. Whereas orthodox forces stressed the German question (confrontation), reformist forces tended to give high priority to arms control (conciliation).

IMAGES OF THE UNITED STATES

The dual "enemy-partner" image of the United States did not arise all of a sudden. Rather, it seems to have developed gradually through a bargaining process with discernible conflict elements.

In early 1958 the only internal U.S. diversity recognized in Soviet commentaries was the dichotomy between the Rockefeller and Morgan monopoly groups. Political leaders were seen as closely associated with, and in essence the tools of, either one of these two dominating financial groupings. While the fundamental interests of the two groupings were hardly distinguishable, the Rockefeller empire was considered to have more immediate interest in a continued arms race than the Morgan group, whose economic interests were said to lie in peaceful domestic development. Consequently, representatives of the Morgan grouping were critical of costly foreign policy adventures and would prefer limited détente, whereas the Rockefeller grouping stood for the continuation of the "cold war." During the first half of 1958 the Rockefeller group was considered to be in control of the government machine generally and State Department in particular.[51] The much publicized controversies between Secretary of State Dulles and Harold Stassen, President Eisenhower's special arms control adviser, were characterized as reflections of this basic Rockefeller–Morgan conflict of interest.[52]

Though there were occasional references in the Soviet press throughout 1958 to individual U.S. leaders advocating East–West negotiations, the explicit distinction between "sober" leaders and "madmen" was yet to make its appearance. It also seems to have entered Khrushchev's thinking rather late.[53] The only differentiation found in his 1958 speeches was between the peace-loving people and the ruling circles "who stubbornly cling to the positions of cold war and a continued arms race"[54] but who would eventually have to abandon their policy due to the growing might of the socialist countries and increasing internal popular pressure.[55]

The dual image seems to have originated in the foreign affairs intelligentsia. The first explicit elaboration of the "realists-madmen" dichotomy appeared in a notable September 1958 *MEMO* article by G. Trofimenko on internal U.S. controversies over foreign policy.[56] In the introduction Trofimenko outlined three types of internal contradictions that may have an impact on the formation of US foreign policy: (1) Rockefeller vs. Morgan, (2) the ruling circles vs. the people, and (3) Republicans vs. Democrats. Dismissing the importance of inter-party divergencies, the author stressed the significance of the Rockefeller–Morgan conflict of interest. Before going into the rulers-ruled dichotomy, Trofimenko made an unannounced and lengthy digression into an analysis of different "tendencies" without relating them to the other contradictions. According to this analysis, the recent Soviet strength epitomized in the Sputnik launching had given rise to contradictory reactions within the United States. On the one hand, the most aggressive imperialist circles especially in Pentagon tried to fan an anti-Soviet hysteria and called for intensified armaments. On the other hand, the Soviet space shot also reinforced another American political tendency: that of "realism." George Kennan, Chester Bowles, Senators Humphrey, Morse, and Fulbright, journalists Walter Lippmann and Norman Cousins as well as the large number of American scientists demanding a test ban were included among the "realists." Trofimenko furthermore concluded that the "realist" tendency was growing in strength.

The ambiguous and poorly integrated character of Trofimenko's article suggests that the elaboration of "realist" tendencies might have been a "trial balloon" at a time when the more orthodox image of rivalling monopoly groupings dominated official discourse.

Mikoyan was the first political leader to propound the theme of "realist" American leaders in public. In a November 1958 speech he stated that "sober voices are heard more and more often in the U.S.A. and among the most diverse circles" and mentioned Senator Fulbright and industrialist Cyrus Eaton as examples.[57] In early January 1959, Mikoyan made an unofficial visit to the United States and returned just in time to give the party congress a report stressing the "longing for peace on the part of the American people and of the majority of businessmen" and also commenting favorably on the U.S. political leadership. Interpreting the absence of references to "containment," "rollback," or "liberation" in American statements as an implicit recognition of peaceful coexistence, Mikoyan made the optimistic estimate that "these statements must be confirmed by deeds, and we have the right to expect such deeds." However, he hastened to caution against "any far-reaching conclusions that the U.S. circles which are interested in fanning the 'cold war' are now in retreat."[58]

Khrushchev, who in his opening speech to the congress had described Mikoyan's U.S. visit as "a manifestation of the American *people's* friendly feelings for the people of the Soviet Union,"[59] in his concluding remarks endorsed Mikoyan's positive view of the American leadership:

We believe that if the President and other U.S. leaders really desire peace, as they told A. I. Mikoyan, they will recognize the necessity for states to coexist in peace and will build their relations with the Soviet Union and other socialist countries on this foundation.[60]

In justification of his optimism Khrushchev referred to his personal experiences of the 1955 Geneva summit.

The meetings and talks which we had in Geneva left a good impression of Mr. Eisenhower. I formed the opinion that, although Mr. Eisenhower is a general, he is not one of those military men who rely on guns for the settlement of knotty problems and who would like to settle all problems by force of arms.[61]

Other speakers at the congress dwelt on the theme of different tendencies in the United States. Aristov said with regard to

American capitalists that "some of them threaten war, while others seek friendship with us. The majority, however, favor an end to the 'cold war' and the development of broad economic and cultural ties between West and East."[62]

Kuusinen stated: "It is to be assumed that the growth of the economic might of socialism will strengthen the positions of those sober thinkers among bourgeois leaders who see the danger of the West's present aggressive policy and favor peaceful coexistence of the two systems."[63]

On the other hand, there were also signs at the congress that the dual image was by no means generally accepted. Khrushchev's and Mikoyan's inclusion of the incumbent U.S. leaders among "realists," however circumscribed it might have been, was particularly controversial. While a number of congress speakers, among them Suslov, simply made no mention of differences within the U.S. leadership, others voiced wary criticism of the idea. Kozlov, for instance, drew totally different conclusions than Kussinen from economic realities: "Lacking confidence in the stability of their economic system, the imperialists are seeking a way out of their economic difficulties not through peaceful competition but through intensifying the arms race, militarizing the economy, and preparing for a new war."[64]

And Marshal Malinovsky, while referring to a "sober current of thought" in Western public opinion, disparaged its impact on Western foreign policy: "[T]he existence of inner contradictions in the aggressive blocs, especially NATO, in no wise reduces the great threat to the peace and security of the peoples. Moreover, the more obvious the failure of the aggressive policy becomes, the greater will become the danger of a military adventure."[65]

That opposition to the idea of "realist" U.S. leaders was rather widespread is suggested by the absence of any reference to it in the congress resolutions, which in an orthodox vein pointed to "the aggressive policy of American imperialism, reflecting the aspirations of U.S. capitalist monopolies to world domination" as the "main source of the war danger" and continued: "The ruling circles of the United States . . . continue to stockpile atomic weapons, reject the peaceful settlement of international problems and constantly provoke armed conflicts in various parts of the world."[66]

Khrushchev, however, continued to emphasize the significance of internal U.S. differences. Speaking at Tula shortly after the congress, for example, he said in regard to the Berlin question: "There are, of course, persons in the West who look at the international situation soberly. . . . With people who take such a position, a soberer position, it might be possible to negotiate an agreement."[67]

Just a few days later, on Soviet Army and Navy Day, Marshals Sokolovsky and Chuikov dissociated themselves from such ideas. Sokolovsky asserted that "the imperialists" indiscriminately were "not realistic enough in their appraisal of the present situation,"[68] and Chuikov further clarified that "aggressive aspirations are not only the fruit of the imagination of certain bourgeois military hotheads, but also the official policy of the ruling circles of the imperialist powers."[69]

An *International Affairs* commentary on the test ban negotiations in April designated American generals closely associated with the armaments industry as the most prominent opponents of a test ban, and added that these groups "enjoy the obvious support of U.S. Congress and the White House."[70] And in a *Pravda* interview of April 10, Khrushchev, when asked about his reaction to the anti-Soviet Eisenhower speech at Gettysburg College a week earlier, had to admit:

Attempts are being made to work people up and to create tension in the atmosphere. One cannot but recognize that President Eisenhower, too, has made a definite contribution here. I say this most regretfully, since I have already had more than one occasion to express my conviction that President Eisenhower has good intentions where peace is concerned.[71]

The April issue of *MEMO* carried a new article by Trofimenko, which reinforced the impression of ambiguity left by his September 1958 article. Though there were references to the dual image, the gist of the article was that current U.S. foreign policy was in the final analysis determined by the monopolies. The two

Trofimenko articles—and some contradictory *MEMO* articles in between [72]—give the impression that the dual image was controversial within the foreign affairs intelligentsia as well.

However, Khrushchev did not abandon the dual image, and the death of U.S. Secretary of State Dulles in May might have lent some credence to his hopes for the emergence of "realist" American leaders. In July, at a time when Vice President Nixon was visiting the Soviet Union and Khrushchev's American journey was being prepared, the first of a series of Lenin documents on cultivating the "pacifist" bourgeoisie were passed to the press, apparently in an effort to endow the dual image with ideological sanction.[73]

July also marked the beginning of a concerted espousal of the dual image in Soviet media. In a *Pravda* review of Walter Lippmann's book "The Communist World and Ours" it was stated: "Every day realistically thinking people in the West recognize more clearly the need for radical changes in the approach to major international problems. It is true that this tendency is not yet dominant, but time works in its favor."[74]

The July issue of *MEMO* included a survey of "current problems of world politics," written by a collective "on the request of the readers," in which the notion of two tendencies in American political life was elaborated in considerable detail. The adventurist, aggressive tendency had dominated up till then, it was said, whereas the other, more realistic tendency had just begun to make its appearance in the ruling circles of the West.[75] An *International Affairs* article expounded the relevancy of this "tendency analysis" to the test ban negotiations:

The outcome of the Geneva talks will largely depend on who gains the upper hand in the ruling circles of the United States: moderate and sober-minded elements or the militaristic forces from the Pentagon and the Atomic Energy Commission, who are clearly linked with the biggest American arms monpolies which are vigorously opposing the ending of atomic and thermo-nuclear weapons tests.[76]

Yet, there remained dissonant voices. *Krasnaya Zvezda*, for one, failed to make any mention of the dual image in its reporting on U.S. foreign policy. In a series of articles in August it emphatically denied any change to the better in U.S. foreign policy and maintained that aggressive monopolists were still, in fact, ruling the country.[77]

Before his departure to America, Khrushchev in a public speech reaffirmed his confidence that President Eisenhower "is prepared to work for the elimination of tension in relations among states" and "understands that the main thing now is to ensure peace throughout the world." Khrushchev dismissed certain "cold war" expressions in a recent Eisenhower press conference as "nothing more than giving former prejudices their due."[78]

In the United States Khrushchev repeated that he had "no doubt whatsoever that the President is sincere in his desire to improve relations between our countries."[79] And upon his return to the Soviet Union, Khrushchev went very far in his propagation of the "realist" tendency in American ruling circles, incarnated in President Eisenhower. He amplified the "realists-madmen" dichotomy, diagnosed that the "realists" were beginning to gain the upper hand, and called attention to the possibility of exploiting the internal American contradictions in the pursuit of Soviet foreign policy goals.

[W]e shall not sit with our arms folded and wait for the dawn, wait to see which way the arrow of international relations will point.[80]

Our task is to deal continuous blows to advocates of the "cold war"—each heavier than the last—in order to isolate them, to pillory them in the eyes of world public opinion. Our most effective weapon in this noble cause is the peaceloving policy of the Soviet government.[81]

Khrushchev's increasing commitment to the dual image seems to have occasioned greater polarization. There were, for instance, marked differences of emphasis in Khrushchev's and Suslov's addresses in Peking at the anniversary of the Chinese Communist Party right after Khrushchev's return from the United States. Whereas Khrushchev underscored the "definite inclination toward a realistic understanding of the situation" on the part of Western political leaders,[82] Suslov struck a different chord. Admitting that the temperature in East–West relations was "rising somewhat," he added:

At the same time it would be naive to think that a further relaxation of international tension will now occur of its own accord. There are still forces in the countries of monopoly capitalism, especially the U.S.A. and West Germany, which are interested in the arms race and in maintaining the "cold war." The dangerous situation in the world remains.[83]

Two weeks later Kozlov, speaking in East Berlin, delivered a thinly veiled criticism of Khrushchev's appraisal of Eisenhower:

The person who today does not recognize the actual existence of two sovereign states on the territory of Germany resembles an ostrich and by his short-sighted policy is not, of course, contributing to a relaxation of international tension.[84]

Krasnaya Zvezda, as before, scrupulously avoided the subject of "realist" Western leaders. Its commentaries on Khrushchev's U.S. visit typically depicted it as a positive event, at the same time pointing out that the continued existence of American aggressive forces and plans should not be forgotten and that seeking peace must not imply slackened Soviet military preparedness.[85] Some articles even maintained that the reactionary, aggressive forces and the enemies of disarmament in the United States had been reactivated after Khrushchev's visit.[86] One article went so far as to deny the traditional Rockefeller–Morgan dichotomy, claiming that "the Morgans, too, remained irreconcilable enemies of peace."[87]

Kuusinen's noted speech on the anniversary of Lenin's birth in April 1960, which constituted an effort to anchor the dual image ideologically, contained a rebuttal of those—inside and outside the Soviet Union—who tended to neglect the significance of the "realist" tendency.

Of course, aggressiveness is attendant upon the character of imperialism. But we must not dogmatically look at just this one side of the matter. We must not be insensible to the appearance of mighty forces militating against war. . . . To be true to Marxism–Leninism today, therefore, it is not enough to repeat the old truth that imperialism is aggressive. The problem is to take full advantage of the new factors operating in favor of peace. . . . The dichotomy in influential bourgeois circles is unquestionably significant for the success of the struggle for peace.[88]

Among those who did acknowledge the existence of "realist" American leaders, there were also shades of difference as to how strong and influential the "realists" were in relation to the "madmen." Khrushchev tended to emphasize the power of the "realist" tendency and disparage the impact of "madmen." In his January 1960 Supreme Soviet speech, he said about the latter that they were "sufficiently influential, and in certain conditions could harm the cause of easing international tension," but "their positions have been undermined, their strength is waning."[89]

A couple of editorials in *International Affairs* echoed Khrushchev's assessment. The November 1959 editorial spoke of a new "spirit of realism and mutual understanding" increasingly prevailing in international relations, and dwelt on the rethinking of "sober" and "realistically-minded" Western political leaders occasioned by the changed relation of forces in the world.[90] According to the December editorial, the United States "re-evaluation of values" also implied a change in civil-military relations: "The generals on active service seem to be disappearing from the political proscenium. The diplomats and the statesmen are coming to the fore, just as it should be in peace time."[91]

The foreign affairs intelligentsia, while sharing the dual image, seems to have been less sanguine about the strength of "sober" forces in the West. A collectively written survey of current international politics in the January 1960 issue of *MEMO* first refuted the argument that the more conciliatory policy of some American leaders might be tactically motivated with a view to the coming election campaign, arguing that the change was part of a long-term process brought about by the changing global balance of power. But then it gave a lengthy description of those influential politicians who had not realized these changes, claimed that U.S. foreign policy was now at the crossroads, and expressed uncertainty as to which tendency would prevail.[92] An article by Trofimenko in the same journal, while explaining contradictory features of recent U.S. foreign policy in terms of the dual image and stressing the decisive influence of aggressive forces on questions of arms control (notably the test ban issue), expressed the same uncertainty about the future course of U.S. foreign policy.[93]

And an article in the April issue concluded that "the process of rethinking on foreign policy among the U.S. ruling circles still proceeds slowly and with difficulty. So far one cannot notice any fundamental change in the attitude of American ruling circles toward the Soviet Union, toward the problems of disarmament, and toward the 'cold war.' "[94]

In conclusion, the official Soviet image of the United States, like that of the test ban issue, seems to have evolved through a bargaining process with Khrushchev becoming increasingly committed to both a test ban and the dual image after his U.S. visit. Whereas he was obviously supported by some other leaders and sub-elites, Khrushchev also faced opposition on both accounts from more orthodox leaders and the military.

TWELVE

Internal Bargaining: Stage II

BACKGROUND

ACCORDING TO most Sovietologists, the U-2 incident and the subsequent break-up of the Paris summit conference heralded a shift in the balance of forces within the Soviet Union. The episode has been described as a "costly setback" to Khrushchev and his détente policy, as a result of which his "prestige and political strength within the Soviet party suffered visibly."[1] The significance of the events of May 1960 has been succinctly summarized by Tatu:

> An embarrassing political reverse (the U-2 incident) served as a catalyst for the latent opposition. Grievances long suffered in silence came tumbling forth, both from the military, who had been by-passed in appropriations, and from the top planners yearning for greater centralization. All their demands, which constituted the background of the struggle for power, found political expression in the Party Presidium where the balance of profits and losses was swiftly drawn. Thus 1960 witnessed a serious blow to Khrushchev's ambitions and forced him to accept some sharing of power. His decline seems definitely to date from this period.[2]

Coincident leadership changes, which can be seen as the denouement of internal political struggles becoming discernible already in late 1959 and early 1960, demonstrated Khrushchev's vulnerability at the time. On May 4, a Central Committee plenary meeting ratified a thoroughgoing reorganization of the CPSU Secretariat and Presidium, the leading decision-making bodies.

Kozlov now entered a Secretariat cut by half—from ten to five members—and was placed in charge of party cadres, thus in effect taking over the number two position in that body.[3] The demoted members (Aristov, Furtseva, Ignatov, Kirichenko, Pospelov, and Brezhnev[4]) were known to have been among Khrushchev's supporters in the leadership crisis of 1957.

These changes deprived Khrushchev of his previous overwhelming and reliable majority in the Secretariat, leaving him with only two supporters (the aging Kuusinen and the less important Mukhitdinov) confronting Kozlov and Suslov. At the same time two Presidium members—Belyaev and Kirichenko—were removed, and three former alternate members—Kosygin, Podgorny, and Polyansky—were promoted to full membership.[5] Although there were cumulating signs of Mikoyan's ill-fortune and loss of status after the U-2 incident, he once again proved his talents for political survival by retaining his Presidium membership. However, according to Tatu, it would take Mikoyan quite some time to regain the privileged position he had occupied in 1959.[6]

Sovietologists tend to agree that, on balance, Kozlov and Suslov were the main beneficiaries of the leadership turnover.[7] While Khrushchev made few public speeches in the months after the U-2 incident, his two main adversaries were all the more active. For instance, in July a Central Committee plenum heard a report on the Bucharest conference, delivered not by Khrushchev, who had led the Soviet delegation to the conference, nor by Podgorny, who had accompanied him, but by Kozlov, who had not even been there.[8] And that same month Suslov, whose advance could be followed in photographs and listings,[9] made an unprecedented series of speeches on regime policy.[10]

The period following the U-2 incident has been characterized as "Khrushchev's struggle"[11] against an "opposition on the offensive"[12] or "a period of conservative ascendancy."[13] Tatu concludes that Khrushchev's "power no longer matched his ambitions,"[14] and Linden attributes Khrushchev's "erratic behavior" to his weakness. "He was not in so secure a position that he could pursue a single and consistent course; he could not ignore the powerful pressures and cross pressures of the internal politics of the Soviet ruling group."[15]

From May 1960 to the 22d CPSU congress in October 1961 the differences between Khrushchev and the opposition were most evident on issues of resource allocation. Already on May 5, 1960, the day after Kozlov and Suslov had entered the Secretariat, Khrushchev referred to "some comrades" who had raised arguments against his pro-consumer policy. On several occasions during the remainder of 1960 both Kozlov and Suslov indicated their preference for heavy industry and defense over consumer welfare.[16] In 1960–61 there were a number of notable promotions of defense industry representatives.[17]

At a Central Committee plenum on agriculture in January 1961, Khrushchev again criticized "some comrades" for their "appetite for metals" and outlined a program for agricultural reform, which was accepted only in part. In the intensified crypto-public debate with the "metal-eaters" during the ensuing months, Khrushchev indicated that the controversy was not limited to domestic issues but touched on basic foreign policy orientations as well.[18]

Khrushchev's dilemma was that whereas he saw détente with the West as necessary for his pro-consumer program, to pursue détente unambiguously in the wake of the U-2 incident would have exposed him to charges of being "soft on capitalism."[19] And the summer of 1961 saw a series of militant Soviet moves: a one-third increase of the military budget, suspension of the 1960 troop cut, erection of the Berlin wall, and resumption of nuclear testing.

The main agenda item of the 22d CPSU congress convening on October 17, 1961, was supposed to be the ratification of a new party program, presented in draft form in June and widely discussed in the months preceding the congress. However, without any advance indication the focus of the party forum was abruptly shifted, and "its prevailing tone was not one of enthusiasm for the bright gleam of the future but rather of rancor and indignation at the sordid past and the intractable present."[20]

"De-Stalinization" and the "group issue" were once again brought to the foreground. The anti-Stalin campaign was carried to its climax with the resolution to remove Stalin's remains from Lenin's mausoleum on the last day of the conference. Before then there had been numerous charges of renewed "anti-party group" activity, the immediate target of which was Molotov, who was said to have criticized the party program as "anti-revolutionary, pacifist, and revisionist" in a letter addressed to the Central Committee. While these attacks seem to have been aimed at other undefeated Khrushchev opponents as well—one Khrushchev follower, for instance, referred to "the Molotovs"—it was far from clear who were among the "guilty by association."[21]

Khrushchev's offensive against his internal opposition was coupled with an equally sudden and ruthless assault on Peking's proxies in Albania with suggestive parallels between the views attributed to Molotov and to the Albanians/Chinese.

The new party program and other congress documents "registered an uneasy balance between the pro-consumer faction and the metal-eaters."[22] On a number of key issues of domestic and foreign policy Khrushchev's innovations were either modified or abandoned, and the party documents bore the marks of compromise.[23]

The congress elections resulted in new leadership changes, reflecting the standoff between Khrushchev and his opponents. A number of Khrushchev's allies were removed from the Presidium (Aristov, Ignatov, Furtseva, and Mukhitdinov among the full members; Kirilenko and Pospelov among the candidates). Mukhitdinov also lost his seat in the Secretariat, where five new members were added (Ilichev, Shelepin, Ponomarev, Demichev, and Spiridonov). Whereas only two of these—Ilichev and Demichev—could be considered staunch Khrushchev supporters, Ponomarev seemed associated with Suslov and Spiridonov with Kozlov.[24]

In the period following the 22d congress the unsettled internal balance of power led to "an unusually high degree of instability and inconsistency in Soviet internal and foreign policy."[25] The deadlocked opponents engaged in factional infighting and innuendo.

The 1960–62 period saw gathering tensions in party-military relations. In April 1960 there was a major reshuffle in the high military command in which, among others, Marshals Sokolovsky and Konev, who had failed to support the demobilization measures at the Supreme Soviet session, were demoted.[26] Military representation in the Central Committee elected by the 22d party congress in 1961 was enlarged from 6 to 14 full members, and from 12 to 17 candidate members. The Stalingrad group made up a majority of these military Central Committee members (23 out of 31).[27] However, the rift between Khrushchev and some ranking members of the Stalingrad group deepened, as the group was split between active supporters of Khrushchev (such as Biryuzov, Moskalenko, Chuikov) and those deviating from Khrushchev's military policy (such as Malinovsky, Zakharov, Grechko).[28] In the summer of 1962 the important volume *Military Strategy*, edited by Marshal Sokolovsky, was published. On the whole, it represented a challenge to some of Khrushchev's strategic ideas.[29]

In brief,

. . . this period was notable for something that was to prove of importance later, namely that when the First Secretary was in serious trouble, Malinovsky, Grechko, and other marshals who were strong Khrushchev supporters, far from hastening to help their protector, kept their distance or even uttered criticism. This attitude was to be theirs also in the crisis of October 1964.[30]

IMAGES OF THE TEST BAN ISSUE

The significance of the U-2 incident for changing Soviet images of the test ban issue can be illustrated by comparing two articles in successive May issues of the *New Times*. The first, sent to the press just before the fateful event, agreed with Western predictions that the summit would facilitate early conclusion of a test ban treaty.[31] The second article, written shortly after the plane was shot down, described U.S. "sabotage of the disarmament and test-stoppage talks" and the violation of Soviet air space as parts of "a single pattern."[32]

Khrushchev, however, apparently did not give up his hopes

for a test ban treaty immediately after the U-2 incident. At a press conference in Paris before leaving the abortive summit, he declared that the Soviet Union would continue the test ban negotiations and was ready to sign an agreement. He furthermore expressed optimism as to the possibility of concluding a treaty "if, as a result of having rubbed their eyes for them near Sverdlovsk, the American imperialists have begun to see better." [33]

On the other hand, Marshal Malinovsky, Khrushchev's escort to the Paris summit, in a speech shortly before their departure to France failed to mention a test ban among his examples of peaceful Soviet foreign policy moves.[34] Marshal Golikov simultaneously made the same omission.[35] Both stressed general and complete disarmament. And by the end of May, Khrushchev seemed to be backing down on the test ban issue. Referring to President Eisenhower's announcement of May 7 foreshadowing underground test resumption, he voiced suspicions that the United States was blocking a decision on test cessation "on which concurrence had almost been achieved." He warned that the Soviet Union would be "forced" to follow suit if the United States resumed testing, and concluded: "We do not want to see that turn of events. The Soviet Union therefore proposes that all means of warfare, and it follows all means of attack, be destroyed."[36]

In other words, disarmament was to take priority of a test ban. This was reflected in other Khrushchev speeches during the summer of 1960 dealing exclusively with GCD.[37] Contrary to his colleagues in the leadership, however, Khrushchev in some public statements tried to keep the test ban issue alive, pointing out that the professed U.S. plans of underground test resumption were the main obstacle to an agreement.[38] A certain disappointment can be detected in his statements, as in the following passage of a speech to Austrian businessmen:

Not very long ago the Soviet Union, USA, and England were about to agree completely on banning nuclear weapon tests. . . . But lately, when there remained, so to speak, a sparrow's step to the signing of an agreement, our partners put forward new obstacles in the road to agreement. Above all, the U.S. government, as you know, announced recently that it intends to resume nuclear weapon tests.[39]

The U.S. test resumption plans were given wide publicity in the Soviet press during the summer of 1960, and Khrushchev's wish to keep the door ajar to a negotiated test ban agreement with the Western powers was apparently not widely shared. For example, at a central party meeting with representatives of the intelligentsia in July, Suslov spoke of the "need to be vigilant and to further improve the country's defenses" and called for "a consistent and unflagging struggle for peace, which must be won through the united efforts of the peoples and not through pleading."[40] The statement implied criticism of Khrushchev's predilection for negotiated settlements with the West; and significantly enough, while Suslov's speech was published in full in *Pravda*, there was only a brief reference to Khrushchev's address to the same forum.[41]

Khrushchev himself on different occasions indicated that his détente policies met with internal opposition.[42] The opponents of détente generally and a test ban in particular seem to have prevailed after the U-2 incident, and during the remainder of 1960 public references to test cessation were few and predominantly negative in tone. Deviations from this trend were rare. A Khrushchev letter to the Women's International League for Peace and Freedom dated October 21 still breathed disappointment that the initial success of the test ban negotiations had not persisted.[43] Around the same time an *Izvestiya* article on Western opposition to disarmament spoke cryptically of "the definite progress achieved in the negotiations at the Geneva conference on the cessation of atomic and hydrogen weapons tests" as being "manifestly unpalatable to the partisans of the nuclear arms race."[44] In a similar vein, Academician Fedorov, who had previously echoed Khrushchev's test ban line, argued that the test ban talks had "brought the positions of the sides considerably closer." About remaining differences he said: "Undoubtedly, important though they are, they are not, in my opinion, the main obstacle on the path to agreement. They rather serve those who do not want such an agreement as a pretext to procrastinate."[45]

Another Soviet scientist active in the Pugwash movement, the chemist A. Topchiev, contributed a noteworthy article to the

November issue of the *Vestnik Akademii Nauk SSSR*, in which he referred to the "urgent necessity of active participation by scientists in the resolution on international problems" and went on to advocate test cessation as a "possible practical step toward reducing the danger of war." Topchiev furthermore argued that control of a test tan agreement was possible at a time when official Soviet propaganda equated control in circumstances short of comprehensive disarmament with espionage.[46]

The impression that the disappointment of Soviet test ban advocates was not exclusively directed toward Western opponents was further strengthened in January 1961, when Soviet diplomats began dropping hints to their American opposites that Khrushchev, failing a success for his "soft-line" policy toward the United States, was likely to be succeeded by Kozlov. It was moreover implied that this would not facilitate arms control negotiations.[47]

On the basis of circumstantial evidence Slusser has advanced the hypothesis that in mid-February 1961 a Presidium meeting was called on the intiative of Khrushchev's opponents, in which the majority presented Khrushchev with the alternative of either obtaining within six months a major concession from the West over Berlin or acceding to Soviet test resumption.[48] Even if Slusser's reconstruction is inconclusive in its details, a number of converging signs suggest that February was a kind of turning point in internal Soviet bargaining on the test ban issue.

A letter from Khrushchev to Norman Cousins and Clarence Pickett, dated February 8, 1961, repeated the Soviet wish to achieve a test ban treaty but at the same time pointed out that it would not solve the major problem of removing the threat of war.[49] After that Khrushchev remained remarkably silent on test cessation until the summer of 1961.

Writing in the March issue of *International Affairs*, the prominent physicist I. Tamm repudiated fears of imagined dangers and risks in disarmament generally and a test ban in particular. He indicated that until "a short time ago" he had seen no urgency in writing about the subject, and his wording strongly suggested that his remarks were not addressed exclusively to *Western* arms control opponents.[50]

In late February no less than four high-ranking military leaders (Malinovsky, Moskalenko, Sokolovsky, and Zahharov) made hostile and well-published speeches on Soviet military superiority.[51] Khrushchev, who had set out on a tour of some of the Soviet Union's principal agricultural regions on January 24, came back to Moscow in mid-February, only to continue his agricultural tour by the end of the month. Whereas before the Moscow break Khrushchev had presented the theme of rivalry with the United States in terms of economic competition in per capita agricultural output, his speeches immediately after the mid-February break contained bellicose boasts about Soviet military strength dominating over the peaceful notes of the rivalry theme.[52]

U.S. Ambassador Llewellyn Thompson, who saw Khrushchev in Novosibirsk on March 9, found him "distant and intransigent" and came away with the impression that the Soviet Union had lost interest in the best ban negotiations.[53] And when the Geneva negotiations were resumed on March 21 after a long recess, the previous standstill following the U-2 incident was superseded by Soviet retractions, beginning with the "troika" proposal.

The Vienna summit in June brought the test ban issue back into focus. On the eve of the Khrushchev-Kennedy meeting, *Izvestiya* printed a long article on test cessation,[54] and the testing issue was included in the summit agenda. The exchange of views in Vienna, however, produced no tangible rapprochement either on this issue or on the more pressing Berlin problem. In his memoirs, Khrushchev has recorded his disappointment in the Vienna summit which "did not create favorable conditions for improving relations." He also recalls his empathy with Kennedy:

I knew his enemies, especially aggressive politicians, would take advantage of him and tease him, saying, "See? You wanted to show off your abilities by meeting Khrushchev and sweet-talking him into an agreement. We've always said the Bolsheviks don't understand the soft language of negotiations; they understand only power politics. They tricked you; they gave your nose a good pull. You got a going-over from them, and you've come back empty-handed and disgraced." That's what I imagined the President expected to hear when he got home.[55]

In view of what is known about the attitudes of Khrushchev's domestic opponents, it is tempting to interpret his reminiscence as a projection of his own situation at the time. Having failed to achieve any tangible détente measure in Vienna, Khrushchev faced an opposition insisting on a tougher line vis-à-vis the West.

While Khrushchev apparently did not totally abandon the idea of a separate test ban immediately after the Vienna summit,[56] from August on references to test cessation dwindled, and the German issue came to dominate his public speeches. Khrushchev had previously tended to place questions of arms control above the German issue,[57] but now his priorities were reversed. "Life" had pushed the German question into the foreground,[58] and it had become "the focal point of all international affairs."[59]

Already on June 21 Khrushchev had hinted at forthcoming measures to strengthen the Soviet armed forces, remarking that the USSR had "developed many devices that require practical verification."[60] Two months later, on August 29, the troop cut initiated in early 1960 was deferred, and the next day the Soviet decision to resume tests was announced. Different interpretations of this chain of events have been offered, among them the notion that these decisions were the outcomes of internal bargaining.

On the basis of a day-to-day Kremlinological analysis, Slusser concludes that these decisions, contravening Khrushchev's policies, interests and intentions, represented the views of his internal opposition.[61] First of all, the decisions were apparently taken in the absence of Khrushchev, who was vacationing at the Black Sea. And when Mr. Tsarapkin was recalled from Geneva "for consultations" on August 24, he flew to Moscow—not to Sochi, where Khrushchev was staying at the time.[62]

Furthermore, the decision to resume testing came at a time when the conference of nonaligned states was in session in Belgrade. Burg and Wiles have noted that most explanations disregarding internal Soviet "polycentrism" fail to account for the timing of the resumption and provide any clues as to why it could not have waited a short time until after the Belgrade conference to avoid the impression of deliberate defiance of nonaligned opinion. They conclude that the date was chosen precisely because the relationship between Khrushchev and the nonaligned leaders was to be marred in an effort to force Khrushchev to revise his coexistence policy.[63]

Among the indications dissociating Khrushchev from the decision to remove tests, the following are noteworthy:[64] (1) Just two weeks after the Soviet test resumption a group of Western "peace marchers" were given permission to travel to the USSR and even to engage in propaganda against nuclear tests at Moscow University. This would hardly have been possible unless someone in a strong power position disapproved of the nuclear tests then in progress. The fact that Mme. Khrushcheva granted an interview with the foreign group gives an indication of who that might have been. (2) Two Soviet writers—A. Korneichuk, who was known to be very close to Khrushchev, and I. Ehrenburg—agreed to a resolution adopted at a disarmament conference in London on September 10, which "appealed to the governments engaged in carrying out atomic tests to stop these tests immediately." (3) An "East European expert" in Belgrade, who did not want this name published because of his position, provided the *New York Times* with the information that the Soviet decision to resume tests was directly linked with a weakening of Khrushchev's internal position which "might accelerate the emergence of a military power group."

Slusser further concludes that the salient feature of Khrushchev's public statements following the test resumption was his distinct lack of enthusiasm and his repeated emphasis on the "forced" character of the move.[65] At the 22d party congress Khrushchev moreover made a point of noting the "collective" character of recent important decisions. "Not one major measure, not one responsible pronouncement has been carried out upon anyone's personal directive; they have all been the result of collective deliberations and collective decisions."[66]

Being interviewed—on his own initiative—by C. L. Sulzberger of the *New York Times* a few days after the testing decision, Khrushchev declared: "We are making nuclear tests. . . . But what the hell do we want with tests? You cannot put a bomb in soup or make an overcoat out of it. Nevertheless we are compelled to test."[67]

If, as the indirect evidence cited above indicates, Khrushchev was opposed to test resumption, who was behind the decision? Khrushchev himself has later referred to pressures from "scientific and military experts" to resume tests and "see if the new improved designs really worked."[68]

Within the scientific community there were, however, signs of cleavages. For instance, while Tamm in the article mentioned above maintained that "clean" bombs were impossible to produce, others, such as Emelyanov, argued the opposite.[69] The argument implied divergent estimates as to the necessity of testing new devices. As it turned out, Soviet testing of "cleaner" bombs did take place in early 1962. On the one hand, the *Vestnik Akademii Nauk SSSR* carried a number of articles and speeches during the spring and summer of 1961 designating nuclear physics as the number one research priority and alluding to plans for large-scale *experimental* research in terms that left much doubt as to whether they had only civilian research in view.[70] On the other hand, Sakharov is known to have made strong protests against test resumption to Khrushchev.[71]

In comparison to the contradictory pressures from scientists, the military involvement in the decision to resume testing seems more unambiguous, though not as well documented. Without offering any evidence, Tatu, in consonance with Khrushchev, asserts that "the marshals had been advocating for a long time the resumption of nuclear testing."[72] Similar statements can easily be found, but available evidence is circumstantial at best.

The *Voenno-istoricheskii zhurnal*, considered to be the forum of traditional elements in the conventional armed forces,[73] in 1960 and 1961 carried several articles underscoring the lessons to be drawn from the outbreak of World War II as to the dangers of low military preparedness.[74] The gradual downward revision of U.S. estimates of Soviet nuclear-missile strength after the U-2 incident probably added weight to this argument.[75] A retrospective article by Marshal Yeremenko[76] cites exactly these two factors—the need for high military preparedness as taught by the World War II experience, and the changed U.S. estimate of Soviet military strength—as the main reasons behind the Soviet decision to resume testing, which would suggest that the military had an important voice in the final decision.

Noteworthy is Slusser's Kremlinological analysis of the front page of *Pravda* of August 30, which carried these news items: in addition to the announcement of the deferred troop cut, which took up most of the page, there was a note on Nkrumah visiting Khrushchev at Yalta and a photo of workers in a Moscow machine construction factory.

Deciphered, the message conveyed by this rebus was plain: the decision on the deferment of the release of troops to the reserves had been taken in the Kremlin while Khrushchev was vacationing on the Black Sea; the men responsible for the decision were those members of the collective leadership who gave top priority to the policy of strengthening Soviet military-industrial power.[77]

Ploss has argued that there was a "political adjunct to the military-industrial complex," noting that the local party newspapers of industrialized areas that featured materials degrading the practicability of arms control after 1960 also attached unusual importance to heavy engineering.[78]

The Soviet test resumption dealt a blow to the test ban negotiations and also ushered in the temporary disappearance of the test ban issue from official Soviet discourse. The Central Committee decree of August 30 on the deferment of the troop cut included a detailed list of Soviet proposals for partial measures "whose implementation would also contribute to the solution of the problem of universal and total disarmament," in which test cessation was conspicuously absent.[79] At the 22d party congress no speaker alluded to a test ban. The previous reference to test cessation in the May Day and revolution anniversary slogans disappeared in October 1961, not to reappear until after the conclusion of the partial test ban treaty.

Interestingly enough, the Soviet proposal of November 28, 1961, for a nationally controlled three-environment ban combined with a moratorium on underground tests until the achievement of

GCD, was fully described and supported in *Krasnaya Zvezda*,[80] a paper that had not been very articulate on the subject of test cessation in the past. This fact suggests the hypothesis that the proposal was the result of a compromise between Khrushchev and other reformists on the one hand, and more orthodox forces, including the military, on the other. While the reformists managed to keep the idea of a separate test ban alive, questions of control and inspection, abhorrent to the military, were evaded. And whereas the reformists could keep hoping for a comprehensive test ban,[81] the military were satisfied to retain the possibility of testing underground.

This hypothesis is supported by the behavior of the main actors during 1962 as well. While Khrushchev was actively propagating a separate test ban, his enthusiasm was not shared by other leaders, and the military in different ways demonstrated its reserve.

Khrushchev again began to place disarmament questions above the German issue. In reply to an explicit question about his priorities by the American publisher Gardner Cowles, Khrushchev in April 1962 described disarmament as "the number one problem" and the German question as "ostensibly subordinate to the disarmament question."[82] The only leader to mention test cessation in the published Supreme Soviet election speeches in March,[83] Khrushchev downgraded the military advantages of continued mutual testing and dwelt on the desirability and practicability of a nationally controlled test ban before dealing with GCD. He also began to deemphasize and gradually abandon the linkage with GCD still remaining in the November 1961 proposal. In a letter to the president of Tokyo University dated March 8, 1962, Khrushchev stated:

The Soviet Government—I want to emphasize this—is very far from wanting the dangerous situation as regards nuclear testing to continue until the Powers finally reach agreement on disarmament. In our opinion, there is every possibility of solving this problem even now without further procrastination.[84]

Speaking in Bulgaria in May, Khrushchev reaffirmed Soviet readiness to sign a nationally controlled test ban treaty without mentioning any linkage with GCD,[85] and in a June correspondence with the Japanese Communist leader Nosaka he was even more explicit: "We are prepared to agree on nuclear weapon test cessation as a separate measure, without waiting until an agreement on general and complete disarmament will be achieved."[86]

In contradistinction to Khrushchev, other voices, especially from the military, tended to stress the link with GCD and be less willing to consider test cessation as a separate measure in its own right. Marshal Yeremenko, writing in *International Affairs*, argued: "The problem of peace is indivisible in the sense that it is impossible to solve it basically with half measures, that is, partial steps towards disarmament. The last few years have given ample proof of this."[87] Further on in the article Yeremenko gave unenthusiastic support to the Soviet agreement to resume test ban negotiations, which "undoubtedly can have a beneficial effect on the disarmament problem as a whole." Yeremenko's main argument was pursued in the following issue of *International Affairs:* "Whatever the subjective motives of the various people who put forward formulas for arms control, a highly important common factor throughout is *denial of the possibility and necessity of general and complete disarmament.*"[88]

Significantly, Khrushchev's above-mentioned letter to Nosaka which put heavy emphasis on a test ban at the expense of GCD was not published in *Krasnaya Zvezda*, whereas another Khrushchev letter written around the same time but dealing exclusively with GCD was, in fact, published.[89]

In a number of his public speeches, defense minister Malinovsky mentioned the test ban negotiations only as proof of Western aggressive intentions,[90] and in June he reverted to the old practice of referring to the banning of nuclear weapons tests *and* production conjointly.[91]

The continued contradictory nature of the scientific involvement in the internal bargaining was epitomized in a *Pravda* article by the president of the USSR Academy of Sciences, M. Keldysh, in July, where he maintained that all Soviet scientists gave their full support to the Soviet proposals for a test ban and at the same time to "all steps taken by our government directed toward the strengthening of the defense capability of our country," an expression frequently used in connection with the Soviet test resumption.[92] Sakharov has recounted that in mid-1962 he made renewed protests against Soviet test series to Khrushchev and also suggested the idea of a three-environment ban excluding underground tests to the minister of the nuclear weapons industry, Slavsky, who is assumed to have conveyed the suggestion to Khrushchev.[93] Topchiev, whose positive interest in test cessation has been noted above, suggested the idea of "black boxes" in a *Pravda* article in September, reporting on a recent Pugwash conference.[94]

On balance, Khrushchev does not appear to have mustered much internal support for his test ban advocacy in 1962. Most leaders simply kept silent on the issue. Gromyko in his Supreme Soviet speech of April 24 gave test cessation low priority, and a series of *International Affairs* editorials and articles on the work of the ENDC during the spring and summer did not refer to the test ban negotiations but concentrated on GCD.[95] The foes of a separate test ban seemed to have prevailed. This impression is reinforced by a curious *Pravda* article on the eve of the Cuban missile crisis devoted to the republished minutes of the 7th party congress of 1918. Pointing out that "scanning the pages . . . one thinks of the present day and of the reality surrounding us," the article went on to describe an acknowledged leader (Lenin) cast into a minority position and fighting to overturn ascendant "left-wing communists" who prefer armed conflict to compromises and peace agreements with imperialism.[96]

IMAGES OF THE UNITED STATES

Khrushchev made several audacious attempts to "save" the dual image immediately after the U-2 incident. In his own retrospective expression: "I went out of my way not to accuse the President in my own statements. . . . As long as President Eisenhower was dissociated from the U-2 affair, we could continue our policy of strengthening Soviet-US relations, which had begun with my talks with Eisenhower."[97]

In his first public comment on the U-2 incident on May 5, Khrushchev reaffirmed his confidence in Eisenhower's "earnest desire for peace" and blamed the event on aggressive circles "that are circumscribing him."[98] Two days later he was even more explicit: "I am quite willing to grant that the President did not know anything about the fact that a plane had been sent into the Soviet Union and had not returned."[99]

Still on May 9 Khrushchev depicted the incident as the work of an "aggressive military clique."[100] Eisenhower, however, assumed full responsibility for the flight, first through his Secretary of State Herter on May 9, and then personally at a press conference two days later; virtually at the same time as Khrushchev, speaking to foreign journalists about the U-2 affair, admitted that the incident had placed him "in a very difficult position" and expressed his disappointment in Eisenhower.[101]

Khrushchev's friendly attitude toward Eisenhower turned into a serious source of weakness for the Soviet Premier and a trump card for his opponents in the internal bargaining process. This became obvious already in connection with Khrushchev's first report to the Supreme Soviet. The Tass agency made a curious addition to its account of Khrushchev's speech. After one passage the following "audience reaction" was inserted: "Shouts of indignation. Voice: 'How can this be squared with Eisenhower's unctuous speeches? This is outright banditry!' "[102]

A comparison of Khrushchev's May 5 report and Marshal Grechko's speech the following day[103] gives further indications of the lines of conflict unearthed by the U-2 affair. First, Grechko made no attempt to dissociate Eisenhower from the incident but spoke of "American imperialists" indiscriminately. Second, whereas Khrushchev depicted the event as an attempt to "weaken our resolve in the struggle for a relaxation of international tension" timed for the summit conference, and underscored that there were no grounds to interpret it as a precursor of war; Grechko cautioned against considering the U-2 flight "in isolation from other similar aggressive actions on the imperialists' part" and drew a picture of imminent war danger, using such expressions as "present-day trumpeters of a new war," "gentlemen who seek to provoke a war," and "those who are seeking to plunge mankind into the abyss of a new war." Third, Khrushchev and Grechko saw divergent implications for Soviet policy toward the West generally and for the pending Paris summit in particular. Khrushchev advocated continuation of a détente policy, exerting "all efforts to reach a solution of urgent questions through negotiation," and promised that "we shall not spare our efforts to reach a mutually acceptable agreement" at the Paris summit. Grechko, on the other hand, underlined the "necessity of strengthening or country's defenses" and expressed his confidence that Khrushchev would go to Paris "to expose and upset the designs of aggressive circles."

Defense Minister Malinovsky in a speech a few days later described the American—and Khrushchevite—version "that the official authorities in Washington had not given their permission for this flight and knew nothing about it" as being beside the point. "It only shows that rudimentary order is lacking in this much-vaunted country and its armed forces if mad, bellicose generals and fanatics of atomic death are acting without control."[104]

Malinovsky accompanied Khrushchev to Paris, which can be seen to symbolize the impact of military viewpoints at the time. And it was evident that the summit conference did not unfold in accordance with Khrushchev's expectations. As late as May 11 Khrushchev had told foreign journalists that he did not believe it necessary to include the question of the U-2 flight in the summit agenda.[105] As it turned out, Khrushchev brought up that very question in his opening speech in Paris, demanding a public apology from Eisenhower before going on with the conference. When no satisfactory reply was forthcoming, the Soviet delegation left Paris on May 19.

Khrushchev's intentions were obviously frustrated in Paris; and while the Soviet delegation was still in Paris *Pravda* made an unprecedented oblique reference to Khrushchev's internal opposition by printing without comments a translation of a Walter Lippmann column arguing that Khrushchev could not neglect the U-2 affair considering, inter alia, "his critics within the Soviet Union."[106]

Returning from Paris, Khrushchev faced increasingly vociferous criticism on account of his dual image of the United States. The military led the way. *Krasnaya Zvezda* blamed "the ruling circles" of the United States for the U-2 incident and the summit failure,[107] and in an obvious snub to Khrushchev stated that "the American 'peace-lovers' have appeared in front of the peoples in all their miserable nudity."[108] Throughout the summer of 1960 there were articles proving that President Eisenhower was, and had always been, an active "cold warrior."[109] Characterizing the present U.S. leaders as frightened, potentially reckless, and "dangerous for the cause of peace" rather than realistic, Malinovsky made it clear that the correct lessons of Camp David were not the ones drawn by Khrushchev:

The lessons of history tell us that the imperialists cannot be taken at their word, regardless of how sweetly they talk. The last lesson, Camp David, is too vivid for us to forget history. No, we do not believe the imperialists. We are convinced that they are only waiting for an opportune occasion to attack the Soviet Union and the other socialist countries, and that all that restrains them is the danger of the complete defeat of imperialism as a system.[110]

Criticism was heard from other quarters as well. All those who had looked askance at the Khrushchev–Eisenhower fraternization of 1959 could now speak out. A cryptic statement in a *New Times* article foreshadowed more outspoken attacks to follow. "*The Soviet people* have always realized and warned that the chief danger to peace follows from the aggressive proclivities of the Pentagon militarists. But not everyone, *particularly in the West*, believed that."[111]

The implication appears to be that even some *Soviet* individuals, not truly representing the people, might have held erroneous beliefs. V. Kochetov, "the acknowledged head of the conservative school in literature,"[112] wrote an article in *Pravda* on May 23 which went very far in pointing out Khrushchev as the target of criticism: "Yes, we wanted to believe Eisenhower, we wanted to believe him for the sake of peace on earth. . . . But unlike certain simple-minded persons (*prostaki*) we were not exactly moved to enthusiasm by the President's foggy, evasive statements."[113]

An article in *International Affairs* by A. Sovetov, a pseudonym associated with authoritative foreign policy statements,[114] represented, in fact, an undisguised homily to Khrushchev. Having noted that the seemingly casual U-2 incident held up a mirror to U.S. foreign policy reflecting "a political line pursued for years or decades," Sovetov went on to say: "Last autumn some people thought that the positions of the bellicose groups in U.S. ruling circles had been sapped and that sober-minded forces were gaining the upper hand. That was a wrong impression."[115]

Sovetov concluded that recent events had proved that the nature of imperialism had not changed and "the only reason why individual imperialist Powers sometimes adopt more flexible methods . . . is because the situation does not allow them to act otherwise." This conclusion was amplified in a simultaneous article in the prestigious party organ *Kommunist*, arguing that the uninterrupted struggle by the imperialists against the Soviet Union "does not cease for one day, for one hour, but becomes more vigorous as the forces and success of the socialist camp grow and as world capitalism becomes more decrepit."[116] Thus not only Khrushchev's characterization of Eisenhower as a man of peace but also his underlying thesis of growing realism in the West as a result of the changing global balance of forces came under attack.

Khrushchev himself, however, was not persuaded by this criticism to abandon altogether his image of Eisenhower or his conception of significant internal divisions within the United States. His anger in Paris had resembled "the anger of the disillusioned lover," as Deutscher has put it.[117] At a press conference before his departure from Paris, Khrushchev again explained the change in Eisenhower's policy from Camp David to U-2 in terms of increased pressure on him by reactionary forces.[118] Speaking in East Berlin on his way back to Moscow, Khrushchev expanded on this explanation, referring to a "hidden and involved struggle between political forces":

In the United States there are powerful and influential circles that are not interested in doing away with tension and the "cold war." They are in the President's entourage, and they are bringing pressure to bear on him."[119]

As on previous occasions, he indicated that these reactionary forces were to be found in Pentagon particularly. Still by the end of May Khrushchev publicly reiterated his opinion that Eisenhower had not known of the U-2 flights and that "the President himself wants peace now too."[120] Another indication that Khrushchev's positive image of Eisenhower was deeply ingrained and little shattered by the U-2 incident is the fact that it recurs in Khrushchev's "last testament." With reference to Eisenhower's behavior at the Paris summit, for example, Khrushchev recollects:

[I]f Eisenhower had followed his own good instincts and used his own considerable intelligence, he would have done the right thing and given in to our demand; he knew it was possible for him to give us the apology and assurances we were asking for. But unfortunately, Eisenhower wasn't the one who determined foreign policy for the U.S. He let himself be pushed around by his Secretary of State, first Dulles and now Herter.[121]

On a number of occasions, Khrushchev publicly stated his hopes for a "realist" recovery in the United States. Already at the Paris summit he said he was convinced that "if not the present government of the U.S.A., then the next one, and if not the next one, then the one after that will understand that there is no alternative to peaceful coexistence of the two systems."[122] And in late June, while admitting that the present U.S. leaders were "apparently not in a position correctly to build relations between states with different social orders," he emphasized that it was in the Soviet interest that the approaching American presidential elections resulted in an administration that would "understand and redeem the errors committed by the present government." He further indicated that the Soviet Union could help to bring about such a result by upholding a détente policy vis-à-vis the United States, whereas adopting a tougher line would be tantamount to favoring "the imperialists who profit from the 'cold war' and the arms race."[123]

Besides this reiterated policy implication—the détente policy must be continued[124]—Khrushchev's retained dual image also affected his interpretation of U.S. behavior in the test ban negotiations. On May 28, he explained the vacillations in the American stand in terms of shifting balances of forces and suggested that Eisenhower's announcement about U.S. underground test resumption plans just prior to the scheduled summit meeting was inspired by "aggressively minded circles."[125] Later in the summer he pointed out Pentagon as the leading force blocking the road to a test ban agreement.[126]

The RB-47 incident in early July, when another U.S. aircraft was shot down over Soviet territory, added fuel to Khrushchev's orthodox opposition. In the words of a *Pravda* commentary, it ought to make "even the politically blind . . . regain their vision."[127] *Krasnaya Zvezda* printed a series of articles throughout the summer on U.S. war preparations, and Suslov made a couple of hostile speeches clearly differing from Khrushchev's in tone, diagnosis and recommendation. The "aggressive American imperialists," who admittedly "took a few steps toward relaxing tension in international relations," were now again treading the old "path of provocation," he said and emphasized the danger of war. Therefore, the Soviet Union, first of all, had to "be vigilant and to further improve the country's defenses."[128]

Even if there was widespread criticism of Khrushchev's dual image, the First Secretary still had some internal support. N. Inozemtsev, a leading IMEMO specialist, in late 1960 published a book on U.S. foreign policy, the manuscript of which was finished in mid-July. Here Inozemtsev dealt with the dual image at great length and explained fluctuations in U.S. foreign policy, especially its behavior in the test ban negotiations, in these terms.[129] However, the foreign affairs intelligentsia kept being divided, as indicated by the collectively written survey of current international problems in the July issue of *MEMO*. While acknowledging the existence of different groupings within the United States, it downgraded the significance of internal divisions and construed the zigzags of U.S. foreign policy—"from 'brinkmanship' to Camp David and back"—as nothing but tactical maneuvers to deceive public opinion.[130]

The only political leader to come out unequivocally in support of Khrushchev at this time was Kuusinen, who maintained that the U-2 incident was initiated by aggressive circles who wanted to provoke the USSR into abandoning its peaceful policy. However, he added, no "temporary cooling of the international atmosphere" could change the basic course of Soviet foreign policy.[131]

An indication that the views of Khrushchev's adversaries dominated over those of his supporters came in early August, when *Pravda* printed an authoritative statement on peaceful coexistence written by party secretary Ponomarev, "Suslov's inseparable companion and associate."[132] The lengthy article included no reference at all to different tendencies or groupings within capitalist countries but, on the contrary, asserted that "the ruling circles of the imperialist countries, above all the U.S.A."—explicitly including President Eisenhower—were totally subordinate to "reactionary imperialist circles." The aggressive nature of imperialism was furthermore said to be sharpening rather than becoming blunted as a result of the changed relation of forces in favor of the socialist camp.[133]

During the latter part of 1960 Khrushchev was reticent on the subject of dual tendencies in the West. Around the time of the American presidential election in late 1960 the diversified image made a gradual reappearance in Soviet official discourse. An October *Izvestiya* article on the test ban negotiations interpreted U.S. policy in terms of an internal struggle in Washington: "The scales of that struggle . . . are tilting in favor of the forces that are seeking the resumption of atomic weapons tests."[134]

A *MEMO* article designated the U.S. defense industry supported by Defense Secretary Gates, AEC President McCone and a group of "nuclear" senators as the main opponents of a test ban.[135] And a review of American books on arms policy in the December issue of *International Affairs*, developed, in more general terms, the notion of a

> . . . struggle between the extremely reckless and the more moderate elements in the ruling camp of imperialist countries, in this case the United States. Such a struggle is an important part of the world-wide process of demarcation between the forces of peace and war, the growing isolation of the reckless forces of imperialism, a process which is a salient feature of our times.[136]

The election of Kennedy was greeted with wary optimism in some Soviet commentaries.[137] For instance, the January 1961 foreign affairs survey of *MEMO* elaborated "some sober and realistic opinions" in Kennedy's pre-election statements, including his commitment to seek an agreement on nuclear test cessation.[138] No such positive comments could be found in *Krasnaya Zvezda*, which in a number of articles before the election demonstrated that both presidential candidates were the tools of monopoly capital and advocates of a continued arms race.[139]

At the turn of the year Khrushchev broke his restraint of the previous months and again spoke unequivocally about the significance of the dual image.

> Two trends are observed in the policy of the capitalist camp vis-à-vis the socialist countries: a bellicose-aggressive one and a more moderate-sober one. V. I. Lenin pointed to the necessity of establishing contact with those bourgeois circles that gravitate toward pacifism, "be it even the poorest kind." . . . He said that in the struggle to preserve peace we must also use sensible representatives of the bourgeoisie. The correctness of these words is confirmed by the events of our times also.[140]

President Kennedy's first months in office were, however, not designed to strengthen the notion of emerging sober forces in the United States but rather provided Khrushchev's orthodox opposition with arguments in the internal bargaining. First, the new administration's budget proposal called for increased defense expenditures. And by its involvement in the Bay of Pigs invasion of April, the Kennedy administration, in the words of a *Krasnaya Zvezda* commentary, "threw off its mask of peacemaker for everyone to see."[141]

Khrushchev obviously had to retreat and for several months did not allude to the dual image in public. After the Vienna summit, he expressed his positive impression of Kennedy in circumscribed terms: "I formed the impression that President Kennedy appreciates the great responsibility that rests with the governments of two such mighty states."[142]

In a radio and TV address of August 7, Khrushchev further expounded the dual image. Elucidating the difference between "the most aggressive imperialist circles" and "sober-minded" persons in the West, he stated his opinion that on questions of peace and war Kennedy "took a sober view of things and displayed definite realism."[143] A few days later he expressed his hopes that "reason will prevail in responsible Western circles, especially those in the United States, and that sabre-rattling will give way to a sober and unprejudiced view of things."[144]

Once again Khrushchev encountered opposition. Malinovsky, for example, struck a different chord in a couple of speeches during the summer. Emphatically denying that "the ruling circles" of the United States had learnt anything from history, he maintained that, in spite of its utterances about peace, the new administration was continuing the old "cold war" policy of military adventures and arms buildup.[145] *Krasnaya Zvezda*, which chose not to make any editorial comment or special articles on the Vienna summit,[146] in connection with Kennedy's UN speech calling for a "peace race" demonstrated that American "peacemakers" were thus far acting as "inveterate war-mongers."[147]

MEMO reflected the divisions within the foreign affairs intelligentsia throughout the summer of 1961, alternatingly publishing orthodox and reformist articles. Thus, whereas the May editorial dwelt on the invariably aggressive nature of U.S. ruling circles, citing the Bay of Pigs as evidence, the next issue carried an article underscoring the existence of certain "clear-sighted representatives of the leading circles of capitalist countries" who tried to adjust to new realities in the world.[148] And while the July survey of foreign affairs in the first half of 1961 recognized no other cleavages in the United States than those between the aggressive ruling circles and the peaceful people, an article in the August issue on the "lobbies" in Washington delineated a multitude of interests and pressures.[149] The summer of 1961 also saw the publication of a book on U.S.–Soviet relations, written by the two scholars V. Korionov and N. Yakovlev, which subscribed to the dual image in unequivocal terms. The whole history of U.S.–Soviet relations was said to be "the history of two tendencies in American political life"—one realistic, working for close and friendly relations; the other reactionary and anti-Soviet, preventing rapprochement. The authors concluded that "the question as to which tendency is gaining the upper hand in U.S. policy is still far from resolved."[150]

The dual image was the subject of an esoteric debate at the 22d party congress. Delivering the collectively sanctioned Central Committee report on the first day of the congress, Khrushchev had to modify somewhat his previous formulations.

When *under the pressure of the masses* the advocates of a more or less moderate policy win the upper hand, a relaxation of international tension occurs, the war clouds are somewhat dissipated. But when *the pressure of the masses relaxes* and the day is carried by those groupings of the bourgeoisie that grow rich on the arms race and see in war a chance for more profit, the international atmosphere becomes aggravated.[151]

This turn of expression, not found in his earlier statements, bears the marks of a compromise between Khrushchev's stress on the existence of different groupings within the U.S. leadership and the orthodox notion that the only significant internal division was between the masses and the rulers.

Kuusinen was, in fact, the only other congress speaker to elaborate the dual image. Asserting that "we are far from regarding the entire present-day bourgeoisie as something unitary and homogeneous," he expounded the difference between "belligerent and aggressive" and "moderately sober" forces. In conformity with the Central Committee report, he added that the compromise struck between these two trends depended on "the pressure of the masses."[152]

No other speaker mentioned the dual image, but several dwelt on the aggressiveness and belligerence of U.S. imperialism. It is also significant that a number of speakers, including Malinovsky, Kozlov, and Gromyko, failed to mention Molotov's foreign policy errors in their castigation of the anti-party group. The most remarkable silence was perhaps that of foreign minister Gromyko, accentuated by the fact that the speaker immediately following him, *Pravda* editor Satyukov, was all the more outspoken and took pains to demonstrate that Molotov and his followers were rehashing the theme of inevitable war and denying the principle of peaceful coexistence. Gromyko's strange omission in what was officially the main foreign policy report to the congress and the contradictory nature of his speech in general can be construed as a reflection of the standoff between Khrushchev and his adversaries,[153] which was also mirrored in the congress resolutions. The party program, for instance, contained no reference to dual tendencies in capitalist countries but declared that peaceful coexistence was "in accord with the vital interests of all mankind except the big monopoly magnates and the *militarists*"[154]—vague enough a formula to give rise to differing interpretations.

And different voices were indeed heard in the months following the congress. The proponents of the dual image were clearly on the defensive. Khrushchev made few major foreign policy statements in general and avoided the subject of different tendencies in the West. IMEMO specialist Inozemtsev, who only about a year earlier had published his views on the significance of dual tendencies in the United States, made just a passing reference to "the more reasonable representatives of the bourgeoisie" in a long January 1962 *Pravda* article on peaceful coexistence.[155] Those who did refer to the dual image hastened to add that the reactionary, aggressive forces were evidently having the decisive word in the formulation of U.S. foreign policy.[156]

Advocates of the orthodox hostile image of the United States were more articulate. In a number of editorials and articles during the first months of 1962, *Krasnaya Zvezda* drove home the thesis that the invariably aggressive U.S. imperialists, unable to realize the consequences of the changed global balance of forces, believed that moribund capitalism would be saved by means of a new world war and were, in fact, harboring plans for such a war.[157] The same theme recurred in Kozlov's and Suslov's mid-March Supreme Soviet election speeches, while most other speakers kept foreign policy issues in the background.[158] And that same month an *International Affairs* article unambiguously implicated Kennedy: "If we put aside the words about 'serious negotiations in a spirit of good will,' which embellish some of the President's speeches, we shall see that his government is concentrating on just one thing— the arms drive."[159]

An article by Stewart Alsop in a late March issue of the *Saturday Evening Post*, in which he attributed to Kennedy the view that "under certain circumstances it is possible we shall take the initiative in nuclear conflict with the Soviet Union" proved a godsend to Khrushchev's orthodox opposition[160] and was exploited to the full especially by the military to corroborate their argument that U.S. policy and politicians were invariably aggressive. Allusions to Kennedy's remarks became legion in military speeches and articles.

Kuusinen, who had previously been a staunch Khrushchev ally in propagating the dual image, made no reference whatsoever to different tendencies in the West in his April Lenin Day speech but instead observed that in the present world situation "the imperialists are forced to conceal their aggressive objectives, to dodge and dissemble."[161] Khrushchev himself had to take Kennedy's statement into consideration. Pointing out that "the President did afterwards try somehow to tone the statement down" (the only Soviet leader recorded to have made that qualification), Khrushchev admitted: "But a word spoken is past recalling. We cannot but reckon with the statement made by Mr. Kennedy."[162]

A shift was discernible within the foreign affairs intelligentsia as well. Dual tendencies within the ruling circles of the United States were the subject of a June *MEMO* article, which took pains to minimize their significance. With reference to the more realistic U.S. leaders it was said: "They are by no means against the arms race; on the contrary, in this respect the views of the adherents of 'firmness' and the advocates of 'flexibility' fully coincide."[163]

The author's conclusion was that no matter which tendency prevailed, the "natural course of events" could not be changed.[164] Another *MEMO* article four months later amplified the strength and active influence of ultra-right, if not fascist, U.S. groupings, especially in the field of foreign policy.[165]

In brief, the 1960–62 period saw the ascendancy of Khrushchev's adversaries, who opposed a test ban and had less diversified and more hostile images of the United States. Khrushchev tried to uphold both his image of Eisenhower and his test ban advocacy after the ill-fated U-2 incident, but came under increasing pressure from orthodox forces, above all the military. After the turn of the year 1960–61 the signs of orthodox prevalence accumulated, with Khrushchev and his followers clearly on the defensive. The 22d party congress in late 1961 registered a compromise of sorts between Khrushchev and his opponents with regard both to the test ban issue and the question of how to assess the United States. Orthodox voices, however, continued to dominate over reformist ones after the congress for the remainder of the studied period.

THIRTEEN

Internal Bargaining: Stage III

BACKGROUND

IT IS a widespread assumption that the Soviet shipment of missiles to Cuba was a Khrushchev initiative and that the First Secretary dominated Soviet decision-making throughout the Caribbean crisis. Specifically, the decision to withdraw missiles from Cuba is generally associated with Khrushchev. According to Western estimates, the decisions of the crisis were made by a narrow circle of leaders including Khrushchev, Mikoyan, Kosygin, Suslov, Brezhnev, and Kozlov, forming a Soviet counterpart to President Kennedy's ExCom.[1]

There were, however, signs of opposition to Khrushchev during and after the crisis. Hyland and Shryock have noted the simultaneity of the temporary Soviet endorsement of the Chinese position after its previous neutral stand in the Sino–Indian border clash and the decision not to run the naval blockade in the Caribbean, which "suggests some horse trading and jockeying within the Kremlin."[2]

On October 26, President Kennedy received a long and emotional letter from Khrushchev, hinting at a Soviet retreat in exchange for a U.S. pledge not to invade Cuba; a suggestion simultaneously conveyed through unofficial channels as well.[3] The following day saw a confusing and contradictory turn of events.

The Moscow papers did not echo Khrushchev's conciliatory line; an American U-2 plane was shot down over Cuba; and a new letter arrived from Khrushchev to Kennedy, this one suggesting Soviet removal of missiles from Cuba in return for the liquidation of American bases in Turkey. While Khrushchev's previous letter bore the marks of being written by him personally, the second message obeyed the rules of protocol and traditional style and was probably collectively drafted.[4] To add to the confusion, *Izvestiya* of that afternoon printed the message proposing the Cuba–Turkey deal on page one but on the next page carried an article characterizing any deal exchanging Cuba for "some American base near Soviet territory," which was allegedly discussed by "some persons in the United States," as a reflection of their "cynical bargaining standard" and "impure conscience." Instead, the author suggested, the United States ought to withdraw all foreign troops and liquidate all foreign bases.[5] To account for this chain of contradictions, Tatu has advanced the hypothesis that the "Turkish" proposal was a compromise between Khrushchev's conciliatory policy and advocates of the hard line reflected in the *Izvestiya* article.[6]

In any case, signs of Khrushchev's diminishing influence accumulated in the wake of the missile crisis. In September and October Khrushchev had launched an offensive on many fronts. A new wave of anti-Stalinism surfaced, reaching a climax with the printing of Yevtushenko's poem "Stalin's Heirs," which warned against the resurgence of old Stalinists and obliquely scorned Kozlov.[7] Solzhenitsyn's novel on Stalin's prison camps, *A Day in the Life of Ivan Denisovich*, was published under Khrushchev's sponsorship. The Liberman debate was begun, and a new Lenin document was found, conveniently stressing the primacy of economics over politics, a line vigorously promoted by Khrushchev. This thesis provided the rationale for a Khrushchev-inspired reorganization of the party apparatus, bifurcating it into separate hierarchies of industrial and agricultural bureaus. Brezhnev's visit to Belgrade in September represented a step toward rapprochement with Yugoslavia.

After the Soviet backdown in Cuba, Khrushchev's offensive

lost momentum. The de-Stalinization campaign came to a halt and gave way to a conservative counterdrive against the Soviet literary and artistic avant-garde. The Liberman debate was shelved, Khrushchev's economic policy came under increasing attack, and a sharp debate over his party reform and the "economics-over-politics" line became visible. There were finally signs of reservations about Khrushchev's active rapprochement with Yugoslavia.[8]

Early 1963 has been characterized as "the time of Khrushchev's greatest weakness,"[9] and his "most serious crisis since 1957."[10] At a meeting in the Kremlin on March 7–8 between top party and government leaders and prominent writers and artists, Khrushchev surrendered major elements of his previous de-Stalinization policies and, along with other speakers, stressed the need for strong party controls in literature and the arts. Western Kremlinologists agree that only strong pressures from the orthodox leaders could have caused such a conspicuous Khrushchev reversal.[11] On March 13 a joint session of the Presidium and the Council of Ministers carried through an economic reorganization, which partially reversed earlier decentralization moves by creating a Supreme National Economic Council. D. Ustinov, a top manager in the arms industry, was appointed its first head, and an important by-product of the reorganization was a mass promotion of defense industry officials and other "metal-eaters" against whom Khrushchev had been fighting ever since 1960.[12] Most Kremlinologists impute to Kozlov a leading role in the orthodox offensive.[13] And in the period after the March 13 session until early April, when Khrushchev was absent from Moscow resting at his Gagra retreat, leadership seemed to be under the growing authority of Kozlov.[14]

Kozlov's sudden illness and incapacitation in mid-April represented another turning point in the internal struggle, enabling Khrushchev to recapture the initiative. An unprecedented *Pravda* "correction" of the May Day slogans three days after they had been published, adding that Yugoslavia was "building socialism," heralded regenerated Khrushchev activity. On April 24 he openly criticized Soviet defense industry of making poor use of its resources and being closed to scrutiny.[15] By the end of the month

Ustinov lost his previous preferential treatment as *first* deputy premier in the press, and in early May a chemical industry official, S. Tikhomirov, was appointed new deputy chairman of Ustinov's Supreme National Economic Council.[16]

Kozlov's illness was officially announced on May 4, and from then on Khrushchev returned to the policy orientation from which he had retreated earlier in the year: de-Stalinization, détente with the West, and a hostile line toward China. In June, Khrushchev launched a new economic program focusing on a massive expansion of the output of chemical fertilizers for agriculture. The first half of 1963 also provided an illustration of "the barometric relationship between the relaxation of international tensions and relaxation of ideological controls over the arts."[17] On April 10, the day before the May Day slogan correction, a Central Committee plenum on ideology scheduled for May 28 was announced. However, simultaneously with the disclosure of Kozlov's heart attack, the postponement of the ideological plenum was announced. And when it finally met in June, it came to focus more on the Sino–Soviet split than on ideological controls.

The June plenum also recorded some shifts in the top leadership. Brezhnev and Podgorny, while remaining members of the Presidium, were appointed Secretaries and apparently came to share the duties and the "successor" spot left by Kozlov. Both were considered to be Khrushchev supporters.[18] Thus, after several months of orthodox inroads, Kozlov's departure from the political scene gave Khrushchev a respite to launch his "last offensive."[19]

As for party-military relations, the available evidence suggests that the military, first, resisted what they regarded as a risky and unnecessary exposure of Soviet weapons and troops in Cuba, and, second, were critical of Khrushchev's conciliatory crisis management.[20] After the Cuban crisis a kind of *modus vivendi* seems to have been established, including the military's acceptance of tighter political controls in return for greater freedom to debate military doctrine.[21] The period as a whole was characterized by abating yet not fully resolved conflict.[22]

IMAGES OF THE TEST BAN ISSUE

In his correspondence with President Kennedy during the Cuban missile crisis, Khrushchev held out the possibility of a test ban agreement as a by-product of a peaceful settlement in the Caribbean. His interest in a test ban was reiterated in another letter to Kennedy in December[23] and was simultaneously communicated through unofficial channels as well. The American journalist Norman Cousins conveyed a message from Khrushchev to Kennedy concerning the urgency of a test ban treaty combined with other measures preventing nuclear proliferation.[24]

Hints were dropped, both in the letter to Kennedy and in the Cousins audience, that the new Soviet line in the test ban negotiations was a Khrushchev initiative that met with some internal resistance. Khrushchev's choice of pronouns when writing to Kennedy about the Soviet acceptance of the "black box" idea is significant: "I tell you frankly that before making this proposal *I* held detailed consultations with the experts and after these consultations *I and my colleagues* in the Government came to the conclusion. . . ."[25] And a personal friend of Khrushchev's told Cousins that the First Secretary needed to produce some specific and effective agreement with the United States in the wake of the Cuban episode in order to persuade those of his colleagues who did not share his assessment of Cuba as a turning point in the "cold war."[26]

Whereas the *New Times* stated editorially in November that a test ban treaty "is now within closer reach than ever before,"[27] test cessation was conspicuously absent from Kosygin's November speech on the revolution anniversary, which focused on GCD achieved through "vigorous and determined" popular struggle rather than negotiation.[28] And while Brezhnev, speaking at the Czechoslovak party congress in December, gave prominence to a test ban as a first priority partial disarmament measure,[29] Kozlov dealt exclusively with GCD and made no mention of test cessation in his address to the Italian Communist Party congress two days earlier.[30]

At the same time there were military voices favoring continued testing. A November editorial of the *Voenno-istoricheskii zhurnal* asserted that in the present situation of imminent U.S. nuclear-missile attack the Soviet Union had no choice but to "reinforce its might, produce the most powerful weapons, and every minute be prepared to retaliate an attack from the aggressors." The 1961 decision to resume nuclear testing was pointed to as a prominent example of such "concern with strengthening the security of our homeland."[31]

The internal debate on test cessation seems to have waned in the first months of 1963. The idea of liquidating foreign bases, first suggested in the collectively written letter to Kennedy during the Cuban crisis, was put in the foreground.[32] In a rare public comment on the test ban issue in late February, Khrushchev sounded pessimistic and was apparently in retreat: "Even on such a question, *which essentially is far from a decisive one*, as halting nuclear weapons tests, we cannot come to an agreement with our partners."[33] In the same speech he explicitly related domestic welfare to defense spending and the failure to achieve an "agreement" with the West, thus implying the desirability of East–West accommodation, if not the feasibility.[34]

In early April Khrushchev gave an interview to Norman Cousins, in which he complained that recent U.S. behavior in the test ban negotiations had furnished ammunition to his critics. He maintained that he had had to persuade his colleagues in the leadership to accept the proposal for 2–3 inspections and was put in a difficult position when this offer, allegedly accepted earlier by the United States through informal channels, was rejected by the U.S. government. Khrushchev emphasized that now he could not and would not go back to his colleagues and ask for further concessions to the West, and also pointed out that he was hard pressed by his atomic scientists to intensify testing and develop new refinements in nuclear weapons.[35]

At the same time Khrushchev expressed his desire to get the test ban negotiations moving, and a turning point seems to have occurred in mid-April. On April 11, the same day as the May Day slogan "correction," *Izvestiya* published with approval a statement by American physicists favoring a test ban.[36] Throughout the following week Western voices in favor of test cessation were featured in the Soviet press. On April 24, Khrushchev received the U.S. and British ambassadors for discussions on the test ban issue, and the next day Averell Harriman arrived in Moscow for a five-day visit. The renewed Soviet activity in regard to test cessation thus coincided with Khrushchev's political recovery after Kozlov's heart attack.

While preparations were being made for the Moscow talks, the military kept signaling their skepticism as to the advisability of an arms control agreement. An April *Voenny Vestnik* editorial warned that, however great the Soviet success in weapons development had been in the recent past, to stop at the achieved level would be tantamount to lagging behind.[37] Marshal Malinovsky displayed his reserve toward a test ban, first, by repeatedly asserting that the Western powers were not likely to accept it[38] and, second, by calling for "a ban on the *manufacture and testing* of atomic weapons."[39]

Indirect evidence of a sharpened internal debate accumulated as the Moscow talks drew near. The decision to hold test ban negotiations in Moscow was announced without any further comments in a brief Tass communiqué, picturing it as an agreement between Khrushchev (not the Soviet government), Kennedy, and Macmillan.[40] The July issue of *International Affairs*, sent to the press on June 22, carried an article about the pending talks, warning against "unjustifiable optimism."[41] The following passages are noteworthy:

Washington, in its quest for a way of evading a complete and final solution of the question, is once again toying with the idea of a *partial nuclear test ban*. . . .

Soviet people take a realistic view of things. They do not overrate the importance of a nuclear test ban, nor do they think it is a cure-all.[42]

Written at a time when Khrushchev was, in fact, dropping diplomatic hints about his willingness to sign a partial treaty, these formulations strongly imply internal opposition among "Soviet people" to Khrushchev's test ban plans.

The mid-year *MEMO* overview of current foreign affairs,

passed to the press five days before the opening of the Moscow talks, curiously enough made no mention whatsoever of the test ban question.[43] And an article in *Kommunist Vooruzhennykh Sil*, going to the press while the negotiations were in progress, conspicuously omitted a test ban from a list of Soviet proposals in the field of disarmament.[44]

After the conclusion of the test ban agreement there were additional signs indicating that it was indeed a Khrushchev initiative and that others in the Soviet Union were unenthusiastic about it. The only Presidium members other than Khrushchev present at the signing of the treaty were Brezhnev, Kirilenko, and Podgorny. "Was it accidental," asks Tatu, "that these four comprised the most pro-Khrushchev group of the Presidium?"[45] The fact that the test ban was listed specifically in the party slogans of November 1963 and May 1964 but *not* November 1964, right after Khrushchev's ouster, provides another indication of the First Secretary's role.[46]

The military reaction to the test ban treaty was eloquent.[47] Marshal Malinovsky did not refer to it in his order of the day on Soviet Navy Day just two days after the agreement had been initialed. Instead, he made the following ambiguous statement in regard to Soviet peace initiatives:

Our government has made concrete proposals for halting the arms race, general and complete disarmament, *a ban on nuclear tests*, the withdrawal of foreign troops from the territory of other countries, the conclusion of a German peace treaty, and *other unsolved issues*.[48]

Thus implying that the test ban issue had, in effect, not been solved, Malinovsky made the strangely inappropriate addition that the reason for this was that the imperialists were heightening international tension and continuing the arms race.

Apart from printing Tass communiqués, *Krasnaya Zvezda* failed to make any comments on the treaty for almost a week, when the rest of the Soviet press displayed verbose enthusiasm. Not until July 31 did it carry an article ostensibly praising the partial test ban, written by a M. Shiryamov with the remarkably low rank of commander (*kapitan pervogo ranga*).[49] In contrast to other Soviet press commentators, Shiryamov pointed out that the Moscow treaty neither excluded all testing, halted the arms race, nor reduced the danger of war. It lasted all the time till August 7 before *Krasnaya Zvezda* made any editorial comment on the test ban, and then it put heavy stress on the opposition to the treaty in NATO countries and China.[50]

The treaty fared no better in other military periodicals. The conservative *Voenno-istoricheskii zhurnal* failed to make any mention of it at all. Not until the October issue did the *Voenny Vestnik* comment on the treaty. And while some articles in the *Kommunist Vooruzhennykh Sil* from late August on made passing and brief references to the test ban, the first article expressing unequivocal and detailed support of the treaty appeared in late September and was written by a civilian.[51]

When the test ban treaty was discussed in the foreign policy committee of the Supreme Soviet on August 31, no military representative took the floor.[52] And at the final ratification debate, veteran Marshal Budenny was the only military speaker. He stressed (a) that the agreement had become possible thanks to the military and economic power of the USSR, (b) that it did not stop the arms race, and (c) that it should not imply less emphasis on the strengthening of Soviet defense might.[53]

One would assume that the defense industry shared the reserved military attitude vis-à-vis the Moscow treaty. Though no direct evidence of this can be found, there are a few suggestive clues. The conservative *Voprosy Ekonomiki* did not comment on the test ban; the August issue instead carried an article emphatically denying any change to the better in contemporary capitalism.[54] Noteworthy is also the editing of a report on Togliatti's comments on the test ban treaty, printed both in *Izvestiya* and *Pravda* on August 27. While the Khrushchevite *Izvestiya* printed the report in full, *Pravda* omitted references to the cost of nuclear armaments and "the heavy burden that it represents for any economic system."[55]

Soviet scientists apparently continued to be divided on the test ban issue. The *Vestnik Akademii Nauk SSSR*, which normally notes major international events, carried no comment on the conclusion of the partial test ban. On August 22 *Pravda* printed an article on the blessings of the test ban, signed by several scientists. Most of them represented medicine and chemistry, but none of them were identified as nuclear physicists.[56]

Interestingly enough, some voices that had previously tended to support a test ban expressed less enthusiasm over the Moscow treaty. We have already noted the dissidence appearing in *International Affairs* and *MEMO* on the eve of the final talks. In addition, the August issue of *MEMO*, sent to the press ten days after the signing of the test ban treaty, included no special article on this event. Instead, an article on NATO's nuclear policy made a highly inappropriate reference to a Soviet government note of April 8 the same year calling, inter alia, for a *comprehensive* test ban.[57] The common denominator of all these dissonant voices was the implicit criticism of the *partial* solution of the test ban issue.

Seen in combination with the military criticism this would suggest that the partial test ban treaty represented a compromise of sorts in the internal bargaining—in other words, a solution that left the involved groupings less than completely satisfied.[58] The reformists, while recognizing the value of the treaty as a first step on the road toward East–West détente, would have considered a comprehensive ban to be of more intrinsic value. The orthodox, while toning down the military significance of the agreement and stressing that it must not prevent further strengthening of Soviet defense capability, would in all probability have preferred no treaty at all.

IMAGES OF THE UNITED STATES

Khrushchev explained Soviet actions and interpreted the peaceful resolution of the Cuban missile crisis in terms of the dual image of the United States. In his December report to the Supreme Soviet, he said:

Among the U.S. ruling circles are politicians who are rightly called "lunatics." The "lunatics" have insisted and continue to insist on unleashing war against the Soviet Union and the countries of the socialist camp as soon as possible. Is it not clear that if we had taken an uncompromising stand we would only have helped the "lunatic" camp to utilize the situation in order to strike at Cuba and unleash a world war?[59]

Adding that "among the ruling circles of the United States there are also persons who appraise the situation more soberly,"[60] he expressed his confidence in the prevalence of sober thinking as an aftermath of the Cuban crisis.

There need be no doubt that the successful struggle for preserving the independence of Cuba, the undeniable winning of this battle by the forces of peace, will force many people to change their view of the development of the international situation and their appraisal of the balance of forces in the international arena. They will have a more realistic conception now of the danger of a nuclear catastrophe.[61]

As an indication of this trend he cited the November U.S. elections, resulting in the defeat of "some of the more aggressive politicians, and first among them such a warmonger as Nixon."[62] Khrushchev also invoked Lenin to prove the possibility and necessity of "reasonable political compromises" with the West, a theme closely associated with the dual image as amplified in a November *New Times* article: "The outcome of the American elections has given the Kennedy Administration a much freer hand to negotiate. . . . So the vote has been a vote for negotiations, for compromise."[63]

The link with the test ban negotiations was spelled out in a *Pravda* article, highlighting the confrontation in Washington between "the partisans of sanity and those of insanity" over the advisability of "constructive negotiations and mutually acceptable compromises":

Sober people in the U.S.A. think that if there is a mutual desire for a reasonable accord, the disarmament negotiations that have resumed in Geneva can finally lead to an agreement on the cessation of dangerous nuclear experiments and on specific measures relating to other disarmament questions.[64]

Khrushchev's interpretation of the Cuban crisis was endorsed by foreign minister Gromyko in the Supreme Soviet debate. Noting the oscillations in U.S. foreign policy between "extreme aggressiveness" and "a saner approach," he concluded: "Both were present in the crisis over Cuba, but here restraint and a sober approach in the end won the upper hand."[65]

However, other Soviet leaders, such as Suslov and Kozlov, spoke of the Cuban missile crisis around the same time without alluding to differences within the U.S. leadership.[66] A November editorial of *MEMO* explained the Caribbean crisis in similar orthodox terms. The only thing that prevented the Americans from going to war over Cuba was the deterrent effect of Soviet military power. Far from recognizing any "sober approach" on the part of the United States, the editorial saw American behavior as proof of the aggressive and "convulsive" foreign policy of crisis-ridden imperialism.[67] Nor did the military press refer to any "sobering" effect of the Cuban confrontation. On the contrary, it was explicitly asserted that Western leaders had not yet drawn the right conclusions from Cuba.[68]

This debate, which implied the question whether Khrushchev had proved himself a "peacemaker" or an "appeaser" in the Cuban crisis,[69] apparently remained unresolved at the turn of the year. In December *International Affairs* stated editorially that it was as yet difficult to assess all the lessons taught by Cuba.[70] And a Sovetov commentary of January 1963 contained both orthodox and reformist formulations.[71]

The first few months of 1963 Khrushchev was evidently on the defensive and did not propagate the dual image with usual vigor. In his speech at the East German party congress of January 17, he made just a brief reference to "sober" Western leaders who realized that issues should be settled through negotiations rather than by war, but hastened to add that "of course one cannot forget for a moment that the forces of reaction and war are hard at work."[72]

Around the same time *Krasnaya Zvezda* explicitly stated that expectations of a more sober U.S. foreign policy after Cuba had not been fulfilled,[73] and Marshal Malinovsky implicitly attacked Khrushchev's idea of emerging "sober" groups in the United States by maintaining that "time has taught the imperialists nothing" and "we have no facts to indicate abandonment by U.S. imperialist circles of a policy of war."[74] In his February Supreme

Soviet election speech, Khrushchev backed down further, using formulations that were strikingly similar to Malinovsky's. Regretting that "life and history have not yet forced the governments of the leading NATO powers to view the world situation realistically and without preconceptions," Khrushchev said that events had shown that "the American imperialists have evidently not renounced the policy of aggression and provocation."[75]

The dual image was still advocated by at least part of the foreign affairs intelligentsia. A February *MEMO* article invoked Lenin, as had Khrushchev done previously, in spelling out the significance of different groupings in the West. The article stressed the need to achieve compromise agreements with the more realistic groups in order to isolate the "madmen" and prevent nuclear war.[76] On the other hand, the collectively written survey of the international situation in the January issue of *MEMO* contained no reference whatsoever to the dual image either in its analysis of the Cuban missile crisis or in other parts.[77]

An interesting fact is that the April issue of *MEMO*, which was sent to the press on April 19 (that is, after Kozlov's stroke), carried another international overview of the kind that had up till then appeared only twice a year, in January and July. This overview, written by a new team of authors, differed markedly from its January counterpart. The existence of different groupings in the United States was a recurrent theme. Specifically, U.S. behavior in the test ban negotiations was explained in terms of an internal political struggle in Washington.[78]

There were additional signs of the recovery of the dual image after Kozlov's disablement. On April 11, *Pravda* reprinted a *Washington Post* article praising Kennedy's "sincere efforts" to reach agreement with the Soviet Union,[79] and in mid-April *Kommunist* published Lenin documents on the need to make concessions to realistic bourgeois forces.[80] No military endorsement of this idea was forthcoming at this time either; on the contrary, the *Voenny Vestnik* stated editorially that "the imperialists recognize no other arguments than force."[81] On the other hand, Ponomarev, generally considered a Suslov associate, repeated Lenin's dictum in his Lenin anniversary speech and called for "sensible agreements with all those who demonstrate that they take a realistic approach to the present alignment of forces and who understand what the consequences of a thermonuclear war would be."[82]

While Ponomarev did not specify who to include among the "realists" and was even unclear as to whether such groups were existing at the time,[83] Khrushchev once again explicitly numbered President Kennedy among "realist" forces: "U.S. President Kennedy has correctly drawn the conclusion that it is necessary to recalculate values, it is necessary to take into account and consider the power of the forces of socialism, it is necessary to change his attitude toward the Soviet Union, and so on."[84]

Malinovsky, on the other hand, clearly associated Kennedy with those imperialists whom "time had taught nothing."[85] And whereas Khrushchev argued that as a result of their decreasing relative strength the imperialists were coming to realize the calamitous consequences of a new war, the defense minister maintained that "in their impotent malice" the imperialists were still "ready to plunge the world into the abyss of a thermonuclear war."[86]

The nuclear test ban did not put an end to this controversy. On the contrary, the divergent attitudes toward the United States were expressed with even greater lucidity in connection with the Moscow treaty. In July and August warnings were heard against drawing too far-reaching conclusions from President Kennedy's conciliatory American University speech of June 10, which was evidently regarded by Khrushchev as a foundation for increased U.S.–Soviet cooperation. The July international survey of *MEMO* demonstrated that "the practical policy of the United States up till now undoubtedly contradicts the peace-loving declarations in the President's speech."[87] And a Sovetov article in *International Affairs*, apparently reflecting the internal Soviet debate, outlined the pro and con arguments concerning the question whether Kennedy's June speech reflected a fundamental "reappraisal" or not.[88] Another indication that the leadership was not united on this issue came in connection with Khrushchev's and Brezhnev's unusually cordial congratulatory telegram to Kennedy on the American Independence Day. The publication of Kennedy's reply, which was "replete with expressions against which a Soviet political conservative would almost instinctively react,"[89] was delayed for several days.

The military, as before, left no doubts about its attitude. *Krasnaya Zvezda*, for instance, chose to highlight the groups opposing the test ban treaty in the ratification debate of the U.S. Congress and concluded that the "dark forces of reaction" were on the offensive.[90] On the other hand, *Pravda* described the same debate as an indication that "in the hard, bitter struggle against foolhardiness, common sense is making its way,"[91] and *MEMO* depicted it as proof of growing "realism" in the United States.[92]

Soviet military journals in general amplified Malinovsky's reiterated conclusion that the imperialists were heightening international tension and continuing the arms race in the wake of the test ban treaty. An article in the August issue of *Voenno-istoricheskii zhurnal* even implied that the danger of war had increased as a result of the Moscow treaty. Cautioning that future wars would probably be preceded by less *overt* "threat periods" than those in the past, the author cited a statement by the French general Gallois as particularly relevant to the contemporary period: "any relaxation of tension or successfully conducted negotiations produce exactly those conditions that an aggressor must create if he wants to have any chance whatsoever to take his victim by surprise."[93]

In brief, the period from Cuba to the Moscow treaty was characterized by intense internal bargaining between Khrushchev and his orthodox adversaries both on the test ban issue and the related issue of how to assess the United States. As before, the military was the group most pronouncedly opposed to Khrushchev, whereas both the scientists and the foreign affairs intelligentsia kept being divided. The zigzags of *MEMO* in 1963 illuminates the divergent opinions within the foreign affairs intelligentsia as well as the close connection between the dual image and test ban advocacy. While the January and July international surveys made no mention either of the dual image or test cessation, the April overview combined an elaborate treatment of different tendencies in the United States with explicit support of a test ban. It is also noteworthy that the three surveys mentioned were written by different teams of authors.

Not until after Kozlov's incapacitation did Khrushchev seem to be able to muster the necessary support to carry through the partial test ban agreement. It is evident, however, that the internal controversies over arms control and the dual image did not terminate with the Moscow treaty.

INTERNAL BARGAINING: SUMMARY

Who were the main actors in internal Soviet bargaining on the test ban issue and what images did they hold? What impact did internal bargaining have on Soviet negotiating behavior at Geneva? These are the basic questions we set before ourselves and should now attempt to answer on the basis of the preceding analysis.

Of the sub-elites studied, both the scientists and the foreign affairs intelligentsia were apparently divided, including orthodox as well as reformist elements. The military, on the other hand, seemed unified in its orthodox outlook and displayed no significant internal divergences. Data on the views of industrial managers are inconclusive but suggest orthodox leanings on the part of heavy industry.

In the top leadership Khrushchev, usually backed by Mikoyan and Kuusinen, can clearly be identified as the leading reformists. The most pronouncedly orthodox leader was Kozlov, mostly in consonance with Suslov, who, however, tended to be more ambiguous and cautious.

The divergent reformist and orthodox images of the United States seemed to be fundamental to the internal bargaining between test ban advocates and opponents. While the reformists argued that the changing global balance of forces impelled U.S. leaders to make more "sober" evaluations and avoid nuclear war, the orthodox maintained that the relative weakening of the U.S. imperialists would make them more desperate and increase the likelihood that they might launch a nuclear attack. The reformists tended to stress the significance of the *internal* U.S. struggle, whereas the orthodox saw the United States as a unitary actor with a distinguishable set of objectives and emphasized the *international* process of deterring an American attack. Arms control, to the reformists, afforded potentials for exploiting the differences within the U.S. leadership to strengthen "sober" forces and achieve détente; the orthodox, on the other hand, stressed the propaganda functions of arms control proposals: They were not directed primarily toward Western ruling circles but toward the peoples. To win more popular support and expose the Western arms control policy rather than seeking compromises with Western leaders were seen to be the main purposes of Soviet proposals. While a test ban agreement fit well into the reformist train of thought, it was more alien to orthodox images.

We have found evidence of continuous bargaining on the test ban issue within the Soviet Union. Moreover, changes in Soviet negotiating behavior at Geneva seem to be correlated with changes in the success and influence of the different groupings in internal Soviet bargaining. The 1960–62 period of intransigent Soviet behavior in the Geneva negotiations coincided with the ascendancy of the orthodox grouping having reservations in regard to a test ban and an "enemy" image of the United States. Conversely, the initial (1958–60) and final (1963) periods of more flexible and conciliatory Soviet behavior at Geneva concurred with greater reformist influence.

Conclusions

In the vernacular of general systems theory, the observer is always confronted with a system, its sub-systems, and their respective environments, and while he may choose as his system any cluster of phenomena from the most minute organism to the universe itself, such choice cannot be merely a function of whim or caprice, habit or familiarity. The responsible scholar must be prepared to evaluate the relative utility—conceptual and methodological—of the various alternatives open to him, and to appraise the manifold implications of the level of analysis finally selected. So it is with international relations.

(SINGER 1961:77)

The actions of one nation affect those of another to the degree that they result in advantages and disadvantages for players in the second nation. The players in one nation who aim to achieve some international objective must attempt to achieve outcomes in their intranational game that add to the advantages of players in the second country who advocate an analogous objective.

(ALLISON 1971:178)

HAVING SCRUTINIZED Soviet bargaining behavior on the test ban issue from three different vantage points, we should now be in a position to address ourselves to the question as to how our three levels of analysis are interrelated.

The main conclusion emanating from our first level of analysis was that Soviet conduct in the test ban negotiations did not corroborate Western assumptions about a typical, unchanging Soviet negotiating behavior. It could moreover be added that such "actor-specific" theories of national negotiating styles[1] contain the same potential dangers as those noted earlier in connection with "mirror images." Insofar as they provide the cognitive basis for negotiators, such assumptions about idiosyncratic behavior may blind them to important nuances and changes in the other actor's negotiating behavior and make them prisoners of their own images. Griffiths' observation on U.S. expectations in a different bargaining context seem to the point: "If they smile, we expect perfidy. If they scowl, we go on guard. Should the Russians choose to inject new elements into their . . . policy . . . the West might therefore fail to recognize the innovation, or to provide an adequate response."[2]

We found that Soviet behavior in the test ban negotiations did indeed change significantly over time and that the changes coincided with shifting Soviet images of the United States. Even though these changes concurred in time with two major turning points in East–West relations, the U-2 incident and the Cuban missile crisis, we concluded that the U.S.–Soviet level of analysis did not provide an exhaustive explanation as to why the shifts occurred just then and took just that direction.

In order to find additional clues we turned to different levels of analysis and examined intra-bloc and internal bargaining. It should be noted that a "micro-level" analysis, correlating each single Soviet move in the test ban negotiations with moves in intra-bloc and internal bargaining, was not possible due to the lack of detailed knowledge about the Sino–Soviet and domestic Soviet decision-making processes. However, on a "macro-level," distinct overall changes in Soviet negotiating behavior at Geneva could be correlated with shifts in the intra-bloc and internal bargaining processes.

Our analysis of intra-bloc bargaining indicated that, though the test ban issue was of vital importance to the development of the Sino–Soviet dispute, the observed changes in Soviet behavior at Geneva cannot readily be explained in terms of changes in direct Chinese influence or pressure on the Soviet Union.

However, the fact that Chinese images of the test ban issue and of U.S. behavior largely coincided with those of the orthodox anti-treaty grouping within the Soviet Union suggests possible *indirect* Chinese influence via links with Khrushchev's opposition. And there are several indications that the Chinese did, indeed, on different occasions make attempts to capitalize on internal Soviet differences.

In the fall of 1960, the Chinese, while making it abundantly clear that they were critical of Khrushchev personally rather than the CPSU as a whole, indicated that Kozlov and Suslov represented more accomodating positions.[3] At the 22d congress of the CPSU in late 1961, Molotov was made the symbol of a kinship between the Peking-led external opposition and the orthodox resistance to Khrushchev at home. The congress also marked the beginning of favoritism toward Kozlov in the Chinese press.[4] After the conclusion of the partial test ban treaty in 1963, the Chinese evidently tried to make political capital out of the dissatisfactions of the Soviet military by pointing out the dangers of Khrushchev's "wrong" military ideas for "the great Soviet people and Red Army" and declaring that Khrushchev "did not hesitate to damage the defense capabilities of the Soviet Union itself" by signing the test ban treaty.[5]

The question is what success such Chinese attempts at interference in the internal Soviet political struggle might have had. Slusser has noted "the evident failure of the Chinese to find real allies within the Soviet leadership" and cites as the main reason for this the Chinese assertions of doctrinal superiority which were

CONCLUSIONS 213

unacceptable to any Soviet leader.[6] Similarly, Conquest argues that

> ... every Soviet leader wishing the support of his fellows must avoid anything that could possibly be interpreted as abandoning the absolute primacy and independence of the Soviet apparatus. In a very real sense, therefore, Chinese support may be a liability to any Soviet grouping.[7]

Tatu concludes that whereas Khrushchev met with effective resistance on several domestic and foreign issues, he was allowed, by and large, to have his way and encountered only slight opposition on the Chinese issue.[8] It is also noteworthy that Suslov in his accusation speech to the Central Committee at the time of Khrushchev's ouster in 1964 did not make Khrushchev responsible for the Sino–Soviet split. There are, in other words, several indications gainsaying any effective indirect Chinese influence via Khrushchev's adversaries in general. Nor have we found any signs suggesting that the Chinese were any more successful on the specific issue of nuclear testing.

Our conclusion that China exercised minimal influence—directly or indirectly—on Soviet behavior in the test ban negotiations is in tune with Sonnenfeldt's assessment:

> In recent years there may have been a tendency to look too much to the Chinese in seeking explanations for Soviet behaviour in the disarmament field, partly because the drama of the evolving Sino–Soviet split was so fascinating that all else seemed to pale in significance and partly because "China" sometimes seemed a convenient explanation for otherwise baffling Soviet moves.[9]

Our analysis of internal Soviet bargaining, on the other hand, showed a coincidence between the changes in Soviet behavior and images at Geneva and the shifting success and influence of pro-treaty and anti-treaty groupings within the Soviet Union. The question then arises of what conclusions can be drawn about the relative weight of inter-state and intra-state factors in explaining Soviet behavior in the test ban negotiations.

In the scholarly debate over the balance between external and internal factors in explanations of foreign policy behavior, two extreme positions can be distinguished. First, there is the traditional inter-state, "billiard-ball" model, which analyzes international politics exclusively in terms of state action/reaction and blackboxes the inner dynamics of state decisions and actions. As noted above, it has been regarded as particularly relevant for the study of Soviet foreign policy; both Soviet official doctrine and the Western concept of "totalitarianism" have ignored domestic sources of Soviet foreign policy.

Recently the state-as-only-actor concept has come under increasing criticism, and an alternative model of "transnational bureaucratic politics" has been proposed, where the focus is shifted to domestic determinants of foreign policy. Specifically, it has frequently been suggested that the U.S.–Soviet arms dialogue might be seen as a transnational rather than international process.

[I]t is two separate internal debates that are of interest, not an external one to which continued reciprocal negotiation is critical. Whatever arms limitation proposals are achieved must survive these extended internal dialogues which any bilateral affirmative decision presupposes.[10]

[T]he "arms race" and "arms control" are not really international phenomena. Instead, both sides act out of domestic political processes which are at most indirectly influenced by the opponent's actions. . . . The same reasoning would suggest that arms control agreements between the superpowers are largely fortuitous occurrences that take place when the political processes on both sides happen to produce simultaneous equivalent outcomes.[11]

We would suggest that a prerequisite for a realistic conception of Soviet foreign policy is to avoid the pitfalls of both extreme positions. Exclusive emphasis on either external or internal factors should be replaced by greater attention to the complex *interplay* between the two.

Our case study of the test ban issue indicates that neither the interstate nor the internal level of analysis alone can tap all relevant dimensions of Soviet foreign policy behavior. Rather, international and domestic events can both be regarded as necessary but not sufficient conditions in explaining Soviet behavior in the test ban negotiations.

Changes in Soviet negotiating behavior were found after the U-2 incident in 1960 and again after the Cuban missile crisis in

1962. If it had not been for the existence of internal divergencies between different groupings, it is unlikely that these international events, in and of themselves, would have triggered major shifts in Soviet behavior. Had there been no internal opposition to Khrushchev, the U-2 incident would hardly have altered his détente line. As for the Cuban crisis, it will be recalled that different conclusions could be drawn—and were, in fact, drawn by different Soviet groupings—from this event; it was far from self-evident that the crisis should result in a more conciliatory Soviet attitude.

Conversely, without these international events it is unlikely that the internal bargaining process would have taken the course it did. The U-2 incident provided fuel to Khrushchev's opponents and served as a catalyst for a change in the internal balance of forces, in the same way as the peaceful resolution of the Cuban crisis was exploited by Khrushchev and his followers to demonstrate the feasibility of détente premised on growing "realism" in the West.

Even if the interplay of international and domestic events was perhaps particularly evident during the Khrushchev era, an analysis of the nexus of external and internal factors seems crucial to an understanding of past, present, or future Soviet foreign policy. Griffiths has, for example, documented the permanence of different images of the West among Soviet leaders ever since Lenin's days, and has demonstrated the significance of internal contradictions in combination with external pressures for Soviet arms control and détente policy throughout the years.[12]

This leads us to a few concluding remarks about the broader theoretical and methodological implications of this study. In theories of international relations, the expanse between stimuli impinging on a state and the state's response has traditionally been "a no-man's land of speculation."[13] We have chosen to tread these precarious domains, employing images as our terrain indicator through three different levels of analysis. We have pointed out some of the dangers and problems involved in such an approach, and confess the rudimentary character of the present method. Yet, granting that our crude tools could be refined, we do claim to have focused on an area of vital importance both to international politics in general and international negotiations in particular.

The objection might be raised that we should concentrate on objective "facts" and ignore subjective "images" in the study of international politics. However, for political behavior, what is "real" is what men perceive to be real. Foreign policy decisions are—and hopefully will continue to be—made by men. Robert Kennedy in his memoirs of the Cuban missile crisis concludes that the final lesson of the crisis was "the importance of placing ourselves in the other country's shoes."[14] This lesson is frequently ignored by decision-makers and analysts alike.

Notes

INTRODUCTION
1. Jönsson 1975.
2. For an elaborate discussion of the notion of "auxiliary games," see Midgaard 1966.
3. Walton and McKersie 1965:281–351, 389–391.
4. Allison 1971.

ONE/CONCEPTUAL FRAMEWORK
1. Rapoport 1960:226–227; Schelling 1967:214 expresses similar views.
2. Rapoport 1960:xii.
3. Forward 1971:49.
4. Coddington 1968:xiv.
5. Shubik 1967:271.
6. Cf. Rapoport 1960:360.
7. McGrath 1966:102.
8. Cf. Deutsch and Krauss 1962:52; Schelling 1963:5–6; Coddington 1968:4–6.
9. Among those who do make a distinction between "negotiation" and "bargaining" there seems to be general agreement as to this view. There are exceptions, however. For definitions giving "bargaining" a more narrow denotation than "negotiation," see, e.g., Cross 1969:7; and Bartos 1967:482.
10. Schelling 1963:21.
11. Cf. *ibid.:*73; Stevens 1963:4.
12. Iklé 1968:119; Etzioni 1969:546.
13. Iklé 1964:43–58.
14. Rapoport 1964:84.
15. *Ibid.:*75.
16. Verba 1961:110.
17. Rosenau 1967:199.
18. Snyder et al. 1962:8.

19. Simon 1957.
20. Kelman 1965:24.
21. Boulding 1956:3–18; de Rivera 1968:19–46; McClelland 1966:8–9. Cf. Holsti's "belief system" (O. R. Holsti 1962), and Frankel's "operational and psychological environment" (Frankel 1963).
22. Cf. Gustafsson 1971:43–47.
23. This is the term used by Festinger in his pioneer work (Festinger 1957). "Cognitive balance" and "cognitive consistency" are synonyms frequently used.
24. Rock 1963:4.
25. Cf. Festinger 1957:3.
26. Deutsch and Merritt 1965:159.
27. O. R. Holsti 1968:22; Jervis 1968:472–473.
28. Cf. Deutsch and Merritt 1965:159; Shapiro and Bonham 1973:150.
29. Cf. Fedder 1964; McGrath 1966:130–131.
30. Rock 1963:12–13; Boulding 1968:2.
31. Brzezinski 1967a:5.
32. Aspaturian 1962:141.
33. Cf. Aspaturian 1962:141; Zimmerman 1969:282–292; Gehlen 1967: 22–42.
34. Cf. Zimmerman 1969:289; Ulam 1958:158; Gehlen 1967:296. Furthermore, Holst contends that arms control is such a question where the cognitive and normative functions of ideology are not operative (Holst 1966:57).
35. Zimmerman 1969:287.
36. Brzezinski 1967a:149.
37. Cf. Triska and Finley 1968:112.
38. *Ibid.*:124–125.
39. Coddington 1968:13–14, 49–57.
40. Cf. Rock 1963:6–15; Stagner 1967:12–13.
41. Cf. Iklé 1964:104; Jensen 1962:108.
42. Cf. the "joker" theory of Spanier and Nogee, which holds that virtually all proposals by the main actors—U.S. and USSR—in the postwar disarmament negotiations have been concessions combined with retractions or "jokers" (Spanier and Nogee 1962:*passim*). Kovalev considers the combination of concessions and retractions to be a characteristic trait of Western negotiation proposals (Kovalev 1968:100).
43. Cf. Rapoport 1960:273.
44. Schelling 1963:122, 160.
45. *Ibid.*:22 ff.
46. Iklé 1964:62; Midgaard 1965:211–215.
47. Schelling 1963:38–39, 146–149.
48. Walton and McKersie 1965:93. As the latter examples show, both the conditions and the threatened or promised action can convey varying degrees of specificity.
49. Schelling 1963:40.

50. Cf. Sjöblom 1968:150–151.
51. Cf. Iklé 1964:76–86; Jervis 1970: 79–88. Fedder points to the common tendency of "confusing communicator and communication credibility" (Fedder 1964:116).
52. Cf. Singer's formula: "threat perception = estimated capability × estimated intent" (Singer 1958:94).
53. Cf. Sjöblom 1968:151.
54. Cf. K. Holsti 1972:198; Schelling 1963:28.
55. Cf. Schelling 1963:34–35; Walton and McKersie 1965:116–121; Iklé 1964:74–75; Jervis 1970:155–173.
56. See, e.g., Rush 1958:88–94; Zagoria 1962b; Dallin and Brzezinski 1963:xxxviii–xliv; Griffith 1970.
57. Cf. Jervis 1970:24.
58. Bauer 1961:223.
59. Cf. George 1959:107–120.
60. Jervis 1970:102–110.

TWO/THE TEST BAN NEGOTIATIONS: AN OVERVIEW

1. For a more detailed analysis of Soviet behavior on each agenda item, see Jönsson 1975.
2. See *SIPRI Yearbook 1968/69*:90–95.
3. *Arms control* can be defined as "all the forms of military cooperation between potential enemies in the interest of reducing the likelihood of war, its scope and violence if it occurs, and the political and economic costs of being prepared for it" (Schelling and Halperin 1961:2).
4. Cf. Mark 1965:18–37.
5. See, e.g., Zoppo 1961:22–37, 58–73.
6. Cf. Mark 1965:12.
7. Members of the Subcommittee were France, the Soviet Union, the United Kingdom, the United States, and Canada.
8. GEN/DNT/PV. 2; cf. PV. 7, 12.
9. See Iklé 1962:3–4.
10. GEN/DNT/PV. 116.
11. See, e.g., GEN/DNT/PV. 22, 32, 47, 63, 125; GEN/DNT/30, 47.
12. *Documents on Disarmament 1945–1959*:1112.
13. *Ibid.*:1591.
14. GEN/DNT/PV. 198.
15. GEN/DNT/PV. 208.
16. *SIPRI Yearbook 1968/69*:242.
17. Members of the ENDC were Brazil, Bulgaria, Burma, Canada, Czechoslovakia, Ethiopia, France, India, Italy, Mexico, Nigeria, Poland, Rumania, Sweden, USSR, United Arab Republic, United Kingdom, and the United States. France never participated in the ENDC.

2. THE TEST BAN NEGOTIATIONS

18. Lall 1964:21.
19. Jacobsen and Stein 1966:376.
20. See Horelick and Rush 1966.
21. Edeen 1966:119.
22. ENDC/PV. 13.
23. ENDC/SC. 1/PV. 2.
24. GEN/DNT/122. Emphasis added.
25. ENDC/PV. 8.
26. For Soviet allusions to the "open skies" proposal and the U-2 incident, see ENDC/PV. 21 and ENDC/SC. 1/PV. 8 respectively.
27. GEN/DNT/PV. 314. Emphasis added.
28. Khrushchev radio and TV address of June 15, 1961, in *Documents on Disarmament 1961*:177.
29. GEN/DNT/PV. 165.
30. GEN/DNT/PV. 300.
31. Kennedy 1969:169.
32. ENDC/SC. 1/PV. 40.
33. ENDC/73.
34. *Ibid.;* ENDC/PV. 100, 101.
35. GEN/DNT/PV. 129.
36. ENDC/SC. 1/PV. 41.
37. Khrushchev speech, Aug. 5, 1963, in *Pravda,* Aug. 6, p. 1.
38. See Holst 1969:150.
39. Soviet government statement, July 22, 1962 (ENDC/51). This view was apparently shared by Western observers (see Zoppo 1963:20).
40. ENDC/PV. 142.
41. ENDC/73.
42. *Documents on Disarmament 1963:*246.

THREE/ A TYPICAL SOVIET NEGOTIATING BEHAVIOR?

1. We have drawn mainly on the following works: Kennan 1946; Leites 1951, 1953, 1961, 1964; Mosely 1951; Dennett and Johnson 1951; Joy 1955; Campbell 1956; Acheson 1959; Kertesz 1959; Hayter 1961; Craig 1962, 1970; Jensen 1962; Wadsworth 1962; Aspaturian 1964; Iklé 1964, 1970; Wright 1964; Wedge and Muromcew 1965; Dean 1966; Pipes 1972; Steibel 1972.
2. U.S. Senate 1969:iii.
3. Dean 1966:43.
4. Steibel 1972.
5. Our analysis covers primarily the following works: Bogdanov 1958; *Diplomaticheskii slovar 1961;* Ladyzhenskii and Blishchenko 1962; Levin 1962; Deborin 1963; Lebedev 1963; Stepanov 1963; Zorin 1964; Kovalev 1968.
6. Cf., e.g., Klineberg 1964:95; Sawyer and Guetzkow 1965:504-505.
7. See White 1965:240-244.

3. SOVIET NEGOTIATING BEHAVIOR? 221

8. Rapoport 1971:120.
9. Bronfenbrenner 1961:46–47; White 1965:244.
10. Bronfenbrenner 1961; White 1965:255.
11. O. R. Holsti 1968:17.
12. Kertesz 1959:141.
13. Leites 1951:47.
14. Mosely 1951:34.
15. It should, of course, be noted that the consensus of Western observers with regard to Soviet expectations may provide a validation of the "mirror-image" theory on a secondary plane: the observers' views of Soviet expectations might very well be parts of the "black" side of their own "mirror image" of the Soviet Union.
16. Wadsworth 1962:15.
17. Dean 1966:34.
18. Steibel 1972:9.
19. Mosely 1951:32.
20. Kertesz 1959:141.
21. Pipes 1972:13.
22. Wadsworth 1962:21–22. Emphasis added.
23. Wright 1964:107. Emphasis added. Wright was chief British negotiator in the test ban negotiations.
24. Wedge and Muromcew 1965:33.
25. See, e.g., Levin 1962:123; Zorin 1964:31; Lebedev 1963:7; *Diplomaticheskii slovar 1961:*466; Kovalev 1968:15.
26. Bogdanov 1958:12.
27. Deborin 1963:51.
28. Stepanov 1963:101.
29. *Ibid.:*102–103.
30. Leites 1953:33; cf. Leites 1961:222.
31. Kennan 1946:5.
32. Wedge and Muromcew 1965:33.
33. Mosely 1951:33.
34. Joy 1955:89.
35. Statement by Th. Wolfe in a discussion included in Aspaturian 1964:281.
36. Joy 1955:89–90.
37. Zoppo 1961:62.
38. Acheson 1959:31.
39. Ladyzhenskii and Blishchenko 1962:70; cf. Zorin 1964:314.
40. Mosely 1951:21.
41. Leites 1951:19.
42. Snyder and Robinson 1961:122.
43. Zoppo 1963:99.
44. Kertesz 1959:144. Emphasis added.

45. Deane 1951:27.
46. Kovalev 1968:74.
47. Kertesz 1959:149.
48. Mosely 1951:9.
49. Zorin 1964:313.
50. Kovalev 1968:17.
51. Mosely 1951:25.
52. Zoppo 1961:42.
53. Craig 1962:369.
54. Dean 1966:45–46.
55. Wedge and Muromcew 1965:31.
56. See, e.g., Dean 1966:45.
57. Iklé 1964:52–55.
58. K. Holsti 1972:189.
59. Hayter 1961:28.
60. Kovalev 1968:41.
61. Zorin 1964:315.
62. Dallin et al. 1964:19.
63. Mosely 1951:34–35.
64. Penrose 1951:145.
65. Jensen 1962:175.
66. Hopmann 1972:234–235.
67. See, e.g., Joy 1955; Steibel 1972.
68. See, e.g., Craig 1970; K. Holsti 1972:202–207.
69. See, e.g., Leites 1961.
70. *Ibid.:*393.
71. Steibel 1972:15.

FOUR/IN SEARCH OF ANSWERS

1. Tucker 1960:229.
2. The labeling of the epoch as "post-imperialist" also served as a justification for the ideological revision. Lenin's analysis of imperialism was no longer applicable and had to be transcended in the name of creative Marxism–Leninism (Zimmerman 1969:135).
3. Zimmerman 1969:131–141.
4. Quoted in Tucker 1963:213.
5. Zimmerman 1969:211–225.
6. Kovalev uses these very words as he comments on "the contemporary stage of international struggle and international cooperation" (Kovalev 1968:36). Cf. Tucker 1963:205–208.
7. *Pravda*, Feb. 18, 1960, p. 4; and March 3, 1960, p. 4.
8. Illuminative in this regard is an *Izvestiya* article of Feb. 5, 1960 (p. 5), relating U.S. press reports to the effect that the results of secret consultations be-

4. IN SEARCH OF ANSWERS

tween the State Department, Pentagon, and AEC concerning planned U.S. compromise proposals in the test ban negotiations had been leaked in a distorted version by the AEC.

9. GEN/DNT/PV. 122.
10. Soviet government statement, Aug. 30, 1961, in *Documents on Disarmament 1961*:342.
11. *Izvestiya*, April 3, 1960, p. 5.
12. *Ibid.*, Nov. 3, 1960, p. 2. Emphasis added.
13. GEN/DNT/PV. 262.
14. As quoted in CDSP (1963), 15(1):11.
15. ENDC/PV. 126.
16. See, e.g., Bloomfield et al. 1966:210–215.
17. ENDC/PV. 116.
18. *Documents on Disarmament 1963*:175.
19. Cf. ENDC/PV. 119, 142, 145; ENDC/SC. 1/PV. 40.
20. See, e.g., ENDC/PV. 116, 123.
21. ENDC/SC. 1/PV. 40. Earlier, during *stage II* (July 1962), it was said about the control-for-intelligence policy: "This position was defended by the Eisenhower Government; this position is also followed by the Kennedy Government." (ENDC/49.)
22. For a detailed analysis, see Clemens and Griffiths 1965:109.
23. GEN/DNT/PV. 27.
24. GEN/DNT/PV. 91.
25. GEN/DNT/PV. 106.
26. GEN/DNT/PV. 46.
27. GEN/DNT/PV. 185, 186.
28. Jensen 1962:142.
29. Cf. Jensen's "propensity to compromise" scores:

	USSR	USA	
Sept.–Dec. 1960	0	4	
Jan. –May 1961	– 5	25	
June –Sept. 1961	–13	10	(Jensen 1962:142.)

30. GEN/DNT/PV. 29.
31. "While at least perfunctory support of GCD is to be expected at all negotiations, heavy or exclusive emphasis on GCD has generally been a signal that Moscow is not ready for serious negotiation in areas of possible agreement." (Bloomfield et al. 1966:145.)
32. GEN/DNT/PV. 270.
33. GEN/DNT/PV. 301.
34. ENDC/SC. 1/PV. 32.
35. Cf. Jacobsen and Stein 1966:281; Mark 1965:85.
36. *Documents on Disarmament 1961*:511.

37. CDSP (1962), 14(18):10–13.
38. Cf. ENDC/PV. 96 and PV. 83.
39. ENDC/PV. 98. Cf. PV. 83, 86, 90; ENDC/SC. 1/PV. 40. Cf. also *Pravda*, Nov. 10, 1962; *Izvestiya*, Nov. 14 and Dec. 26, 1962.
40. ENDC/PV. 90. Cf. PV. 101; *Pravda*, Dec. 11, 1962 and Jan. 26, 1963.
41. ENDC/PV. 101.
42. Jensen 1968:152–153.
43. Jensen 1962:142.
44. Cf. the Soviet failure to exploit the "troika" proposal in the UN context to obtain more influence in the Secretariat (see, e.g., Iklé 1964:234).
45. ENDC/PV. 94; ENDC/SC. 1/PV. 50.
46. ENDC/73.
47. Introduced at Geneva on Feb. 23, 1959; published on Dec. 26, 1958 (*Pravda*) and Jan. 4, 1959 (*Izvestiya*).
48. Introduced at Geneva on Nov. 13, 1962; published on Nov. 10, 1962 (*Pravda*).
49. GEN/DNT/PV. 211.
50. GEN/DNT/PV. 206, 208, 210.
51. GEN/DNT/PV. 234.
52. Zoppo 1962:89–94.
53. ENDC/SC. 1/PV. 37; cf. PV. 18, 41.
54. ENDC/SC. 1/PV. 29.
55. ENDC/SC. 1/PV. 14.
56. ENDC/PV. 74.
57. Dean 1966:35.
58. ENDC/SC. 1/PV. 48; cf. PV. 49.
59. ENDC/SC. 1/PV. 14.
60. GEN/DNT/PV. 5; cf. PV. 4.
61. GEN/DNT/PV. 65.
62. ENDC/SC. 1/PV. 46.
63. GEN/DNT/PV. 57.
64. Kovalev 1968:18.
65. Clemens and Griffiths 1965:116.
66. Cf. *ibid*.
67. See, e.g., Welch 1970; Welch and Triska 1971.
68. de Rivera 1968:392.
69. Pipes 1972:1.

FIVE/SINO-SOVIET RELATIONS AS BARGAINING SITUATION

1. For explicit elaborations, see, e.g., Brzezinski 1962 and Zagoria 1962a:3–25.
2. See London 1962:412.

6. INTRA-BLOC BARGAINING: STAGE I

3. Brzezinski 1962:404.
4. Zagoria 1962a:11–12. The expression is attributed to George Kennan.
5. *Ibid.*:8.
6. Zagoria 1964:xix.
7. See, e.g., Griffith 1964:20; Whiting 1962:389; Brzezinski 1967b:406.
8. Cf. Brzezinski 1962:394; Zagoria 1962a:384; Deutscher 1970:208.
9. *Kuang-min Jih-pao*, Feb. 2, 1958, as quoted in Hsieh 1962:86.
10. Brzezinski 1962:395.
11. Lowenthal 1959:15.
12. Clemens 1967:155.
13. Text of the treaty in R. Garthoff 1966a:214–215.
14. Lowenthal 1959:14.
15. The expression is used by Ploss (see Ploss 1965:225).

SIX/ INTRA-BLOC BARGAINING: STAGE I

1. SCMP (1750):51. Emphasis added.
2. See, e.g., Halperin 1967:134–136; Clemens 1968:27.
3. SCMP (1571):40, as quoted in Halperin 1967:119.
4. *Jen-min Jih-pao*, Dec. 30, 1957, in SCMP (1686):3.
5. Chou En-lai at the 21st CPSU Congress, Jan. 28, 1959, in *Stenograficheskii otchet*, 1:157.
6. Yu Chao-li on Lenin Anniversary, March 30, 1960, in SCMP (2233):11.
7. In addition to the examples quoted, see SCMP (1832):1–2; SCMP (1838):57; SCMP (1893):12; SCMP (1953):36; *Peking Review* 1959 (20):21; URS, 1960 (18):37.
8. Chinese government statement of Aug. 15, 1963, in Griffith 1964:352.
9. The details of the Chinese position will be further elaborated below.
10. SCMP (1847):42.
11. SCMP (1753):45.
12. *Ibid.*:43–44.
13. See Halperin 1967:137–138.
14. See, e.g., SCMP (1838):56.
15. Hsieh 1960:8–11; Hsieh 1962:155–157.
16. Chinese government statement of Aug. 15, 1963, in Griffith 1964:351.
17. See Ford 1964:160–161.
18. SCMP (1786), as quoted in Ford 1964:162. Emphasis added by Ford.
19. That this development was not entirely painless is indicated by the unprecedented eight-week session of the Military Committee of the CPC Central Committee May–July, which is believed to have been "the scene of a bitter and protracted debate between the modernizers and the traditionalists." (Zagoria 1962a:191.)
20. Ford 1964:162–163.
21. Cf. Hsieh 1960:2–3; Ford 1964:163; Clemens 1968:18.

22. SCMP (1831), as quoted in Ford 1964:163. Emphasis added by Ford.
23. Chinese government statement of Aug. 15, 1963, in Griffith 1964:351.
24. See Charles 1961.
25. See Clemens 1968:20–22.
26. Cf. Zagoria 1962a:160–167.
27. See, e.g., SCMP (1897):7.
28. Cf. the discussion of the implications of the "peaceful coexistence" doctrine in chapter 4.
29. *Jen-min Jih-pao* editorial, Nov. 12, 1958, in SCMP (1897):7.
30. *Jen-min Jih-pao*, Oct. 31, 1958, in CB (534):1.
31. *Jen-min Jih-pao* editorial, Nov. 12, 1958, in SCMP (1897):8.
32. Sung Tu, "Answers to Readers' Queries on War and Peace," *Chung-kuo Ching-nien*, Feb. 16, 1960, in SCMM (207):2.
33. The publication of this theme started in late 1958, and was to become frequently reiterated ever since.
34. Yu Chao-li, "Peaceful Competition: An Inevitable Trend," *Peking Review* 1959 (33):6.
35. See, e.g., the editorial "Behind the U.S. Smokescreen of Peace," *Peking Review* 1959 (50):3.
36. See, e.g., SCMM (190):11.
37. *Jen-min Jih-pao* editorial, Jan. 21, 1960, in SCMP (2185):47.
38. Sung Tu, "Answers to Readers," p. 3.
39. *Jen-min Jih-pao* editorial, Jan. 21, 1960, in SCMP (2185):51. Emphasis added.
40. CB (617):12.
41. *Jen-min Jih-pao* editorial, Jan. 16, 1960, in SCMP (2181):43.
42. *Ta-kung Pao*, Jan. 14, 1958, in SCMP (1693):21.
43. SCMP (1811):39.
44. See, e.g., SCMP (1846):51; *Peking Review* 1958 (28):22.
45. *Ta-kung Pao*, Dec. 28, 1958, in SCMP (1924):44.
46. *Jen-min Jih-pao*, Jan. 2, 1960, in URS (18):38.
47. See, e.g., *Peking Review* 1960 (1):25, and (8):20.
48. *Jen-min Jih-pao*, Jan. 10, 1960, in SCMP (2177):38.
49. *Shih-chieh Chih-shih*, June 5, 1959, in SCMM (178):2.
50. *Kuo-chi Wen-ti Yen-chiu*, Oct. 3, 1959, in SCMM (190):4.
51. Whiting 1961:1.
52. Lu Ting-yi, "Get United Under Lenin's Revolutionary Banner," in SCMP (2246):10.
53. Hsieh 1968:9.
54. *Kuo-chi Wen-ti Yen-chiu*, Oct. 3, 1959, in URS (17):386.
55. *Jen-min Jih-pao* editorial, Nov. 12, 1958, in SCMP (1897):8.
56. See Editor's Note, URS (17):371; Zagoria 1962a:206. For further statements to the same effect after mid-1958, see, e.g., Ford 1964:169.
57. Lu Ting-yi report, in SCMP (2246):11.

58. Zagoria 1962a:198.
59. For an account of Sino–Soviet behavior in the crisis, see *ibid.*:195–199.
60. *Ibid.*:206–217.
61. See, e.g., Hsieh 1962; Ford 1964:168.
62. The traumatic character of the events mentioned above is indicated by the fact that they all loom large in the post-1963 Sino–Soviet open polemics (see, e.g., Griffith 1964).
63. *Jen-min Jih-pao* editorial, Aug. 14, 1958, in SCMP (1832):3.
64. Sung Tu, "Answers to Readers," p. 6.
65. Chou En-lai to National People's Congress, Feb. 10, 1958, in CB (492):8.
66. Lu Ting-yi report, April 22, 1960, in SCMP (2246):10.
67. *Kuang-ming Jih-pao* editorial, July 4, 1958, in SCMP (1807):6.
68. *Jen-min Jih-pao* editorial, Sept. 1, 1958, in SCMP (1847):42.
69. *Peking Review* 1958 (28):22.
70. The most elaborate discussion of this "puzzle" is found in Clemens 1968:chs. 1–2.
71. See Halperin 1967:141–143; Hinton 1967:176.
72. For a more detailed criticism, see Clemens 1968:33–35.
73. Brzezinski 1976b:377. Brzezinski also notes the parallel with the simultaneous U.S. problems with regard to France.
74. Chinese statement of Sept. 8, 1963, in Griffith 1964:399.
75. Cf. Hsieh 1960:5, 8; Hsieh 1962:170.
76. Cf. Hsieh 1960:4.
77. Crankshaw 1965:92.
78. SCMP (2185):4.
79. *Pravda*, Jan. 15, 1960.
80. Chinese government statement of Aug. 15, 1963, in Griffith 1964:351.
81. See, e.g., Halperin 1967:141–142; Clemens 1968:19.
82. Chinese government statement of Sept. 1, 1963, in Griffith 1964:374.
83. Cf. Brzezinski 1967b:301.
84. Soviet government statement of Sept. 21, 1963, in Griffith 1964:434.
85. Brzezinski 1967b:379.
86. See, e.g., Crankshaw 1965:52–61.

SEVEN/INTRA-BLOC BARGAINING: STAGE II

1. Brzezinski 1967b:368.
2. Brzezinski 1962:396.
3. Griffith 1964:37.
4. Cf. Dallin and Brzezinski 1963:xxx–xxxi.
5. See Lowenthal 1962:18; Zagoria 1962a:325.
6. See Gelman 1964:10.
7. Zagoria 1962a:337; cf. Yin 1971:6.

8. See Griffith 1964: *passim*.
9. See, e.g., Griffith 1962; Crankshaw 1965:97–110.
10. Text of the Moscow Declaration in Hudson et al. 1962:177–205.
11. See, e.g., Zagoria 1962a:343–369.
12. See Griffith 1963.
13. Sung Tu, "Answers to Readers' Queries on War and Peace," *Chung-kuo Ching-nien*, Feb. 16, 1960, in SCMM (207):1–7.
14. *Ibid.*:4.
15. Liu Chang-sheng speech, in CB (621):5.
16. *Jen-min Jih-pao* editorial, April 3, 1962, in SCMP (2715):26.
17. *Ibid.*
18. Cf., e.g., SCMP (2291):36; (2471):42; (2559):39.
19. See, e.g., SCMP (2399):4; (2715):24; (2814):25.
20. For details, see Young 1967:16.
21. Some statements indicate that China was in favor of the spread of nuclear weapons to other non-socialist "peace-loving" countries as well, although this point was never elaborated in any detail. See, e.g., SCMP (2648):38; cf. Young 1967:24–26.
22. Liu Chang-sheng speech, June 8, 1960, in CB (621):6. Emphasis added.
23. *Jen-min Jih-pao*, Sept, 18, 1962, in SCMP (2826):35. Emphasis added.
24. Crankshaw 1965:116.
25. *Jen-min Jih-pao*, Sept, 12, 1962, in SCMP (2820):31.
26. Wen Wei-ming, "A Dangerous Step," *Peking Review* 1962 (26):12.
27. Chinese government statement of Aug. 15, 1963, in Griffith 1964:351.
28. *Peking Review* 1960 (20):5.
29. *Hung-chi*, June 16, 1960, and *Pravda*, June 22, 1960, respectively, as quoted in Zagoria 1962a:ix–x.
30. *Jen-min Jih-pao* editorial, May 13, 1960, in SCMP (2261):35.
31. *Hung-chi*, June 16, 1960, in SCMM (215):8.
32. *Jen-min Jih-pao* editorial, May 28, 1960, in SCMP (2271):50.
33. *Hung-chi*, June 16, 1960, in SCMM (215):7.
34. *Kuang-ming Jih-pao*, Nov. 11, 1960, in SCMP (2380):31.
35. As quoted in *Jen-min Jih-pao* editorial, May 5, 1961; in SCMP (2490):12.
36. Cf. SCMM (270):8; SCMP (2554):30.
37. *Jen-min Jih-pao* editorial, May 8, 1961, in SCMP (2496):41.
38. See, e.g., *Peking Review* 1962 (37):8–9.
39. *Jen-min Jih-pao* editorial, Sept. 17, 1962, in SCMP (2823):24.
40. *Jen-min Jih-pao*, Sept, 18, 1962, in SCMP (2826):35.
41. *Jen-min Jih-pao* editorial, June 7, 1960, in SCMP (2277):32.
42. *Jen-min Jih-pao*, Sept. 12, 1962, in SCMP (2820):30.
43. *Hung-chi*, Jan. 1, 1961, in SCMM (244):1.
44. As quoted in *Peking Review* 1960 (23):8. Cf. similar statements in SCMP (2291):35; CB (621):6; SCMP (2274):41.
45. See, e.g., *Jen-min Jih-pao* editorial, Sept. 8, 1960, in SCMP (2337):36.
46. *Hung-chi*, June 16, 1960, in SCMM (215):7. Emphasis added.

47. Liu Chang-sheng speech, June 8, 1960, in CB (621):6.
48. *Jen-min Jih-pao*, June 21, 1960, in URS (19):390.
49. See *China News Analysis* (376):2.
50. *Jen-min Jih-pao*, Feb. 19, 1962, in SCMP (2685):33.
51. See, e.g., Lowenthal 1962:22–23; Hsieh 1964:101. The question of direct Chinese impact on Soviet negotiating behavior will be discussed below in chapter 9.
52. Zagoria 1962a:379.

EIGHT/INTRA-BLOC BARGAINING: STAGE III
1. Griffith 1964:143.
2. Cf. *ibid.*:156.
3. Chinese government statement of Aug. 15, 1963, in *ibid.*: 351.
4. Soviet government statement of Aug. 21, 1963, in *ibid.*:361.
5. See, e.g., SCMP (2901):26–27; *Peking Review* 1962 (52):21; SCMM (355):19; cf. Halperin 1965:50–51.
6. See *Jen-min Jih-pao* editorial, July 19, 1963, in SCMP (3025):30.
7. See, e.g., Griffith 1964:361.
8. *Jen-min Jih-pao*, Aug. 10, 1963, in SCMP (3040):27.
9. Chinese government statement of Aug. 15, 1963, in Griffith 1964:341.
10. SCMP (3031):30.
11. *Jen-min Jih-pao* editorial, Dec. 31, 1962, in CB (702):3.
12. Wi Hsiu-chuan speech, Jan. 18, 1963, in SCMP (2904): 22.
13. *Chung-kuo Ching-nien*, Feb. 10, 1963, in SCMM (355):18.
14. Cf. *Jen-min Jih-pao* editorial, Aug. 2, 1963, in SCMP (3034):38; Chinese government statement of Aug. 15, 1963, in Griffith 1964:344–345.
15. *Jen-min Jih-pao* editorial, Dec. 31, 1962, in CB (702):3.
16. *Hung-chi*, May 1, 1963, in SCMM (366):11.
17. "Two Different Lines on the Question of War and Peace," in Griffith 1964:481.
18. Chen Yi speech, Nov. 7, 1962, in SCMP (2858):20.
19. *Hung-chi*, Jan. 1, 1963, in SCMM (347):16.
20. Liao Cheng-chih speech, Dec. 19, 1962, in SCMP (2886):25.
21. "Two Different Lines on the Question of War and Peace," in Griffith 1964:489.
22. Chinese government statement of Sept. 1, 1963, in *ibid.*:386.
23. See, e.g., *ibid.*:65; SCMM (347):4; CB (706):78.
24. See, e.g., CB (702):4; Griffith 1964:490.
25. CPC June 14, 1963, letter, in Griffith 1964:276.
26. *Jen-min Jih-pao* editorial, March 8, 1963, in SCMP (2936):31; cf., e.g., SCMP (2929):28.
27. This should be seen in the context of the Chinese interpretation of the crisis primarily in terms of a U.S.–Cuban rather than U.S.–Soviet confrontation.
28. *Chung-kuo Ching-nien*, Nov. 13, 1962, in SCMP (2874):15.

29. *Jen-min Jih-pao* editorial, Dec. 15, 1962, in CB (701):7.
30. *Jen-min Jih-pao,* June 21, 1963, in SCMP (3007):37.
31. *Jen-min Jih-pao* editorial, Aug. 2, 1963, in SCMP (3034):26.
32. See *Hung-chi,* Sept. 6, 1963, in SCMM (383):7–11.

NINE/INTRA-BLOC BARGAINING: CONCLUSIONS
1. See above, pp. 14–15.
2. Clemens 1968:216.
3. Cf. above, pp. 13–14.
4. Cf. Clemens 1964; Griffiths 1967.
5. Adapted from Gasteyger 1964:20.
6. Soviet government statement of Aug. 21, 1963, in Griffith 1964:362.
7. Cf. Hsieh 1965:12–13; Young 1967:28–46.
8. Cf., e.g., Lowenthal 1962:13; Zagoria 1962a:238.
9. SCMP (2940):31.
10. Crankshaw 1965:44.
11. See, e.g., Lowenthal 1959:15; Clemens 1968:245.
12. Clemens 1965:215.
13. For an elaboration of this point, see, e.g., Zimmerman 1971.
14. Brzezinski and Huntington 1967:388.
15. *Ibid.:*389.
16. Cf. Halperin and Perkins 1965:14.
17. Lieberman 1967.
18. O. R. Holsti 1966.
19. Griffith 1964:29; Brzezinski 1967b:378; and Clemens 1968:28 all regard mid-1959 as a watershed in Sino–Soviet relations generally, after which the dispute was irreparable and the stage was set for a head-on confrontation.
20. For an explicit Chinese statement about the deterioration of Sino–Soviet relations in spite of the "positive" changes in Soviet policy, see Griffith 1964:400–401.
21. *Ibid.:*417–419.
22. See Schecter 1963.
23. D. Garthoff 1972:177.

TEN/SOVIET POLICY MAKING
AS BARGAINING SITUATION
1. For a discussion of the possible interrelationship of Soviet official doctrine and the concept of "totalitarianism," see Dallin 1973:564.
2. Lodge 1969:115.
3. Cf. Griffiths 1971a:356–357.
4. Glassman 1968:393.
5. Linden 1966:7.

6. Cf. Fingar 1973; Dinerstein 1968:35.
7. See, e.g., Brzezinski 1967a:116–117; Dallin 1969:45.
8. Linden 1966:16–19.
9. Cf. Kolkowicz 1971; Wolfe 1968. The "Stalingrad group" consisted of the men around Khrushchev at the Stalingrad front in World War II, the "Stavka" of the men around Marshal Zhukov at the Supreme Headquarters staff in Moscow.
10. Aspaturian 1971:530–543; Aspaturian 1972.
11. Wolfe 1968; cf. Morozow 1971:101.
12. See, e.g., Fleron 1970:120–121; Stewart 1969; Griffiths 1971a:339–342; Ploss 1968:78.
13. Griffiths 1971a:342.
14. Kolkowicz 1966:2; Paul 1971:180.
15. Schwartz and Keech 1968; Paul 1971; Morozow 1971:87; Gallagher and Spielmann 1972:29–30.
16. Stewart 1969:42; cf. Griffiths 1971a:342.
17. Linden 1966:21.
18. Cf. Kolkowicz et al. 1970:39.
19. Kolkowicz 1971:136.
20. Kolkowicz et al. 1970:14.
21. Aspaturian 1971:537.
22. *Ibid.*:526–547.
23. Cf. *ibid.*:546.
24. Aspaturian 1972:18; Lee 1972:74.
25. See, e.g., Aspaturian 1972:13–19; Morozow 1971:96–98.
26. Wolfe 1973:37.
27. Such a blunt indicator as numerical representation in the Central Committee testifies to their potentially high influence. See Aspaturian 1972:17; Morozow 1971:96.
28. Khrushchev letter to Twickenham Council for the Abolition of Nuclear Weapons, in *International Affairs* 1958 (3):4.
29. Jacobsen and Stein 1966:279; Ploss 1968:97.
30. Cousins 1964:58.
31. The term is used by Wolfe 1973:31–32.
32. Zimmerman 1969:10.
33. Lodge 1969:5.

ELEVEN/INTERNAL BARGAINING: STAGE I
1. Conquest 1967; Slusser 1967.
2. Linden 1966.
3. Cf. *ibid.*: 40; Slusser 1967:194.
4. Cf. Conquest 1967:363–381; Linden 1966:72–77.
5. See Linden 1966:58–89; Ploss 1965:113–153.

6. See Slusser 1967:200–203; Ploss 1965:181–183.
7. Linden 1966:94; Conquest 1967:391–392; Tatu 1969:80–84.
8. Kolkowicz 1967:*passim*, see esp. his "tension chart," p. 371.
9. *Ibid*.:135–150, 253–259.
10. *Ibid*.:150–153; Gallagher 1964.
11. Slusser 1967:202.
12. Linden 1966:70.
13. *Krasnaya Zvezda*, April 2, 1958, p. 1.
14. *Ibid*., April 3, 1958, p. 1.
15. In CDSP (1958), 10(18):17. Emphasis added.
16. *Krasnaya Zvezda*, July 1, 1958, p. 4.
17. Judy 1971:213. *Pravda* on July 30, 1959 accused *Voprosy Ekonomiki* of neglecting agriculture. See CDSP (1959), 11(30):19.
18. The examples cited were a non-aggression pact, the banning of nuclear weapons, general and complete disarmament, and a European friendship and cooperation treaty. P. Figurnov, "The World System of Socialism on the Rise," *Voprosy Ekonomiki* 1958 (8):5.
19. Whereas one article (A. Loshchakov, "The Militant Program of a Fight for Peace and Socialism," *Voprosy Ekonomiki* 1958 (11):23) mentioned no concrete examples, the other (L. Volodarskii, "The Soviet Economy on the Rise," *ibid*.: 6–12) listed the 1955 troop cut, the refraining from foreign bases, and the gradual reduction of the military budget as examples of Soviet disarmament initiatives.
20. Sakharov 1974:32; cf. Khrushchev 1974:69–70.
21. Kurchatov died in 1961, and an obituary in *Pravda* (Sept. 24, 1961) stressed his close relations with Khrushchev (in CDSP (1961), 13(39):15–16, 39).
22. H. E. Salisbury's Foreword to Sakharov 1974:10.
23. Sakharov and Kurchatov were the only nuclear physicists associated with weapons research who contributed to an anthology on the dangers of nuclear tests in 1959 (Lebedinskii 1959).
24. See *Bulletin of the Atomic Scientists* 1957 (9):314–317.
25. *Pravda*, Dec. 27, 1958, pp. 6–7.
26. Gruliow 1960:58.
27. *Ibid*.:95, 163.
28. *Ibid*.:152.
29. According to the official record, he was interrupted by applause only once when he made a joke about U.S. espionage designs. See Gruliow 1960:205–206.
30. *Ibid*.:214. Emphasis added.
31. Khrushchev's speech in *Pravda*, Feb. 25, 1959, p. 3. For other election speeches, see *Pravda*, Feb. 19–28, 1959.
32. *Vestnik Akademii Nauk SSSR* 1959(4):50.
33. See especially *Krasnaya Zvezda*, Feb. 10, 1959, p. 4; and Feb. 11, 1959, p. 4.

11. INTERNAL BARGAINING: STAGE I 233

34. *Ibid.*, Feb. 13, p. 1. Emphasis added.
35. *Pravda*, Feb. 22, 1959, in CDSP (1959), 11(8):11.
36. According to *Pravda* reports, Kozlov did not touch on test cessation in his speeches either in the United States in July, or in connection with Nixon's Soviet visit in early August, or in East Germany in October.
37. Cf. CDSP (1958), 10(15):27 and (42):9; *ibid.* (1959), 11(15):16 and (40):7.
38. In CDSP (1959), 11(44):5.
39. *Vestnik Akademii Nauk SSSR* 1959(10):11–16.
40. In CDSP (1960), 12(2):7–8.
41. Cf., e.g., his interview with an Argentine newspaper (*Pravda*, Jan. 4, 1960), his letter to the World Federation of Scientific Workers (*Pravda*, Feb. 6, 1960), and his March 14 letter to the European Federation against Atomic Armament (Khrushchev 1961a, 1:231–232).
42. A perusal of CDSP and *New Times* for the period mentioned sustains this.
43. Khrushchev 1961a, 1:363.
44. *Ibid.*:279, 326, 362–363.
45. *Ibid.*:246–247.
46. *Ibid.*:356.
47. *Ibid.*:415.
48. N. Arkadyev, "Disarmament: Eve-of-Summit Survey," *New Times* 1960 (20):7–8.
49. See *Pravda*, Jan. 15–16, 1960.
50. CDSP (1960), 12(15):15. Emphasis added.
51. For elaborate statements of this image, see, e.g., *New Times* 1958 (5): 5–7; *ibid.* (30):10–13; *MEMO* 1958 (9):109–111.
52. See, e.g., *Pravda*, Jan. 5, 8, 15, and Feb. 9, 1958; *Izvestiya*, March 3, 1958.
53. This conclusion tallies with Khrushchev's retrospective testimony of his relative ignorance about U.S. affairs prior to his American visit in 1959. Khrushchev 1974:371–372.
54. Khrushchev 1959:356.
55. *Ibid.*:594.
56. G. Trofimenko, "The Struggle in the U.S.A. on Foreign Policy Questions," *MEMO* 1958 (9):106–116.
57. CDSP (1958), 10(45):5.
58. Gruliow 1960:130.
59. *Ibid.*:61. Emphasis added.
60. *Ibid.*:203.
61. *Ibid.*:203.
62. *Ibid.*:121.
63. *Ibid.*:159.
64. *Ibid.*:153.
65. *Ibid.*:152.

66. *Ibid.*:214.
67. CDSP (1959), 11(6–7):18.
68. *Ibid.* (8):11.
69. *Ibid.* (8):12.
70. A. Stroganov, "Nuclear Testing: Pentagon Opposes Agreement," *International Affairs* 1959(4):93–94.
71. CDSP (1959), 11 (15):3.
72. Cf., e.g., *MEMO* 1958 (11):24–25; 1959 (3):68–82.
73. Cf. Bloomfield et al. 1966:118.
74. *Pravda*, July 7, 1959, in CDSP (1959), 11(27):23.
75. *MEMO* 1959 (7):12–16.
76. K. Semyonov, "Obstructive Tactics Continue," *International Affairs* 1959 (8):13.
77. *Krasnaya Zvezda*, Aug. 18, 22, and 25, 1959, respectively; p. 4 of each issue.
78. Speech at Veshenskaya, Aug. 31, 1959, in CDSP (1959), 11(35):5.
79. Khrushchev 1960b:191.
80. Speech of Sept. 28, 1959, in *New Times* 1959 (40):40.
81. Supreme Soviet speech of Jan. 14, 1960, in CDSP (1960), 11(2):8.
82. CDSP (1959), 11(39):21.
83. *Ibid.*:17.
84. CDSP (1959), 11(40):11.
85. Cf., e.g., *Krasnaya Zvezda*, Sept. 30, Oct. 13, 21, Nov. 19, Dec. 15, 1959.
86. Cf. *ibid.*, Oct. 21 and 29, p. 4.
87. *Ibid.*, March 24, 1960, p. 4.
88. CDSP (1960), 12(17):10.
89. *Ibid.* (2):7, 8.
90. *International Affairs* 1959 (11):3–6.
91. *Ibid.* (12):3.
92. *MEMO* 1960 (1):10–11.
93. G. Trofimenko, "Realism and U.S. Foreign Policy," *MEMO* 1960 (3):29–42.
94. S. Menshikov, "The Discussion on Foreign Policy in the U.S.A.," *MEMO* 1961 (4):114.

TWELVE/INTERNAL BARGAINING: STAGE II
1. Linden 1966:90–91. Cf. Tatu 1969:100.
2. Tatu 1969:122.
3. Cf. *ibid.*:85; Linden 1966:96.
4. Kirichenko's removal had already been announced a few months earlier. Brezhnev, who replaced Voroshilov as chairman of the Supreme Soviet in the May 4 reshuffle, was "released" from his work in the Secretariat in July 1960.

12. INTERNAL BARGAINING: STAGE II

5. Tatu classifies Podgorny and Polyansky as Khrushchev "allies" though not "clients," and Kosygin as "independent" (Tatu 1969:91–99). For a similar assessment, see Linden 1966:96–97.
6. Tatu 1969:84.
7. See, e.g., Linden 1966:97; Ploss 1965:184; Tatu 1969:100,110.
8. Tatu 1969:110; Linden 1966:97–98.
9. Gehlen 1971:61.
10. Linden 1966:98–100.
11. Hahn 1972:10.
12. Slusser 1967:200.
13. Gehlen 1967:81.
14. Tatu 1969:114.
15. Linden 1966:116.
16. *Ibid.*:105–106.
17. In the summer of 1960 V. N. Novikov, a senior arms industry manager, replaced Kosygin as Gosplan chairman, and was succeeded as head of the RSFSR Gosplan by K. M. Gerasimov, belonging to the same group (Tatu 1969:118). About a year later, another arms industry executive, V. M. Ryabikov, already promoted in 1960, was appointed First Vice-President of Gosplan. At the same time K. N. Rudnev, an engineer working in the field of armaments, became chairman of the newly created scientific research coordinating committee; and M. V. Keldysh, formerly director of a secret research project in the area of missile and space technology, was elected president of the Academy of Sciences (cf. Tatu 1969:137; Sosnovy 1964:491).
18. Linden 1966:106–107; cf. Ploss 1965: 216–234.
19. Cf. Linden 1966:114.
20. Slusser 1973:286. Cf. Linden 1966:118.
21. Cf. Tatu 1969:147; Slusser 1973:403.
22. Linden 1966:129.
23. See, e.g., *ibid:*129–131; Slusser 1973:461–465; Tatu 1969:172–175; Ploss 1963:214–215; Ploss 1965:236–238; Ploss 1971:214–215.
24. Cf. Tatu 1969:193–207; Slusser 1967:212–213; Slusser 1973:459–461; Ploss 1965:239.
25. Slusser 1973:466. Cf. Ploss 1963; Tatu 1969:208–255; Linden 1966:133–145 for similar diagnoses.
26. See, e.g., Tatu 1969:70–74.
27. R. Garthoff 1966b:55–56.
28. Kolkowicz 1967:265.
29. *Ibid.*:266.
30. Tatu 1969:79.
31. *New Times* 1960 (20):8.
32. *Ibid.* (21):7.
33. Statement at press conference in Paris, May 18, 1960, in CDSP (1960), 12(20):8; and Khrushchev 1961a, 1:562.

12. INTERNAL BARGAINING: STAGE II

34. *Pravda*, May 10, 1960, pp. 2–3.
35. *Krasnaya Zvezda*, May 9, 1960, pp. 2–3.
36. Speech at workers' conference, May 28, 1960, in CDSP (1960), 12(22):7.
37. See, e.g., Khrushchev 1961a, 1:586–587 and 2:77–83; CDSP (1960), 12(25):7.
38. Cf. Khrushchev 1961a, 2:32–33, 102.
39. *Ibid.*: 102.
40. CDSP (1960), 12(29):31.
41. *Pravda*, July 18, 1960, pp. 1–2.
42. In a May 28 speech, Khrushchev dealt at length with Kremlinological speculation in the West about military opposition to the Premier. Though discarding it as "fictions" and "lies," Khrushchev made a remarkable deviation from accepted Soviet practice by referring at all to Western speculations about internal Kremlin affairs. See CDSP (1960), 12(22):8. At a luncheon given by Cyrus Eaton in September, Khrushchev made candid complaints about military pressures for increased allocations (Khrushchev 1961b:81). When the American producer David Susskind in an October TV interview with Khrushchev suggested that some of the Premier's colleagues might be for a more militaristic approach toward the West, Khrushchev did not outright deny this but made an evasive reply (Khrushchev 1961b:151).
43. Khrushchev 1961a, 2:580–581.
44. *Izvestiya*, Oct. 9, 1960, in CDSP (1960), 12(41):27.
45. *International Affairs* 1961 (1):89.
46. *Vestnik Akademii Nauk SSSR* 1960 (11):3–8.
47. *Survey of International Affairs, 1961*, p. 212; cf. Slusser 1972:289.
48. Slusser 1972.
49. *Pravda*, Feb. 15, 1961, p. 1.
50. *International Affairs* 1961 (3):64–66.
51. *Survey of International Affairs, 1961*, p. 217.
52. Slusser 1972:285.
53. *Survey of International Affairs, 1961*, pp. 217–218.
54. *Izvestiya*, June 1, 1961, p. 2.
55. Khrushchev 1974:499.
56. See, especially, Khrushchev 1963, 1:249.
57. Khrushchev's priorities were explicitly stated on April 2, 1960 (Khrushchev 1961a, 1:363). As late as June 15, 1961, he placed questions of arms control above the German issue (Khrushchev 1963, 1:169–173).
58. Khrushchev 1963, 1:401.
59. *Ibid.*: 359.
60. Speech on anniversary of Nazi attack, June 21, 1961, in CDSP (1961), 13(25):9.
61. Slusser 1973:157–170.
62. *Ibid.*: 148.

12. INTERNAL BARGAINING: STAGE II   237

63. Burg and Wiles 1971:223; cf. Linden 1966:115.
64. Burg and Wiles 1971:220–226.
65. Slusser 1973:286.
66. Saikowski and Gruliow 1962:200.
67. As quoted in Slusser 1973:205.
68. Khrushchev 1974:68–69. It should be noted that Khrushchev at times seems to confuse the 1958 and the 1961 test series in his recollections.
69. See *New Times* 1961 (32):9.
70. See, especially, *Vestnik Akademii Nauk SSSR* 1961 (3):13; (4):27; (7):48.
71. Sakharov 1974:32–33.
72. Tatu 1969:171.
73. Kolkowicz 1967:160–161.
74. See, in particular, *Voenno-istoricheskii zhurnal* 1960 (6):96; 1961 (7):3–14.
75. For example, Dinerstein suggests that the specificity and insistent tone of the Kennedy administration superiority claims, as contrasted with the more general statements of the Eisenhower administration, "of course strengthened the position of anti-Khrushchevites in the Soviet Union." Dinerstein 1968:49.
76. *International Affairs* 1962 (1):27–31.
77. Slusser 1973:160–161.
78. Ploss 1964:25.
79. CDSP (1961), 13(35):9.
80. *Krasnaya Zvezda*, Dec. 2, 1961, p. 3.
81. For instance, an *Izvestiya* article (Dec. 20, 1961, p. 5) by the geophysicist M. Sadovsky argued the imminent possibility of detecting and identifying low-yield underground explosions without any international control network. CDSP (1961), 13(51):28.
82. CDSP (1962), 14(17):20.
83. See *Pravda*, March 13–16, 1962. Khrushchev's speech in CDSP (1962), 14(13):3–9.
84. *International Affairs* 1962 (4):4.
85. CDSP (1962), 14(20):5.
86. *Pravda*, June 29, 1962, p. 1.
87. *International Affairs* 1962 (1):30.
88. S. Yefimov, "Disarmament or the Arms Race?" *ibid.* (2):4. Emphasis in original.
89. *Krasnaya Zvezda*, June 28, 1962, p. 1. The failure to publish Khrushchev's letter to Nosaka is all the more notable as a Tass report on the Japanese reaction to the letter was, in fact, published on June 30.
90. See, e.g., *Pravda*, Feb. 23 and May 1, 1962.
91. CDSP (1962), 14(25):15.
92. *Pravda*, July 9, 1962.
93. Sakharov 1974:33–34.
94. Pravda, Sept. 16, 1962. An expanded version of his report appeared in the *Vestnik Akademii Nauk SSSR*, however not until the November issue.

12. INTERNAL BARGAINING: STAGE II

95. Cf. CDSP (1962), 14(18):10–13; *International Affairs* 1962(4–8).
96. *Pravda*, Oct. 21, 1962, pp. 2–3. Ploss has noted the article and interprets it as an effort "to dramatize in esoteric fashion Khrushchev's differences with domestic as well as foreign Communist bosses who prefer an 'armed truce' to any 'demoralizing' search for an accommodation with the West" (Ploss 1963:460).
97. Khrushchev 1974:447.
98. Speech to the Supreme Soviet, May 5, 1960, in CDSP (1960), 12(18):17.
99. Speech to the Supreme Soviet, May 7, 1960, in CDSP (1960), 12(19):6.
100. Speech at Czechoslovak embassy, May 9, 1960, in CDSP (1960), 12(19):23.
101. CDSP (1960), 12(19):29.
102. *Ibid.* (18):17. Tatu, who was present at the Supreme Soviet session recalls no such exclamation being made by any deputy (Tatu 1969:58).
103. Khrushchev's report in CDSP (1960), 12(18):4–19, 44; Grechko's speech in *ibid.* (19):11–12.
104. Speech on anniversary of Victory Day, May 9, 1960, in CDSP (1960), 12(19):21.
105. *Ibid.*:29.
106. See Tatu 1969:63–64.
107. *Krasnaya Zvezda*, May 18, 1960, p. 1.
108. *Ibid.*, June 2, 1960, p. 1.
109. See, e.g., *ibid.*, June 16 and 30, Aug. 8, 1960.
110. Speech at workers' conference, May 30, in CDSP (1960), 12(22):13.
111. V. Korionov, "Strength Policies on Trial," *New Times* 1960 (21):6. Emphasis added.
112. Tatu 1969:65.
113. As quoted in *ibid.*:66.
114. Cf. Zimmerman 1969:16.
115. A. Sovetov, "The Present Situation: Conclusions and Prospects," *International Affairs* 1960(7):8.
116. *Kommunist* 1960 (11), in CDSP (1960), 12(31):3.
117. Deutscher 1970:198.
118. Khrushchev 1961a, 1:572.
119. CDSP (1960), 12(21):3.
120. Speech at workers' conference, May 28, 1960, in CDSP (1960), 12(22):22.
121. Khrushchev 1974:455.
122. CDSP (1960), 12(20):5.
123. Speech at Rumanian Party Congress, June 21, 1960, in CDSP (1960), 12(25):7.
124. Cf., e.g., *ibid.* (21):3; (22):4.
125. *Ibid.* (22):4.
126. Khrushchev 1961a, 2:163–164.

12. INTERNAL BARGAINING: STAGE II   239

127. *Pravda*, July 15, 1960, p. 5, in CDSP (1960), 12(28):25.
128. Speech at meeting with representatives of the intelligentsia, July 17, 1960, in CDSP (1960), 12(29):31.
129. Inozemtsev 1960; see especially p. 691.
130. *MEMO* 1960 (7):7–8.
131. *Pravda*, July 21, 1960.
132. Slusser 1973:461; cf. Tatu 1969:203–204.
133. B. Ponomarev, "Peaceful Coexistence Is a Vital Necessity," *Pravda*, Aug. 12, 1960, in CDSP (1960), 12(32):3–5.
134. *Izvestiya*, Oct. 9, 1960, in CDSP (1960), 12(41):28.
135. S. Menshikov, "The War Industry and U.S. Foreign Policy," *MEMO* 1960 (11):35.
136. L. Gromov, V. Strigachov, "The Arms Race: Dangers and Consequences," *International Affairs* 1960 (12):18.
137. See, e.g., *MEMO* 1960 (12):45; *International Affairs* 1961 (1):50–54.
138. *MEMO* 1961 (1):32–33.
139. Cf. *Krasnaya Zvezda*, Oct. 30, 1960, p. 3; Nov. 3, p. 3.
140. N. S. Khrushchev, "For New Victories of the World Communist Movement," *Kommunist* 1961 (1) and *Pravda*, Jan. 25, 1961, in CDSP (1961), 13(4):11.
141. *Krasnaya Zvezda*, May 5, 1961, p. 4.
142. Radio and TV address on the Vienna summit, June 15, 1961, in CDSP (1961), 13(24):8.
143. *Ibid.* (32):5.
144. Khrushchev 1963, 1:348.
145. Cf. his speech on anniversary of Nazi attack, June 21, 1961, in CDSP (1961), 13(25):4–5; speech of July 8, 1961, in *Pravda*, July 9, 1961, p. 2.
146. Its scanty coverage of the Vienna summit stood in curious contrast to its broad coverage of Sukarno's visit directly after Khrushchev's return from Vienna.
147. *Krasnaya Zvezda*, Sept, 29, 1961, p. 4.
148. Cf. *MEMO* 1961 (5):7–8, and (6):14.
149. Cf. *ibid.*, (7) and (8):119–127.
150. Korionov and Yakovlev 1961; see, especially, pp. 6–7.
151. Saikowski and Gruliow 1962:49. Emphasis added.
152. *Ibid.*:179.
153. This interpretation differs from Slusser's which focuses on the orthodox notes of Gromyko's speech and sees it as an indication of his advocacy of a harder line vis-à-vis the West (Slusser 1973:395).
154. Saikowski and Gruliow 1962:14. Emphasis added.
155. *Pravda*, Jan. 17, 1962, in CDSP (1962), 14(3):26.
156. Cf., e.g., *MEMO* 1962 (3):99; *International Affairs* 1962 (1):25.
157. Cf., especially, *Krasnaya Zvezda*, Jan. 28, 1962, p. 1; Feb. 16, 1962, p. 4.

158. Suslov's speech in *Pravda*, March 13, 1962, p. 3; Kozlov's in *Pravda*, March 16, 1962, p. 2.
159. B. Marushkin, "Where Are the 'New Frontiers'?" *International Affairs* 1962 (3):17.
160. Cf. Slusser 1967:215.
161. *Pravda*, April 24, 1962, p. 2.
162. Speech in Sofia, May 19, 1962, in CDSP (1962), 14(20):7.
163. A. Galkin, "The Foreign Policy of Moribund Imperialism," *MEMO* 1962 (6):11.
164. *Ibid.*:13.
165. B. Dmitriev, "U.S.A.—the Threat from the Right," *MEMO* 1962 (10):27–38.

THIRTEEN/INTERNAL BARGAINING: STAGE III

1. U.S. Senate 1963:25. Cf. Tatu, who also includes Polyansky in this inner circle, with Khrushchev, Brezhnev, Kozlov, and Kosygin playing the major role (Tatu 1969:272).
2. Hyland and Shryock 1968:58.
3. Kennedy 1969:86–91.
4. See, e.g., *ibid.*:93–94.
5. Tatu 1969:268.
6. *Ibid.*:270.
7. *Pravda*, Oct. 21, 1962, in CDSP (1962), 14(40):5. The following lines, in particular, allude to Kozlov: "Evidently not for nothing do Stalin's heirs today suffer heart attacks. They, once his lieutenants, do not like these times."
8. Cf., e.g., Linden 1966:146–173; Tatu 1969:273–311; Reddaway 1971:243–244; Frankland 1966:197–198.
9. Reddaway 1971:244.
10. Tatu 1969:229.
11. Cf., e.g., Linden 1966:160; Tatu 1969:313.
12. See, especially, Tatu 1969:328–332.
13. See, e.g., *ibid.*:332–336; *Linden* 1966:165; Slusser 1967:224–232.
14. Cf. Tatu 1969:337; Slusser 1967:231–232.
15. *Pravda*, April 24, 1963, as quoted in Kolkowicz 1967:292–293.
16. Cf. Tatu 1969:344–345; Hahn 1972:110.
17. Aspaturian 1971:547.
18. Cf. Linden 1966:178; Tatu 1969:349–351; Slusser 1967:239.
19. Linden 1966:174.
20. Cf. Kolkowicz 1967:171–173; Allison 1971:234.
21. Kolkowicz 1967:278.
22. *Ibid.*:371.
23. ENDC/73; also in CDSP (1963), 15(3):10.
24. Cousins 1971:32.

13. INTERNAL BARGAINING: STAGE III

25. ENDC/73.
26. Cousins 1971:27.
27. *New Times* 1962 (47):1.
28. Speech at revolution anniversary, Nov. 6, 1962, in CDSP (1962), 14(45):7-8.
29. *Pravda*, Dec. 6, 1962.
30. *Ibid.*, Dec. 4, 1962.
31. *Voenno-istoricheskii zhurnal* 1962 (11):8-9.
32. See, e.g., *MEMO* 1963 (1):10; *International Affairs* 1963 (1):11-18.
33. Supreme Soviet election speech, Feb. 27, 1963, in CDSP (1963), 15(9):9.
34. Cf. Hyland and Shryock 1968:85.
35. Cousins 1964.
36. CDSP (1963), 15(15):26.
37. *Voenny Vestnik* 1963 (4):8.
38. Cf. CDSP (1963), 15(8):10; (19):26.
39. May Day speech, May 1, 1963, in CDSP (1963), 15(18):29.
40. CDSP (1963), 15(23):20.
41. Commentator, "Strange 'Lull,'" *International Affairs* 1963 (7):63.
42. *Ibid.*:63-64. Emphasis added.
43. *MEMO* 1963 (7):63-85.
44. A. Kirillov, "Peaceful Coexistence—a Form of Class Struggle," *Kommunist Vooruzhennykh Sil* 1963 (15):26.
45. Tatu 1969:352.
46. Cf. D. Garthoff 1972:156.
47. Cf. Conquest 1965:186-187; Kolkowicz et al. 1970:14-15; D. Garthoff 1972:158-162.
48. *Pravda*, July 28, 1963. Emphasis added.
49. *Krasnaya Zvezda*, July 31, 1963, p. 4. It is an interesting coincidence that the same Shiryamov also wrote the belated and reluctant *Krasnaya Zvezda* endorsement of the peaceful resolution of the Cuban missile crisis nine months earlier (Nov. 1, 1962, p. 1).
50. *Krasnaya Zvezda*, Aug. 7, 1963, p. 1.
51. V. Vershinin, "The General Line of Soviet Foreign Policy," *Kommunist Vooruzhennykh Sil* 1963 (19):8-16.
52. *Pravda*, Sept. 1, 1963, p. 3.
53. *Ibid.*, Sept. 25, 1963.
54. G. Khromushin, "Anti-communism—the Main Content of Imperialist Ideology," *Voprosy Ekonomiki* 1963 (8):43-52.
55. Cf. Gehlen 1967:84-85.
56. *Pravda*, Aug. 22, 1963, p. 4.
57. M. Lvov: "NATO's Nuclear Policy—Contradictions and Discords," *MEMO* 1963 (8):33. The very last paragraph of the article expresses support of the Moscow treaty (p. 35). The paragraph appears to have been added in the last minute.

58. Cf. the analysis of the November 28, 1961 proposal in the previous chapter.
59. CDSP (1962), 14(51):6.
60. *Ibid.*
61. CDSP (1962), 14(52):5.
62. *Ibid.* An identical interpretation of the U.S. election results was given in *Pravda,* Nov. 11, 1962, p. 5.
63. B. Izakov, "The Negotiations Continue . . . ," *New Times* 1962 (46):11.
64. *Pravda,* Nov. 29, 1962, in CDSP (1962), 14(48):28.
65. CDSP (1963), 15(1):11.
66. Cf. Suslov's Nov. 6, 1962 speech, in *Pravda,* Nov. 7, 1962; and Kozlov's Dec. 3, 1962 speech at the Italian CP congress, in *Pravda,* Dec. 4, 1962.
67. *MEMO* 1962 (11):3–6.
68. Cf., e.g., *Krasnaya Zvezda,* Dec. 18 and 31, 1962, p. 4.
69. Deutscher 1970:243.
70. *International Affairs* 1962 (12):75.
71. A. Sovetov, "Old Year, New Year . . . ," *International Affairs* 1963 (1):3–10.
72. CDSP (1963), 15(4):13.
73. *Krasnaya Zvezda,* Jan. 19, 1963, p. 3.
74. Speech on Armed Forces anniversary, Feb. 22, 1963, in CDSP (1963), 15(8):10.
75. CDSP (1963), 15(9):9,11.
76. I. Sokolov, "The Main Problem of Today," *MEMO* 1963 (2):23.
77. *MEMO* 1963 (1):3–21.
78. *Ibid.* (4):57–74.
79. *Pravda,* April 11, 1963, p. 3.
80. Cf. Hyland and Shryock 1968:86.
81. *Voenny Vestnik* 1963 (4):7.
82. Lenin Day speech, in CDSP (1963), 15(16):8.
83. His diagnosis that contemporary "doomed capitalism is carrying to extremes its contempt for the vital interests of humanity" does not bespeak any "realism" (*ibid.*).
84. Speech at Central Committee plenum, June 21, 1963, in CDSP (1963), 15(24):6.
85. *Pravda,* May 9, 1963, in CDSP (1963), 15(19):25.
86. May Day speech, May 1, 1963, in CDSP (1963), 15(18):29.
87. *MEMO* 1963 (7):71.
88. A. Sovetov, " 'New' Trends and the Realities," *International Affairs* 1963 (8):42–48.
89. D. Garthoff 1972:142–143.
90. *Krasnaya Zvezda,* Aug. 16, 1963, in CDSP (1963), 15(33):17–19.
91. *Pravda,* Aug. 20, 1963, in CDSP (1963), 15(33):18.
92. *MEMO* 1963 (10):80.

93. S. Lipitskii, "Actions of the Aggressor in the Threat Period of War," *Voenno-istoricheskii zhurnal* 1963 (8):24.

CONCLUSIONS

1. Cf. Jönsson 1978.
2. Griffiths 1973:5.
3. Cf. Linden 1966:100.
4. *Ibid.*:131–133.
5. *Jen-min Jih-pao*, Nov. 18, 1963, as quoted in Asparaturian 1971:539 and Reddaway 1971:253, respectively.
6. Slusser 1967:206.
7. Conquest 1967:390.
8. Tatu 1969:105.
9. Sonnenfeldt 1966:123.
10. Stone 1967:30–31.
11. Griffiths 1971b:656.
12. See, e.g., Griffiths 1967; Griffiths 1973.
13. Jervis 1967:368.
14. Kennedy 1969:124.

Bibliography

PRIMARY SOURCES

East-West Bargaining

Documents on Disarmament 1954–1959, 1960, 1961, 1962, 1963. Washington, D.C.: Department of State Publications, 1960, 1961, 1962, 1963, 1964.

Conference of the Eighteen-Nation Committee on Disarmament. Geneva.
  ENDC/1–103. Documents.
  ENDC/PV. 1–147. Verbatim records of meetings 1–147.
  ENDC/SC. 1/PV. 1–50. Verbatim records of meetings 1–50 of the Subcommittee on a treaty for the discontinuance of nuclear weapon tests.

Conference on the Discontinuance of Nuclear Weapon Tests. Geneva.
  GEN/DNT/1–127. Documents.
  GEN/DNT/PV. 1–353. Official verbatim records of meetings 1–353.

Intra-Bloc Bargaining

CB. Current Background. Hong Kong: U.S. Consulate General.
Peking Review
SCMM. Selections from China Mainland Magazines. Hong Kong: U.S. Consulate General.
SCMP. Survey of China Mainland Press. Hong Kong: U.S. Consulate General.
URS. Union Research Service. Hong Kong.

Internal Bargaining

CDSP. *Current Digest of the Soviet Press*.
Gruliow, L., ed. 1960. *Current Soviet Policies III: The Documentary Record*

of the Extraordinary 21st Communist Party Congress. New York: Columbia University Press.
International Affairs. Moscow.
Izvestiya.
Khrushchev, N. S. 1959. *For Victory in the Peaceful Competition with Capitalism (K pobede v mirnom sorevnovanii s kapitalizmom)*. Moscow: Foreign Languages Publishing House.
—— 1960a. *World Without Arms, World Without Wars (Mir bez oruzhiya—mir bez voin)*. Moscow: Foreign Languages Publishing House.
—— 1960b. *Khrushchev in America (Zhit v mire i druzhbe!)*. New York: Crosscurrents Press.
—— 1961a. *O vneshnei politike Sovetskogo Soyuza, 1960 god* (Soviet Foreign Policy, 1960). 2 vols. Moscow: Gosudarstvennoe izdatelstvo politicheskoi literatury.
—— 1961b. *Disarmament and Colonial Freedom (Za mir, za razoruzhenie, za svobodu narodov!)* London: Lawrence and Wishart.
—— 1963. *Communism—Peace and Happiness for the Peoples. (Kommunizm—mir i schaste narodov)*, 2 vols. Moscow: Foreign Languages Publishing House.
Kommunist.
Kommunist Vooruzhennykh Sil (Communist of the Armed Forces).
Krasnaya Zvezda (Red Star).
MEMO. Mirovaya ekonomika i mezhdunarodnye otnosheniya (World Economy and International relations).
New Times.
Pravda.
Saikowski, C. and L. Gruliow, eds. 1962. *Current Soviet Policies IV: The Documentary Record of the 22d Congress of the Communist Party of the Soviet Union*. New York: Columbia University Press.
Stenograficheskii otchet 1959: Vneocherednoi XXI sezd kommunisticheskoi partii Sovetskogo Soyuza (Stenographic record of the extraordinary 21st CPSU congress). 2 vols. Moscow: Gospolitizdat.
Stenograficheskii otchet 1962: XXII sezd kommunisticheskoi partii Sovetskogo Soyuza (Stenographic record of the 22d CPSU congress). 3 vols. Moscow: Gospolitizdat.
Vestnik Akademii Nauk SSSR (Bulletin of the USSR Academy of Sciences).
Voenno-istoricheskii zhurnal (Journal of Military History).
Voenny Vestnik (Military Bulletin).
Voprosy Ekonomiki (Economic Questions).

OTHER REFERENCES

Acheson, D. 1959. "On Dealing with Russia," reprinted in U.S. Senate 1969, q.v.
Allison, G. T. 1971. *Essence of Decision*. Boston: Little, Brown.
Aspaturian, V. V. 1962. "Soviet Foreign Policy," in R. C. Macridis, ed., *Foreign Policy in World Politics*. Englewood Cliffs, N.J.: Prentice-Hall.
―― 1964. "Diplomacy in the Mirror of Soviet Scholarship," in J. Keep and L. Brisby, eds., *Contemporary History in the Soviet Mirror*. London: Allen and Unwin.
―― 1971. *Process and Power in Soviet Foreign Policy*. Boston: Little, Brown.
―― 1972. "The Soviet Military-Industrial Complex—Does It Exist?" *Journal of International Affairs*, 26(1).
Bartos, O. J. 1967. "How Predictable Are Negotiations?" *Journal of Conflict Resolution*, 11(4).
Bauer, R. A. 1961. "Problems of Perception and the Relations between the United States and the Soviet Union," *Journal of Conflict Resolution*, 5(3).
Bloomfield, L. P., W. C. Clemens, and F. Griffiths. 1966. *Khrushchev and the Arms Race*. Cambridge, Mass.: MIT Press.
Bogdanov, O. V. 1958. *Peregovory—osnova mirnogo uregulirovaniya mezhdunarodnykh problem* (Negotiations—the basis for peaceful settlement of international problems). Moscow: Izdatelstvo "Znanie."
Boulding, K. E. 1956. *The Image*. Ann Arbor: University of Michigan Press.
―― 1968. "The Learning and Reality-Testing Process in the International System," in J. C. Farrell and A. P. Smith, eds., *Image and Reality in World Politics*. New York: Columbia University Press.
Bronfenbrenner, U. 1961. "The Mirror Image in Soviet-American Relations; A Social Psychologist's Report," *Journal of Social Issues*, 17(3).
Brzezinski, Z. K. 1962. "The Problematics of Sino-Soviet Bargaining," in K. London, ed., *Unity and Contradiction*. New York: Praeger.
―― 1967a. *Ideology and Power in Soviet Politics*. New York: Praeger.
―― 1967b. *The Soviet Bloc: Unity and Conflict*. Rev. ed. Cambridge, Mass.: Harvard University Press.
Brzezinski, Z. K. and S. P. Huntington. 1967. *Political Power: USA/USSR*. New York: Viking Press.
Burg, D. and P. Wiles. 1971. "Khrushchev's Power Position—Polycentrism Within the Soviet Ruling Group," in S. I. Ploss, ed., *The Soviet Political Process*. Waltham, Mass.: Ginn.

Campbell, J. C. 1956. "Negotiation with the Soviets: Some Lessons of the War Period," *Foreign Affairs*, 34(2).
Charles, D. A. 1961. "The Dismissal of Marshal P'eng Teh-huai," *China Quarterly*, no. 8.
China News Analysis. Hong Kong.
Clemens, W. C., Jr. 1964. "Lenin on Disarmament," *Slavic Review*, 23(3).
—— 1965. "The Sino–Soviet Dispute: Dogma and Dialectics on Disarmament," *International Affairs* (London), 41(2).
—— 1967. "The Nuclear Test Ban and Sino–Soviet Relations," in M. H. Halperin, ed., *Sino–Soviet Relations and Arms Control*. Cambridge, Mass.: MIT Press.
—— 1968. *The Arms Race and Sino–Soviet Relations*. Stanford: Hoover Institution.
Clemens, W. C., Jr. and F. Griffiths. 1965. "The Soviet Position on Arms Control and Disarmament: Negotiations and Propaganda, 1954–1964." Cambridge, Mass.: Center for International Studies, MIT.
Coddington, A. 1968. *Theories of the Bargaining Process*. London: George Allen and Unwin.
Conquest, R. 1965. *Russia After Khrushchev*. New York: Praeger.
—— 1967. *Power and Policy in the U.S.S.R.* New York: Harper and Row.
Cousins, N. 1964. "Notes on a 1963 Visit With Khrushchev," *Saturday Review*, Nov. 7.
—— 1971. "The Improbable Triumvirate: Khrushchev, Kennedy, and Pope John," *Saturday Review*, Oct. 30.
Craig, G. A. 1962. "Techniques of Negotiation," in I. J. Lederer, ed., *Russian Foreign Policy: Essays in Historical Perspective*. New Haven: Yale University Press.
—— 1970. "Totalitarian Approaches to Diplomatic Negotiations," in F. A. Sondermann, W. C. Olson, and D. S. McLellan, eds., *The Theory and Practice of International Relations*. Englewood Cliffs, N.J.: Prentice-Hall.
Crankshaw, E. 1965. *The New Cold War: Moscow v. Pekin*. Harmondsworth: Penguin.
—— 1966. *Khrushchev*. London: Collins.
Cross, J. G. 1969. *The Economics of Bargaining*. New York: Basic Books.
Dallin, A. 1969. "Soviet Foreign Policy and Domestic Politics: A Framework for Analysis," in E. P. Hoffman and F. J. Fleron, Jr., eds., *The Conduct of Soviet Foreign Policy*. Chicago: Aldine-Atherton.

—— 1973. "Bias and Blunders in American Studies on the USSR," *Slavic Review*, 32(3).
Dallin, A. and Z. K. Brzezinski. 1963. "Introduction: Issues and Methods," in A. Dallin, ed., *Diversity in International Communism: A Documentary Record, 1961–1963*. New York: Columbia University Press.
Dallin A. et al. 1964. *The Soviet Union and Disarmament*. New York: Praeger.
Dean, A. H. 1966. *Test Ban and Disarmament: The Path of Negotiation*. New York: Harper and Row.
Deane, J. R. 1951. "Negotiating on Military Assistance, 1943–1945," in Dennett and Johnson 1951, q. v.
Deborin, T. A. 1963. "Novyi istoricheskii etap v razvitii sovetskoi vneshnei politiki i diplomatii" (The new historical stage in Soviet foreign policy and diplomacy), in V. Z. Lebedev, ed., *O sovremennoi sovetskoi diplomatii* (Contemporary Soviet diplomacy). Moscow: Izdatelstvo IMO.
Dennett, R. and J. E. Johnson, eds. 1951. *Negotiating with the Russians*. New York: World Peace Foundation.
Deutsch, K. W. and R. L. Merritt. 1965. "Effects of Events on National and International Images," in H. C. Kelman, ed., *International Behavior: A Social-Psychological Analysis*. New York: Holt, Rinehart and Winston.
Deutsch, M. and R. M. Krauss. 1962. "Studies of Interpersonal Bargaining," *Journal of Conflict Resolution*, 6(1).
Deutscher, I. 1970. *Russia, China, and the West*. Harmondsworth: Penguin.
Dinerstein, H. S. 1968. *Fifty Years of Soviet Foreign Policy*. Baltimore, Md.: Johns Hopkins University Press.
Diplomaticheskii slovar (Diplomatic dictionary). 1961–64. 3 vols. Moscow: Gospolitizdat.
Edeen, A. 1966. "Den strategiska debatten i Sovjetunionen" (The strategic debate in the Soviet Union), in *SOU 1966:18 Strategi i väst och öst* (Strategy in West and East). Stockholm: Esselte.
Etzioni, A. 1969. "Social-Psychological Aspects of International Relations," in G. Lindzey, and E. Aronson, eds., *Handbook of Social Psychology*, vol. 5. Reading, Mass.: Addison-Wesley.
Fedder, E. H. 1964. "Communication and American–Soviet Negotiating Behavior," *Background*, 8(2).
Festinger, L. 1957. *A Theory of Cognitive Dissonance*. Evanston, Ill.: Row, Peterson.

Fingar, T. 1973. "Issues, Interest Groups and Linkages Between Foreign and Domestic Policy in the Soviet Union." Stanford: unpublished paper.

Fleron, F. J., Jr. 1970. "Representation of Career Types in Soviet Political Leadership," in R. B. Farrell, ed., *Political Leadership in Eastern Europe and the Soviet Union*. Chicago: Aldine.

Ford, H. P. 1964. "Modern Weapons and the Sino-Soviet Estrangement," *China Quarterly*, no. 18.

Forward, N. 1971. *The Field of Nations*. London: Macmillan.

Frankel, J. 1963. *The Making of Foreign Policy*. London: Oxford University Press.

Frankland, M. 1966. *Khrushchev*. Harmondsworth: Penguin.

Gallagher, M. P. 1964. "Military Manpower: A Case Study," *Problems of Communism*, 13(3).

Gallagher, M. P. and K. F. Spielmann, Jr. 1972. *Soviet Decision-Making for Defense*. New York: Praeger.

Garthoff, D. F. 1972. "The Domestic Dimension of Soviet Foreign Policy. The Kremlin Debate on the Test Ban: October 1962, to October 1963." Baltimore, Md.: Ph.D. Dissertation, Johns Hopkins University.

Garthoff, R. L., ed. 1966a. *Sino–Soviet Military Relations*. New York: Praeger.

——— 1966b. *Soviet Military Policy: A Historical Analysis*. New York: Praeger.

Gasteyger, C. 1964. "Krieg und Abrüstung in sowjetischer Sicht," in *Strategie und Abrüstung der Sowjetunion*. Frankfurt/M.: Alfred Metzner.

Gehlen, M. P. 1967. *The Politics of Coexistence*. Bloomington: Indiana University Press.

——— 1971. "Group Theory and the Study of Soviet Politics," in S. I. Ploss, ed., *The Soviet Political Process*. Waltham, Mass.: Ginn.

Gelman, H. 1964. "The Conflict: A Survey," *Problems of Communism*, 13(2).

George, A. L. 1959. *Propaganda Analysis*. Evanstone, Ill.: Row, Peterson.

Glassman, J. D. 1968. "Soviet Foreign Policy Decision-Making," in *Columbia Essays in International Affairs*, vol. III. New York: Columbia University Press.

Goriainov, M. and I. Glagoliev. 1965. "Notes concerning Research on Peace and Disarmament in the U.S.S.R.," *International Social Science Journal*, 17(3).

Griffith, W. E. 1962. "The November 1960 Moscow Meeting: A Preliminary Reconstruction," *China Quarterly*, no. 11.
—— 1963. *Albania and the Sino–Soviet Rift*. Cambridge, Mass.: MIT Press.
—— 1964. *The Sino–Soviet Rift*. Cambridge, Mass.: MIT Press.
—— 1970. "On Esoteric Communications," *Studies in Comparative Communism*, 3(1).
Griffiths, F., 1967. "Inner Tensions in the Soviet Approach to 'Disarmament,' " *International Journal*, 22(4).
—— 1971a. "A Tendency Analysis of Soviet Policy-Making," in H. G. Skilling and F. Griffiths, eds., *Interest Groups in Soviet Politics*. Princeton: Princeton University Press.
—— 1971b. "Transnational Politics and Arms Control," *International Journal*, 26(4).
—— 1973. *Genoa plus 51: Changing Soviet Objectives in Europe*. Toronto: Canadian Institute of International Affairs.
Gustafsson, L. 1971. *Förhandlingar* (Negotiations). Stockholm: Prisma.
Hahn, W. G. 1972. *The Politics of Soviet Agriculture, 1960–1970*. Baltimore, Md.: Johns Hopkins University Press.
Halperin, M. H. 1965. *China and the Bomb*. London: Pall Mall.
—— 1967. "Sino–Soviet Nuclear Relations, 1957–1960," in M. H. Halperin, ed., *Sino-Soviet Relations and Arms Control*. Cambridge, Mass.: MIT Press.
Halperin, M. H. and D. H. Perkins. 1965. *Communist China and Arms Control*. New York: Praeger.
Hayter, W. 1961. *The Diplomacy of the Great Powers*. New York: Macmillan.
Hinton, H. C. 1967. "The Chinese Attitude," in M. H. Halperin, ed., *Sino–Soviet Relations and Arms Control*. Cambridge, Mass.: MIT Press.
Holst, J. J. 1966. "Soviet International Conduct and the Prospects of Arms Control," *Cooperation and Conflict*, 1(1).
—— 1969. "Missile Defense: The Soviet Union and the Arms Race," in J. J. Holst, and W. Schneider, Jr., eds., *Why ABM?* New York: Pergamon.
Holsti, K. J. 1972. *International Politics: A Framework for Analysis*. Englewood Cliffs, N.J.: Prentice-Hall.
Holsti, O. R. 1962. "The Belief System and National Images: A Case Study," *Journal of Conflict Resolution*, 6(3).
—— 1966. "External Conflict and Internal Consensus: The Sino–Soviet

Case," in P. J. Stone et al., *The General Inquirer*. Cambridge, Mass.: MIT Press.

—— 1968. "Cognitive Dynamics and Images of the Enemy," in J. C. Farrell, and A. P. Smith, eds., *Image and Reality in World Politics*. New York: Columbia University Press.

Hopmann, P. T. 1972. "Internal and External Influences on Bargaining in Arms Control Negotiations: The Partial Test Ban," in B. M. Russett, ed. *Peace, War, and Numbers*. Beverly Hills: Sage.

Horelick, A. L. and M. Rush 1966. *Strategic Power and Soviet Foreign Policy*. Chicago: University of Chicago Press.

Hsieh, A. L. 1960. "The Chinese Genie: Peking's Role in the Nuclear Test Ban Negotiations." Santa Monica: RAND report P-2022.

—— 1962. *Communist China's Strategy in the Nuclear Era*. Englewood Cliffs, N.J.: Prentice-Hall.

—— 1964 "The Sino-Soviet Nuclear Dialogue: 1963," *Journal of Conflict Resolution*, 8(2).

—— 1965. Foreword to the Japanese edition of *Communist China's Strategy in the Nuclear Era* "Implications of the Chinese Nuclear Detonations." Santa Monica: RAND report P-3152.

—— 1968. "Communist China's Military Policies, Doctrine, and Strategy." Lecture presented at the National Defense College, Tokyo, September 17, 1968. Santa Monica: RAND report P-3960.

Hudson, G. F., R. Lowenthal, and R. MacFarquhar 1962. *The Sino-Soviet Dispute*. New York: Praeger.

Hyland, W. and R. W. Shryock 1968. *The Fall of Khrushchev*. New York: Funk and Wagnalls.

Iklé. F. C. 1962. "Alternative Approaches to the International Organization of Disarmament." Santa Monica: RAND report R-391-ARPA.

—— 1964. *How Nations Negotiate*. New York: Praeger.

—— 1968. "Negotiation," in *International Encyclopedia of the Social Sciences*, vol. 11. New York: Macmillan and Free Press.

—— 1970. "American Shortcomings in Negotiating with Communist Powers." Memorandum prepared for Subcommittee on National Security and International Operations of Committee on Government Operations, U.S. Senate. Washington: Government Printing Office.

Inozemtsev, N. 1960. *Vneshnyaya politika SShA v epokhu imperializma* (U.S. foreign policy in the epoch of imperialism). Moscow: Gospolitizdat.

Jacobsen, H. K. and E. Stein 1966. *Diplomats, Scientists, and Politicians:*

The United States and the Nuclear Test Ban Negotiations. Ann Arbor: University of Michigan Press.
Jensen, L. 1962. "The Postwar Disarmament Negotiations: A Study in American–Soviet Bargaining Behavior." Ann Arbor: Ph.D. dissertation, University of Michigan.
—— 1968. "Approach-Avoidance Bargaining in the Test Ban Negotiations," *International Studies Quarterly*, 12(2).
Jervis, R. 1967. "The Cost of the Scientific Study of Politics: An Examination of the Stanford Content Analysis Studies," *International Studies Quarterly*, 11(4).
—— 1968. "Hypotheses on Misperception," *World Politics*, 20(3).
—— 1970. *The Logic of Images in International Relations.* Princeton: Princeton University Press.
Jönsson, C. 1975. *The Soviet Union and the Test Ban: A Study in Soviet Negotiating Behavior.* Lund: Studentlitteratur.
—— 1978. "Situation-Specific vs. Actor-Specific Approaches to International Bargaining." Paper presented to European Consortium for Political Research workshop on "International Decision-Making Processes," in Grenoble, France, April 1978.
Joy, C. T. 1955. *How Communists Negotiate.* New York: Macmillan.
Judy, R. W. 1971. "The Economists," in H. G. Skilling and F. Griffiths, eds., *Interest Groups in Soviet Politics.* Princeton: Princeton University Press.
Kelman, H. C. 1965. "Social-Psychological Approaches to the Study of International Relations: Definition of Scope," in H. C. Kelman, ed., *International Behavior: A Social-Psychological Analysis.* New York: Holt, Rinehart and Winston.
Kennan, G. F. 1946. "The Technique for Dealing with Russia," reprinted in U.S. Senate 1969, q.v.
Kennedy, R. F. 1969. *Thirteen Days: A Memoir of the Cuban Missile Crisis.* New York: Signet.
Kertesz, S. D. 1959. "American and Soviet Negotiating Behavior," in S. D. Kertesz and M. A. Fitzsimons, eds., *Diplomacy in a Changing World.* Notre Dame: University of Notre Dame Press.
Khrushchev, N. S. 1974. *Khrushchev Remembers: The Last Testament.* London: André Deutsch.
Klineberg, O. 1964. *The Human Dimension in International Relations.* New York: Holt, Rinehart and Winston.
Kolkowicz, R. 1966. "The Red 'Hawks' on the Rationality of Nuclear War." Santa Monica: RAND memorandum RM-4899-PR.

―― 1967. *The Soviet Military and the Communist Party.* Princeton: Princeton University Press.
―― 1971. "The Military," in H. G. Skilling and F. Griffiths, eds., *Interest Groups in Soviet Politics.* Princeton: Princeton University Press.
―― et al. 1970. *The Soviet Union and Arms Control: A Superpower Dilemma.* Baltimore, Md.: Johns Hopkins University Press.
Korionov, V. and N. Yakovlev. 1961. *SSSR i SShA dolzhny zhit v mire* (USSR and U.S. must live in peace). Moscow: Gospolitizdat.
Kovalev, A. 1968. *Azbuka diplomatii* (ABC of diplomacy). Moscow: Izdatelstvo IMO.
Ladyzhenskii, A. M. and I. P. Blishchenko. 1962. *Mirnye sredstva razresheniya sporov mezhdu gosudarstvami* (Peaceful means of resolving interstate disputes). Moscow: Gosyurizdat.
Lall, A. 1964. *Negotiating Disarmament.* Ithaca, N.Y.: Center for International Studies, Cornell University.
Lebedev, V. Z. 1963. "Osnovnye cherty sovetskoi diplomatii na sovremennom etape" (Principal features of Soviet diplomacy in the contemporary stage), in V. Z. Lebedev, ed., *O sovremennoi sovetskoi diplomatii* (Contemporary Soviet diplomacy). Moscow: Izdatelstvo IMO.
Lebedinskii, A. V., ed. 1959. *Sovetskie uchenye ob opasnosti ispytanii yadernogo oruzhiya* (Soviet scholars on the dangers of nuclear weapons tests). Moscow: Izdatelstvo Glavnogo upravleniyu po ispolzovaniyu atomnoi energii pri Sovete ministrov SSSR.
Lee, W. T. 1972. "The 'Politico-Military-Industrial Complex' of the U.S.S.R.," *Journal of International Affairs,* 26(1).
Leites, N. 1951. *The Operational Code of the Politburo.* New York: McGraw-Hill.
―― 1953. *A Study of Bolshevism.* Glencoe, Ill.: Free Press.
―― 1961. "Styles in Negotiation: East and West on Arms Control, 1958–1961." Santa Monica: RAND memorandum RM-2838-ARPA.
―― 1964. "Kremlin Moods." Santa Monica: RAND memorandum RM-3535-ISA.
Levin, D. B. 1962. *Diplomatiya: ee sushchnost, metody i formy* (Diplomacy: its essence, methods, and forms). Moscow: Sotsekgiz.
Lieberman, B. 1967. "The Sino–Soviet Pair: Coalition Behavior from 1921 to 1965," in M. H. Halperin, ed., *Sino–Soviet Relations and Arms Control.* Cambridge, Mass.: MIT Press.
Linden, C. A. 1966. *Khrushchev and the Soviet Leadership 1957–1964.* Baltimore, Md.: Johns Hopkins University Press.

Lodge, M. C. 1969. *Soviet Elite Attitudes Since Stalin.* Columbus, Ohio: Merrill.
London, K. 1962. "Sino–Soviet Relations in the Context of the 'World Socialist System,'" in K. London, ed., *Unity and Contradiction.* New York: Praeger.
Lowenthal, R. 1959. "Shifts and Rifts in the Russo–Chinese Alliance," *Problems of Communism,* 8(1).
—— 1962. "Diplomacy and Revolution: The Dialectics of a Dispute," in Hudson et al. 1962, q.v.
March, J. G. and H. A. Simon. 1958. *Organizations.* New York: Wiley.
Mark, D. E. 1965. *Die Einstellung der Kernwaffenversuche; Probleme und Ergebnisse der bisherigen Verhandlungen.* Frankfurt/M.: Alfred Metzner.
McClelland, C. A. 1966. *Theory and the International System.* New York: Macmillan.
McGrath, J. E. 1966. "A Social Psychological Approach to the Study of Negotiation," in R. V. Bowers, ed., *Studies on Behavior in Organizations.* Athens: University of Georgia Press.
Midgaard, K. 1965. *Strategisk tenkning* (Strategic thinking). Oslo: Norsk Utenrikspolitisk Institutt.
—— 1966. "Auxiliary Games and the Modes of a Game," *Cooperation and Conflict,* 1(1).
Morozow, M. 1971. *Das sowjetische Establishment.* Stuttgart: Seewald.
Mosely, P. E. 1951. "Some Soviet Techniques of Negotiation," reprinted in P. E. Mosely, *The Kremlin and World Politics.* New York: Vintage, 1960.
Nicolson, H. 1954. *The Evolution of Diplomacy.* New York: Collier.
Paul, D. W. 1971. "Soviet Foreign Policy and the Invasion of Czechoslovakia: A Theory and a Case Study," *International Studies Quarterly,* 15(2).
Penrose, E. F. 1951. "Negotiating on Refugees and Displaced Persons, 1946," in Dennett and Johnson 1951, q.v.
Pipes, R. 1972. "Some Operational Principles of Soviet Foreign Policy." Memorandum prepared for Subcommittee on National Security and International Operations of Committee on Governmental Operations, U.S. Senate. Washington, D.C.: Government Printing Office.
Ploss, S. I. 1963. "The Uncertainty of Soviet Foreign Policy," *World Politics,* 15(3).
—— 1964. "The Soviet Leadership between Cold War and Détente." Philadelphia: University of Pennsylvania, Foreign Policy Research Institute.

—— 1965. *Conflict and Decision-Making in Soviet Russia.* Princeton: Princeton University Press.
—— 1968. "Interest Groups," in A. Kassof, ed., *Prospects for Soviet Society.* New York: Praeger.
—— 1971. "Deadlock in the Party Presidium," in S. I. Ploss, ed., *The Soviet Political Process.* Waltham, Mass.: Ginn.
Rapoport, A. 1960. *Fights, Games, and Debates.* Ann Arbor: University of Michigan Press.
—— 1964. *Strategy and Conscience.* New York: Harper and Row.
—— 1971. *The Big Two: Soviet-American Perceptions of Foreign Policy.* New York: Pegasus.
Reddaway, P. B. 1971. "The Fall of Khrushchev—A Tentative Analysis," in S. I. Ploss, ed., *The Soviet Political Process.* Waltham, Mass.: Ginn.
de Rivera, J. H. 1968. *The Psychological Dimension of Foreign Policy.* Columbus, Ohio: Merrill.
Rock, V. P. 1963. "Human Behavior and the Control of Conflict." Washington: Institute for Defense Analyses.
Rosenau, J. N. 1967. "The Premises and Promises of Decision-Making Analysis," in J. C. Charlesworth, ed., *Contemporary Political Analysis.* New York: Free Press.
Rush, M. 1958. *The Rise of Khrushchev.* Washington, D.C.: Public Affairs Press.
Sakharov, A. D. 1974. *Sakharov Speaks.* London: Collins and Harvill Press.
Sawyer, J. and H. Guetzkow. 1965. "Bargaining and Negotiation in International Relations," in H. C. Kelman, ed., *International Behavior: A Social-Psychological Analysis.* New York: Holt, Rinehart and Winston.
Schecter, J. L. 1963. "Khrushchev's Image inside China," *China Quarterly,* no. 14.
Schelling, T. C. 1963. *The Strategy of Conflict.* New York: Oxford University Press.
—— 1967. "What Is Game Theory?" in J. C. Charlesworth, ed., *Contemporary Political Analysis.* New York: Free Press.
Schelling, T. C. and M. Halperin. 1961. *Strategy and Arms Control.* New York: Twentieth Century Fund.
Schwartz, J. J. and W. R. Keech. 1968. "Group Influence and the Policy Process in the Soviet Union," *American Political Science Review,* 62(3).
Shapiro, M. J. and G. M. Bonham. 1973. "Cognitive Process and

Foreign Policy Decision-Making," *International Studies Quarterly,* 17(2).
Shubik, M. 1967. "The Uses of Game Theory," in J. C. Charlesworth, ed., *Contemporary Political Analysis.* New York: Free Press.
Simon, H. A. 1957. *Models of Man, Social and Rational.* New York: Wiley.
Singer, J. D. 1958. "Threat-Perception and the Armament-Tension Dilemma," *Journal of Conflict Resolution,* 2(1).
—— 1961. "The Level-of-Analysis Problem in International Relations," in K. Knorr and S. Verba, eds., *The International System: Theoretical Essays.* Princeton: Princeton University Press.
SIPRI Yearbook of World Armaments and Disarmament 1968/69. 1969. Stockholm: Almqvist and Wiksell.
Sjöblom, G. 1968. *Party Strategies in a Multiparty System.* Lund: Studentlitteratur.
Slusser, R. M. 1967. "America, China, and the Hydra-Headed Opposition: The Dynamics of Soviet Foreign Policy," in P. H. Juviler and H. W. Morton, eds., *Soviet Policy-Making.* New York: Praeger.
—— 1972. "The Presidium Meeting of February, 1961: A Reconstruction," in A. and J. Rabinowitch, eds., *Revolution and Politics in Russia.* Bloomington: Indiana University Press.
—— 1973. *The Berlin Crisis of 1961: Soviet–American Relations and the Struggle for Power in the Kremlin.* Baltimore, Md.: Johns Hopkins University Press.
Snyder, R. C. and J. A. Robinson. 1961. *National and International Decision-Making.* New York: Institute for International Order.
Snyder, R. C. et al. 1962. *Foreign Policy Decision Making.* New York: Free Press.
Sonnenfeldt, H. 1966. "The Chinese Factor in Soviet Disarmament Policy," *China Quarterly,* no. 26.
Sosnovy, T. 1964. "The Soviet Military Budget," *Foreign Affairs,* 42(3).
Spanier, J. and J. Nogee. 1962. *The Politics of Disarmament.* New York: Praeger.
Stagner, R. 1967. *Psychological Aspects of International Conflict.* Belmont, Calif.: Wadsworth.
Steibel, G. L. 1972. *How Can We Negotiate with the Communists?* New York: National Strategy Information Center.
Stepanov, A. I. 1963. "V. I. Lenin o kompromissakh vo vneshnei politike i sovremennost" (V. I. Lenin on compromises in foreign policy and the present time), in V. Z. Lebedev, ed., *O sovremennoi sovetskoi*

diplomatii (Contemporary Soviet diplomacy). Moscow: Izdatelstvo IMO.
Stevens, C. M. 1963. *Strategy and Collective Bargaining Negotiation.* New York: McGraw-Hill.
Stewart, P. D. 1969. "Soviet Interest Groups and the Policy Process: The Repeal of Production Education," *World Politics,* 22(1).
Stone, J. J. 1967. *Strategic Persuasion: Arms Limitation through Dialogue.* New York: Columbia University Press.
Sullivan, M. P. 1971. "International Bargaining Behavior," *International Studies Quarterly,* 15(3).
Survey of International Affairs, 1961. 1965. London: Oxford University Press.
Tatu, M. 1969. *Power in the Kremlin.* London: Collins.
Triska, J. F. and D. D. Finley. 1968. *Soviet Foreign Policy.* New York: Macmillan.
Tucker, R. C. 1960. "The Psychology of Soviet Foreign Policy," in A. Dallin, ed., *Soviet Conduct in World Affairs.* New York: Columbia University Press.
—— 1963. *The Soviet Political Mind.* New York: Praeger.
Ulam, A. B. 1958. "Soviet Ideology and Soviet Foreign Policy," *World Politics,* 11(2).
U.S. Senate. 1963. "Staffing Procedures and Problems in the Soviet Union." Report prepared for Subcommittee on National Security Staffing and Operations of Committee on Government Operations, U.S. Senate. Washington, D.C.: Government Printing Office.
—— 1969. "The Soviet Approach to Negotiation." Selected writings compiled by the Subcommittee on National Security and International Operations of the Committee on Government Operations, U.S. Senate. Washington, D.C.: Government Printing Office.
Verba, S. 1961. "Assumptions of Rationality and Non-Rationality in Models of the International System," in K. Knorr and S. Verba, eds., *The International System: Theoretical Essays.* Princeton: Princeton University Press.
Wadsworth, J. J. 1962. *The Price for Peace.* New York: Praeger.
Walton, R. E. and R. B. McKersie. 1965. *A Behavioral Theory of Labor Negotiations.* New York: McGraw-Hill.
Wedge, B. and C. Muromcew. 1965. "Psychological Factors in Soviet Disarmament Negotiation," *Journal of Conflict Resolution,* 9(1).
Welch, W. 1970. *American Images of Soviet Foreign Policy.* New Haven: Yale University Press.
Welch, W. and J. F. Triska. 1971. "Soviet Foreign Policy Studies and Foreign Policy Models," *World Politics,* 23(4).

White, R. K. 1965. "Images in the Context of International Conflict: Soviet Perceptions of the U.S. and the U.S.S.R.," in H. C. Kelman, ed., *International Behavior: A Social-Psychological Analysis*. New York: Holt, Rinehart and Winston.

Whiting, A. S. 1961. "Moscow and Peking; Suspended Dialogue?" *Current Scene* (Hong Kong), 1(4).

—— 1962. "Conflict Resolution in the Sino–Soviet Alliance," in K. London, ed., *Unity and Contradiction*. New York: Praeger.

Wolfe, T. W. 1968. "The Military," in A. Kassof, ed., *Prospects for Soviet Society*. New York: Praeger.

—— 1973. "Soviet Interests in SALT," in W. R. Kintner and R. L. Pfaltzgraff, Jr., eds., *SALT: Implications for Arms Control in the 1970s*. Pittsburgh: University of Pittsburgh Press.

Wright, M. 1964. *Disarm and Verify: An Explanation of the Central Difficulties and of National Policies*. London: Chatto and Windus.

Yin, J. 1971. *Sino–Soviet Dialogue on the Problem of War*. The Hague: M. Nijhoff.

Young, O. R. 1967. "Chinese Views on the Spread of Nuclear Weapons," in M. H. Halperin, ed., *Sino–Soviet Relations and Arms Control*. Cambridge, Mass.: MIT Press.

Zagoria, D. S. 1962a. *The Sino–Soviet Conflict 1956–1961*. Princeton: Princeton University Press.

—— 1962b. "Talmudism and Communist Communications." Santa Monica: RAND paper P-2631.

—— 1964. *The Sino–Soviet Conflict 1956–1961*. 2d ed., with new introduction. New York: Atheneum.

Zimmerman, W. 1969. *Soviet Perspectives on International Relations 1956–1967*. Princeton: Princeton University Press.

—— 1971. "The Soviet Union," in S. L. Spiegel and K. N. Waltz, eds., *Conflict in World Politics*. Cambridge, Mass.: Winthrop.

Zoppo, C. E. 1961. "The Issue of Nuclear Test Cessation at the London Disarmament Conference of 1957: A Study in East–West Negotiations." Santa Monica: RAND report RM-2821-ARPA.

—— 1962. "Technical and Political Aspects of Arms Control Negotiation: The 1958 Experts' Conference." Santa Monica: RAND report RM-3286-ARPA.

—— 1963. "The Test Ban: A Study in Arms Control Negotiation." New York: Ph.D. dissertation, Columbia University.

Zorin, V. A. 1964. *Osnovy diplomaticheskoi sluzhby* (Foundations of diplomatic service). Moscow: Izdatelstvo IMO.

Index

Acheson, D. A., 94
"Agreement in principle," 50-51, 71-74
Albania, 103, 106, 126, 165
Allison, G. T., 4, 133, 209
Alsop, S., 188
"Anti-party group," 143, 144, 165, 187
Aristov, A. P., 154, 163, 165
Asian atom-free zone, 87, 89, 100
Aspaturian, V. V., 138, 140
Atomic Energy Commission (AEC), 57, 59, 60, 70, 157, 184

Bargaining: definition, 9; tacit, 9, 18, 20, 129
Bargaining situation, 8-12, 20; nuclear testing as, 22-24; Sino-Soviet relations as, 81-85, 129; Soviet policy making as, 135-42
Bay of Pigs invasion (1961), 110, 185, 186
Belyaev, N. L., 144, 163
"Bikini incident" (1954), 24-25
Biryuzov, S. S., 166
Bogdanov, O. V., 45
Bowles, C. B., 153
Brezhnev, L. I., 163, 191, 192, 194, 195, 198, 204
Bronfenbrenner, U., 43
Brzezinski, Z. K., 13, 83, 128
Bucharest conference (1960), 103, 105, 109, 112, 131, 163
Budenny, S. M., 199

Bulganin, N. A., 143, 144
Bulgaria, 115, 175
Burg, D., 171

Canada, 25
Central Intelligence Agency (CIA), 60
Chou En-lai, 86, 87, 89, 103
Chuikov, V. I., 156, 166
Churchill, W. C., 76
Clemens, W. C., Jr., 75, 83, 123, 127
Commitments, 17-20, 21, 49, 50; Soviet, 31, 42, 48-51, 66-74, 141
Communist Party of China (CPC), letters to CPSU, 103, 116
Communist Party of the Soviet Union (CPSU): 20th congress (1956), 55; letters to CPC, 79, 116, 127; 21st congress (1959), 87, 89, 144, 147-49, 154-56; 22d congress (1961), 103, 164-65, 166, 172, 174, 187-88, 190, 212; Presidium, 139, 144, 162, 163, 165, 169, 193, 198; Central Committee, 143, 149, 162, 164, 165, 166, 174, 187, 194, 213; Secretariat, 163, 164, 165, 194
Compromises: Soviet views of, 44-46, 61-64, 150, 177, 201, 203, 207; Chinese views of, 97, 121; in intra-bloc bargaining, 82; in internal bargaining, 165, 175, 190, 192, 200
Concessions, 16, 19, 30, 31, 45, 47; Soviet, 27, 28, 34, 35, 36, 61-62, 64,

INDEX

Concessions (*Continued*)
  65, 67, 69, 76; as signs of weakness, 46-47, 64-65
Congo, 34
Conquest, R., 213
Control of test ban, 25, 26, 27, 36, 68, 74; national vs. international, 24, 28-29, 33, 34, 58, 65, 67, 69, 70, 76; control posts, 27, 35, 61, 66, 68, 70, 71, 72-73; on-site inspections, 27, 35-36, 61, 64, 65-66, 67, 68, 69, 70, 72-73, 196; impartial vs. reciprocal, 28, 29-30, 34, 73; Control Commission, 29-30, 61, 66, 72-73; administrator, 35, 61, 65, 67, 69; "black boxes," 35, 64, 65, 66, 67, 68, 70, 73, 177, 195
Cousins, N., 141, 153, 169, 195, 196
Cowles, G., 175
Crankshaw, E., 79, 108
Credibility, 14, 18-20, 21, 49, 69-70
Cuba, 110, 119
Cuban missile crisis (1962), 4, 59, 177, 195, 196, 216; and the test ban negotiations, 26, 35, 37, 38, 60, 63, 68, 76, 78, 131, 132, 211; and intra-bloc bargaining, 115, 116, 118, 119, 120-21; and internal bargaining, 191-92, 194, 200-3, 214-15
Czechoslovakia, 25, 115, 195

Dean, A. H., 36, 41, 43, 71
Deborin, T. A., 45
Demichev, P. N., 165
de Rivera, J. H., 77
Détente: and test ban, 24, 37, 38, 76, 200; as issue in intra-bloc bargaining, 84, 92, 121, 132, 151; as issue in internal bargaining, 137, 140, 144, 145, 162, 164, 168, 171, 179, 182, 194, 207, 215
Deterrence, 9, 56, 95, 109, 145
Deutscher, I., 181

Disarmament: and test ban, 24, 25, 38, 63; Soviet proposals for linkage with test ban, 32, 33-34, 35, 62, 65, 67, 107, 169, 174-76; Chinese views of, 88, 93, 106-7, 111, 118; comparison of Soviet and Chinese views of, 124-25, 128; as issue in internal bargaining, 133, 147, 148, 149, 150, 151, 167, 169, 175, 176, 177, 195, 198
Dulles, J. F., 94, 152, 157, 182

East Germany, 115, 202
Eaton, C., 154
Ehrenburg, I., 172
Eighteen-Nation Committee on Disarmament (ENDC), 32, 33, 35, 38, 52, 60, 63, 71, 74, 111, 113, 114, 177
Eisenhower, D. D.: on test ban, 25, 30, 31; Soviet views of, 57-58, 60, 154, 156, 158-59, 167, 177-84, 189; Chinese views of, 94-95, 109, 110, 111, 112, 119
Emelyanov, V., 173
Encouragements, 17
"Esoteric communication," 20, 87, 104, 151
Expectations, 13, 15-17; of outcome, Soviet, 28, 29, 34, 36, 42, 44-46, 61-64, 76; of U.S. behavior, Soviet, 28, 29, 30, 34, 37, 42-44, 55-61, 64, 76
Experts' conference (1958), 25, 27, 70, 72, 86, 149; Soviet references to, 27, 28; Chinese references to, 89, 93, 97-98

Fedorov, E. K., 36, 149, 150, 168
Finley, D. D., 14
France, 25, 128; Soviet references to, 32, 59, 62, 65, 150; Chinese references to, 89, 117
Fulbright, J. W., 153, 154
Furtseva, Ye. A., 163, 165

INDEX

Gallois, P., 205
Game theory, 7-8, 10, 11, 12, 16; "subgame," 3, 10; "auxiliary game," 3, 135; "supergame," 9-10, 38, 42, 51, 53, 74; zero-sum games, 10, 57, 64, 82; "mixed-motive" games, 10, 57, 64
Gates, T. W., 184
Glagoliev, I., 133
Golikov, F. I., 167
Goriainov, M., 133
Great Britain: participation in test ban negotiations, 25, 32, 33, 36, 53; Soviet references to, 58, 59, 151, 167; Chinese references to, 88, 89, 94, 98
Grechko, A. A., 166, 178-79
Griffith, W. E., 79
Griffiths, F., 75, 211, 215
Gromyko, A., 59, 63, 148, 177, 187, 201

Hailsham, Q. H., 116
Hammarskjöld, D., 34
Harriman, W. A., 116, 197
"Head-against-stone-wall" technique, 48-49, 67-69
Herter, C., 94, 112, 178, 182
Holsti, O. R., 130, 131
Hopmann, P. T., 53
Humphrey, H. H., 57, 153
Hungary, 102, 115
Huntington, S. P., 128
Hyland, W., 191

Ideology, 13-15, 42, 55-56, 82, 123-24, 136
Ignatov, N. G., 163, 165
Iklé, F. C., 10, 51
Ilichev, L. F., 165
Images, 11-15, 18, 215, 216; of self, Soviet, 42-43; "mirror images," 43, 211; of the U.S., Soviet, 43, 56-61, 75, 77-78, 152-61, 177-90, 200-7; of the U.S., Chinese, 84-85, 91-98, 108-13, 118-21; of test ban issue, Chinese, 84, 88-91, 106-8, 117-18; comparison of Soviet and Chinese, 98-102, 113-14, 121-22, 123-27; of test ban issue, Soviet, 145-52, 166-77, 195-200
Informal meetings, 49-50, 70-71
Inozemtsev, N. N., 183, 188
Institute of World Economy and International Relations (IMEMO), 141, 183, 188
Iraq, 96
Italy, 115, 195

Japan, 89
Jensen, L., 53, 62, 64
Jordan, 96
Joy, C. T., 47

Kaganovich, M. M., 143
Keldysh, M. V., 176
Kennan, G. F., 153
Kennedy, J. F., 35, 38, 66, 191, 195, 196, 197; Soviet views of, 60, 170, 185-86, 188-89, 201, 203-4; Chinese views of, 108, 110-11, 113, 114, 119, 122
Kennedy, R. F., 216
Khrushchev, N. S., *passim*; on test ban, 25, 32, 33, 35, 38, 66, 86, 89, 147-51, 166-77, 195-200; image of the U.S., 55-56, 60, 109, 110, 126, 153-61, 177-90, 200-7, 215; visit to Peking (1958), 84, 86, 96; visit to Peking (1959), 87, 88, 94; U.S. visit (1959), 87, 92, 94, 97, 100, 144, 150, 158, 159; Chinese attitudes to, 93, 96, 101, 113, 114, 119, 122, 131, 212
Khrushcheva, N. P., 172
Kirichenko, A. I., 144, 163
Kirilenko, A. P., 165, 198
Kochetov, V. A., 180
Konev, I. S., 166

Korea, 43, 112; South, 89
Korionov, V., 186
Korneichuk, A. E., 172
Kosygin, A. N., 163, 191, 195
Kovalev, A., 1, 75
Kozlov, F. R., 144, 163, 164, 165, 169, 187, 191, 192, 193, 206; on disarmament, 149, 195; image of the U.S., 155, 159, 188, 202; heart attack (1963), 193, 194, 197, 203, 206; and Sino-Soviet split, 212
Kuomintang, 82, 129
Kurchatov, I. V., 147, 148, 151
Kuusinen, O. V., 163, 206; image of the U.S., 155, 159, 183-84, 187, 189
Kuznetsov, V. V., 36

Laos, 112
Lavrentev, A. A., 148
Lebanon, 96
Leites, N., 42, 46, 54
Lemin, I., 39
Lenin, V. I., 14, 96, 123, 135, 137, 159, 177, 192, 215; on Soviet diplomacy, 39; on disarmament, 124; on "pacifist bourgeoisie," 157, 185, 203; on compromises, 201
Liberman, Y. G., 192, 193
Linden, C. A., 137, 139, 163
Lippmann, W., 153, 157, 179
Liu Shao-chi, 91, 112
Lodge, M. C., 142
London Disarmament Conference (1957), 28, 88
Lowenthal, R., 83

McCloy, J. J., 141
McCone, J., 184
McGrath, J. E., 8
McKersie, R. B., 3
Macmillan, H., 197
Malenkov, G. M., 143
Malinovsky, R. Ya., 148, 166, 170, 187; on test ban, 146, 167, 176, 197,
198; image of the U.S., 155, 179, 180, 186, 202, 204, 205
Mao Tse-tung, 86, 92, 96, 102, 103, 109, 112
March, J. G., 5
Marshall, G. C., 94
Marx, K., 135
Metternich, K. von, 21
Mikoyan, A. I., 144, 163, 191, 206; on test ban, 145; image of the U.S., 154, 155
Molotov, V. M., 143, 144, 165, 187, 212
Morgan group, 152, 153, 159
Morse, W. M., 153
Moscow conference of Communist parties (1960), 103, 105, 108, 112
Moscow talks (July 1963), 20, 36, 75, 116, 197
Moscow treaty (1963), 26, 37, 116; Soviet view of, 38, 198-200, 204-6; Chinese views of, 118, 122, 128
Mosely, P. E., 41, 47
Moskalenko, K. S., 166, 170
Mukhitdinov, N. A., 163, 165
Muromcew, C., 45

NATO, 60, 155, 199, 200, 203; MLF (Multilateral Force) plans, 117, 125
Negotiation, definition, 9
"New seismic data," 27, 29, 30, 58, 70
Nicolson, H., 39
Nixon, R. M., 157, 201
Nkrumah, K., 174
Nosaka, S., 176

Partial test ban: U.S. proposals for, 27, 32-33; Soviet proposals for, 33-34, 36, 38, 67, 68; and intra-bloc bargaining, 118; and internal bargaining, 177, 197, 200
"Peaceful coexistence," 45, 55-57, 60-61, 105, 126, 154, 187, 188
Peng Teh-huai, 87, 91

INDEX

Pentagon, 57, 59, 60, 70, 111, 153, 157, 180, 182, 183
Pickett, C., 169
Pipes, R., 77
Ploss, S. I., 174
Podgorny, N. I., 163, 194, 198
Poland, 25, 102
Polyansky, D. S., 163
Ponomarev, B. N., 165, 184, 203, 204
Pospelov, P. N., 163, 165
"Prisoner's dilemma," 23, 24
Proliferation of nuclear weapons: and test ban, 24, 195; as issue in intra-bloc bargaining, 89, 104, 107-8, 114, 115, 117, 124-26, 131
Promises, 17, 19; Soviet, 69
Propaganda, 10, 51-53, 54, 74-75, 107, 207
Proposals, 16-18, 31
Pugwash conferences, 147, 177

RAND Corporation, 70
Rapoport, A., 7, 42
"Red herring" technique, 47, 65-66
Retractions, 16, 47; Soviet, 31-32, 62, 65-66, 69, 76, 170
Rockefeller group, 152, 153, 159
Rumania, 25, 103
Rusk, D., 122

Sakharov, A. D., 147, 173, 177
Satyukov, P. A., 187
Schelling, T. C., 17, 19
Shelepin, A. N., 165
Shiryamov, M., 198
Shryock, R. W., 191
Simon, H. A., 5, 11
Singer, J. D., 209
Sino-Indian border incidents, 87, 97, 101, 115, 116, 121, 191
Sino-Soviet talks (July 1963), 116-17
Sino-Soviet Treaty of Friendship, Alliance, and Mutual Assistance, 84
Slavsky, Ye. P., 177

Slusser, R. M., 1, 169, 171, 172, 174, 212
Snyder, R. C., 11
Sokolovsky, V. D., 148, 149, 156, 166, 170
Solzhenitsyn, A. L., 192
Sonnenfeldt, H., 213
Soviet Academy of Sciences, 141, 147, 149, 176
Soviet test resumption (1961), 32, 37, 63, 86, 103, 164, 171-74, 196
Spiridonov, I. V., 165
Stalin, J. V., 45, 55, 81, 82, 104, 127, 136, 137, 165, 192
"Stalingrad group," 138, 145, 166
Stassen, H., 152
Steibel, G. L., 41, 54
Stepanov, A. I., 45, 46
Stevenson, A. E., 57
Stewart, P. D., 139
Sullivan, M. P., 5
Sulzberger, C. L., 172
Summit meetings: Paris (1960), 31, 103, 151, 162, 167, 179, 182; Vienna (1961), 32, 33, 103, 113, 170, 185, 186; Geneva (1955), 154
Supreme Soviet: speeches before, 59, 63, 100, 145, 150, 160, 177, 178, 200; election speeches, 145, 175, 188, 202-3; debates, 146, 147-48, 151, 166, 199, 201
Suslov, M. A., 144, 163, 164, 165, 184, 191, 203, 206; image of the U.S., 155, 158, 183, 188, 202; on negotiations with the West, 168; and Sino-Soviet split, 212, 213

Taiwan, 89
Taiwan Strait crisis (1958), 86, 96, 100, 101
Talleyrand, C. M., 50
Tamm, I. E., 169, 173
Tatu, M., 162, 163, 173, 192, 198, 213
Thompson, L., 170

Threats, 17, 19; Soviet, 28, 32, 69
Tikhomirov, S. M., 194
Tito, J. B., 111
Topchiev, A. V., 168-69, 177
Triska, J. F., 14
Trofimenko, G., 153, 156-57, 160
"Troika," Soviet proposal for, 32, 34, 62, 65, 67, 69, 170
Truman, H. S., 60
Tsarapkin, S. K., 27, 28, 31, 35, 58, 59, 60, 61, 63, 69, 70, 71, 72, 171
Turkey, 192

U-2 incident (1960): and the test ban negotiations, 26, 31, 33, 34, 58, 76, 78, 170, 211; and intra-bloc bargaining, 103, 108-9, 110, 111, 119; and internal bargaining, 151, 162-64, 166-68, 177-84, 189, 214-15
U-2 incident, Chinese (1962), 111, 114
United Nations (UN), 25, 32, 62, 186
U.S.-Chinese ambassadorial talks, 86, 98, 112
U.S.-Soviet interests in test ban, 24, 58, 59

Ustinov, D. F., 193, 194

Veto, Soviet demands for, 30, 34, 66, 67

Wadsworth, J. J., 43
Walton, R. E., 3
Warnings, 17; Soviet, 28
Warsaw Pact, 86, 87, 100
Wedge, B., 45
West Germany, 43, 89, 125, 146, 159
Wiesner, J. B., 36
Wiles, P., 171
Wolfe, T. W., 138

Yakovlev, N., 186
Yeremenko, A. I., 173, 176
Yevtushenko, Ye. A., 192
Yugoslavia, 106, 126, 192, 193

Zagoria, D. S., 82, 96, 114
Zakharov, M. V., 166, 170
Zhukov, G. K., 144, 145
Zimmerman, W., 14, 141
Zorin, V. A., 33, 52, 59, 60, 63, 71

Augsburg College
George Sverdrup Library
Minneapolis, Minnesota 55454